INCREDIBLE MYSTERIES and LEGENDS of the SEA

by Edward Rowe Snow

Illustrated

The vastness and terror of the sea have inspired generations of storytellers and been the source of countless mysteries and legends. Some of these tales have a foundation in fact or are based on the reports of eyewitnesses, but nevertheless stretch credulity. In this volume Edward Rowe Snow tells twenty-two of these stories, including tales of mermaids and mermen, of frozen people who have revived and lived, of a shipwrecked sailor's miraculous climb up a sheer cliff face, of a young woman walled up alive.

There are other stories of incredible courage and endurance, of pirates, shipwrecks, and men lost overboard at sea. Also included are accounts of the strange fate of Theodosia Burr, the proud daughter of Aaron Burr, and of Stephen Hopkins, the former piratical mutineer who came to America on the *Mayflower*.

Edward Rowe Snow, who lives in Marshfield, Massachusetts, has long been known for his stories of the sea.

INCREDIBLE MYSTERIES
AND
LEGENDS OF THE SEA

INCREDIBLE MYSTERIES AND LEGENDS OF THE SEA

Edward Rowe Snow

ILLUSTRATED

DODD, MEAD & COMPANY

NEW YORK

Library of Congress Catalog Card Number: 67-26146

Printed in the United States of America
by The Cornwall Press, Inc., Cornwall, N. Y.

TO

ARTHUR J. CUNNINGHAM

PRESIDENT OF THE MASSACHUSETTS MARINE
HISTORICAL LEAGUE

Introduction

The sea and shore have fascinated me since the early days of my life. This is due in part to my ancestors, for with one exception, in eight generations the men from whom I am descended were all sea captains. Another reason is my Massachusetts birthplace, Cottage Hill in Winthrop. The town of Winthrop is a peninsula, practically surrounded by the ocean, and there I spent many years of my youth canoeing, sailing, and often exploring the islands, forts, and lighthouses off Winthrop's shores.

The present volume is a result of research that began more than a third of a century ago, research concerning many stories that taxed my credulity. In other books I have already told many unusual tales, for example the story of Jerome, the unfortunate mute who in 1863 was put ashore at Digby Neck, Nova Scotia, with his legs cut off almost at the hips; the story of the *Mary Celeste,* found abandoned at sea in 1872 with all ten people aboard missing, not one of whom was ever seen again; and the story of the strange "money pit" at Oak Island, which has withstood all efforts of treasure seekers to solve its secret since its discovery in 1795.

The four chapters in this book that probably will be hardest for you to believe are "Mermaids and Mermen," "Frozen

People," "Lawson's Incredible Climb," and "Walled Up Alive." Another story that had extreme interest for me in searching for background material is the unusual life of Stephen Hopkins, my piratical ancestor. Hopkins was wrecked at Bermuda aboard the *Sea Venture* in 1609 and later became a passenger on the *Mayflower* in 1620. Incidentally, the name Stephen Hopkins is the only one both in the Mayflower Compact in 1620 and the Declaration of Independence in 1776.

I also enjoyed compiling the weird tale of the enchanted silo with its horrible visitor, as well as that of the ship found abandoned at sea with a wild animal as its sole occupant.

Although many of the accounts in this volume at first glance border on the improbable, the reader should study carefully all the known facts included in each chapter. To aid you along the paths of understanding I have included every last vestige of information that I have been able to ferret out in each case.

Do not misunderstand me. I am not suggesting that you should believe every detail presented in each chapter. I merely ask that you do what I did: respect the beliefs of those sincere individuals who recorded what they were certain they saw or experienced. Of course, one doesn't necessarily have to agree with them. How many of our ancestors would believe in our radios, television, airplanes, and astronautical flights?

I am grateful to the following organizations: The Boston Athenaeum; the Boston Public Library; the Bostonian Society; the Massachusetts Historical Society; the Massachusetts Marine Historical League; the Mariners Museum at Newport News, Virginia; the Lynn Public Library; the Thomas Crane Public Library, Quincy; the National Archives; the Harvard College Library; the Peabody Museum; the Essex Institute; the American Antiquarian Society; the Woods Hole Oceanographic Institution; the U. S. Navy; and the U. S. Coast

Guard. I particularly want to thank *Yankee Magazine* for permission to include "America's First Canal," which originally appeared in that magazine in somewhat different form in March 1966.

John R. Herbert of Quincy also has done much to further the preparation of my works, and at this time I express my deep gratitude for his interest in my career.

Down through the years my wife, Anna-Myrle, has been more than anxious to help in the formation of each book as it was put together. It has meant working through many, many nights, especially at index time, and this volume is no exception.

In addition to those who prefer to remain anonymous, I thank the following people:

Eric Brandsema
Helen Bresnahan
Mary Brown
Sister Jean de Chantal
Arthur J. Cunningham
Thomas Curtis
Lt. William Devine
Walter Spahr Ehrenfeld
Dr. "Rocky" Flanders
Alexander Frith
Judson Hale
Marie Hansen
Bradford Hathaway
Barbara Hayward
John R. Herbert
Melina Herron
Caroline E. Jakeman
Thomas Johnson
Joseph Kolb
Gary Kosciusko
Eileen Lardner

William F. McIntire
Muriel A. McKenzie
Joel O'Brien
Ida Payzant
William Pyne
Laurence Rideout
Robb Sagendorph
James Shannon
Alice Rowe Snow
Annabel Snow
Dorothy Caroline Snow
Edward Donald Snow
Winthrop J. Snow
Janet Sumner
Sarah Stein
Bror Tamm
Captain Warner K. Thompson, Jr.
Mrs. Terry Tucker
Dr. Henry Wilkinson
Charles R. O. Wood
Will E. Zuill

Contents

Illustrations

Following page 78

INCREDIBLE MYSTERIES
AND
LEGENDS OF THE SEA

1

Lawson's Incredible Climb

Rattling and stinging against the plexiglas, the snow melted to form tiny rivulets which slithered in neat little rows along the windshield surface of the airplane and flipped off into space. Pilot Doug Stults and I were high over the ocean on our trip from Pennfield, New Brunswick, attempting to land at Grand Manan Island, which is out to sea from West Quoddy Head Light at the entrance to the Bay of Fundy. The weather unfortunately didn't look too encouraging.

We knew we were approaching Grand Manan, but the snowstorm into which we had flown gave us no visibility at all, and we went up to a safe 700 feet to avoid the 350-foot cliffs of the island ahead. Then suddenly the storm ended and we could see Grand Manan directly below us.

We dropped down for a perfect landing on the cleared field at Grand Manan Island and came to a stop 400 feet later, at a point where the pine trees were massed on both sides of us.

Doug told me that Mr. Small, the owner of the field, would probably come to meet us. Soon we heard an ancient truck chugging its way up the steep road that leads to the airfield.

The truck wheezed to a stop, and a middle-aged Canadian climbed out. "I'm Oscar Small," he began, "and I suppose you are Snow. We were waiting for you all day yesterday, but you never did come. It was nice and sunny here in the morning—where were you?"

"If you'd been over on the mainland you'd have known why we didn't leave," I answered. "It was thick fog all day long, and not a plane flew in New Brunswick."

"Well, now that you're here, what is it that interests you?"

"I want to try to get the real story of the *Lord Ashburton* wreck," I said, "and I'm especially anxious to learn the truth about the man who is said to have climbed a three-hundred-foot cliff."

"Why, that was old Lawson, the shoemaker," answered Mr. Small. "I knew him before he died and he told me the story many times. Seems to me we've got something about it at the house. Let's go down there and see what we find."

Later I examined Mr. Small's pictures of the island while he found the documents and clippings he had saved concerning the wreck. The material confused me more than ever, for the papers and articles didn't agree with one another or with the previous story I had heard. We spent half an hour discussing the various sources of information, and the many conflicting accounts. Mr. Small then drove me over to the graveyard where the victims of the *Ashburton* disaster were buried. After studying the inscription and photographing the monument, we drove over to the headland several miles away where the ship had been wrecked in 1857.

After I had obtained every possible bit of information on the *Ashburton,* Doug Stults flew back with me to the mainland. Reaching St. John, I hastened to examine the local papers. As I had hoped, they yielded further valuable information. A month later more facts came in from George H. Russell, and then I felt that I had a complete story of what had happened. The following account is as detailed and accurate as it can be at this late date, one hundred and ten years after the disaster.

On November 17, 1856, the *Lord Ashburton,* a ship of one thousand tons, sailed in ballast from Toulon, France, with a ship's company of twenty-nine, bound for Saint John, New Brunswick. After an uneventful voyage across the North Atlantic, Captain Owen Crerar of Pictou, Nova Scotia, drew abeam of Cape Sable Island. It was Christmas afternoon when the *Ashburton* entered the Bay of Fundy. When he sighted Grand Manan Island a little later, Captain Crerar was confident that he would reach port within a few days. But terrific headwinds soon began to form, and shortly afterward the violence of the gale drove the *Lord Ashburton* * off her course. Captain Crerar was forced to put out to sea for safety.

Again and again the captain tried to reach his destination, but each time the wind forced him back. On no less than four occasions he sighted the high cliffs of the island that was to prove his doom, and each time the changing wind drove him out to sea again. The weather grew colder and colder with ice building up on the ship and her rigging. Crashing against the *Ashburton,* the waves sent chilling spray forty feet high—spray which froze into ice within a few moments.

On Saturday night, January 17, 1857, Captain Crerar sighted Partridge Island Light at the entrance to St. John Harbor, and hoped that his worries were over. Nevertheless, the threatening cliffs of Grand Manan Island remained a constant danger. When the wind changed again and came in strong from the northeast, the captain began to wonder if he would ever reach port. Then it started to snow again, in a

---

* Built by Briggs in 1843 at Brandy Cove, St. Andrew, New Brunswick, she was registered at 1009 tons. She was 155.6 feet long, 30.1 feet in breadth, and 22.9 deep. Officially numbered 23919, her letters were NPTL.

heavy, smothering downfall which soon blotted out all sea-marks and landmarks, and the waves began to build up in size and strength. Before midnight all the men on the doomed ship knew that a great northeast snowstorm had set in, and their thoughts turned to their families. A few hours before, they had been within easy distance of port and now they were shut off from all contact with home by the gale.

With the coming of dawn, a terrible sight presented itself. The ocean was a seething mass of foam and waves battered by a high shrieking wind, and the snow was thicker than ever. There was no way of determining the ship's location, although every one of the twenty-nine sailors knew that the northeast gale was pushing them inevitably in the general direction of the cliffs of Grand Manan. Sunday afternoon passed without any appreciable letup in the storm, and all hands waited with anxiety for the darkness which soon settled over the area. Midnight passed, and still the storm continued.

Toward one o'clock in the morning, the lookout aboard the *Lord Ashburton* heard the distant sound of breakers and warned the captain of what lay ahead. However, there was nothing that could be done, and the ship sailed on through the gale toward certain destruction. The booming of the distant surf grew louder and louder, and came to the ears of the sailors even above the roar of the wind and the sea. Then, with a final lunge, the proud ship struck the rocks at the foot of the cliff, hitting the boulders at a point abreast of her forechain. Captain Crerar shouted out: "My God, my God, we are all gone!"

The chief officers ordered the boats lowered away, but the commands were futile, for no small boat could survive in that maelstrom of surf, rocks, wind, and shattering timbers. Going over on her beam ends, the *Ashburton* lost her foremast and mainmast, with the mizzenmast soon following. Gathered together on the starboard quarter, the captain and crew had no idea that black January night what part of the island they had struck. Each man prayed in his own way that somehow he might get ashore alive.

The seas swept in across the deck, and almost every successive wave claimed its human victim. Soon there were only ten men aboard the ship. Those ten survivors, watching their chances, decided to let themselves down into the surf in the partial lee created by the ship's quarter. One by one they leaped into the surging waves. Some attached themselves to broken fragments from the *Ashburton*, while others boldly struck out for shore.

James Lawson, a young native of Bornholm, Denmark, was among those who attempted to swim to land. After a terrific struggle against the waves and debris, he found himself nearing the shore, but suddenly he was caught in the powerful undertow. Desperate, he attempted to free himself but was drawn inexorably beneath the waves. When he rose to the surface again, he could hear his drowning shipmates shouting all around him, but he could help neither himself nor the others nearby.

A wave pushed him high on the rocky beach. Managing to struggle to his feet, Lawson started for the rocks just ahead, but the next wave engulfed him and drew him into deep water again. Time after time, he was tossed ashore by one wave and snatched out into the sea by another. One moment he would believe himself safe, and the next he'd lose his footing and be well over his head. He might have had an easier time if the tide had been going out, but now the water was coming in.

Finally a wave mightier than all its predecessors overwhelmed Lawson and rushed with him toward the rocky cliff. A moment later the billow dashed him against the ledges. Stunned, he hung desperately to an abutment there. Before the next wave could catch him, Lawson struggled to reach a point higher up the abutment, just above the reach of the tide. After resting, he attempted to stand, but the effort was too great. He needed to collect his strength, but by the time he could do so, the tide came in and caught him again at the base of the great cliff. Finding a projecting pinnacle, Lawson grasped it with both hands.

Every wave surged against him. Soon waist-deep in the surf, he clung tenaciously to the pinnacle. Fighting a losing battle with the oncoming tide, Lawson cried aloud in desperation. To his amazement, his cry was answered by a shipmate who had managed to get ashore from the wreck. The sailor, up on the ledge, worked his way over to grasp Lawson and help him to climb onto a projecting shelf a few feet above the high-tide mark. There Lawson rested until dawn.

When the sun came up, he saw that his friend had disappeared. Though Lawson did not know it, the man had gone just around the bend of the cliff, where five others from the wreck were huddled on the narrow ledge.

The cliff towered three hundred feet above Lawson, and he knew that unless he climbed to the top to get aid, he would freeze before night fell. He had lost his shoes and socks in his fight to gain the shore, and he realized that even as he began his climb his feet were freezing.

The northeast storm was bringing ever-increasing winds, but in their terrific surges up the cliff they actually helped Lawson as they swirled around him. The winds, which hit the Grand Manan cliff that January day at sixty and seventy miles an hour, were to figure prominently in the miracle that Lawson was accomplishing.

Climbing steadily for several score feet, Lawson stopped to rest when he had reached the more difficult part of the cliff. Then he glanced again above him at the towering precipice. Determined to reach the top, he stood up, and the force of the wind seemed to flatten him against the rock. As he again began to work his way up the smooth face of the promontory, he found that the wind was so strong that he could support his weight by grasping tiny crevices and ledges that without the hurricane pushing him would not be sufficient to help him climb. Inch by inch he ascended, leaving behind a trail of blood from his torn feet.

Three quarters of the way up he reached a sheer fifteen-foot wall, flat as the side of a ship, with no handholds at all. He knew that he could not scale it. Clinging to a crevice 225 feet in the air with the unbroken surface of the cliff above him, he almost gave up. At first he felt that his last hope was gone and that his life was about to end.

Then the stubborn Dane remembered a jutting ledge about twenty-five feet below, and began to retrace his steps slowly and carefully. Eventually he inched his aching body to the ledge, and then worked his way for thirty feet along it. Here he discovered a trail of minute crevices leading upward. The wind was now blowing no less than eighty miles an hour, literally pushing him up the cliff. Foot by foot, inch by inch, using the new trail, he neared the summit. At last the top of the cliff was just ahead. The last few feet were much easier to scale and finally he achieved his goal. Collapsing at the top of the three-hundred-foot cliff, he fell unconscious.

Half an hour later Lawson revived. Rested considerably, he was able to get to his feet, but ahead were deep snowdrifts. Doggedly he struggled through them until, a short distance away, he saw a barn. Step by step he dragged his bleeding feet, eventually reaching the building to pull open the door and collapse in a pile of hay. Almost at once he fell into a deep sleep of exhaustion.

An hour later the snow stopped falling, and the wind swung around to the north. This was the customary signal for James Tatton, who lived nearby, to hike out to the headland and scan the ocean. Many of us enjoy doing that very thing today.

But it was fortunate for Lawson that Tatton took his usual after-storm walk that January 19, for he came across bloody footsteps in the snow and followed them to the barn. There he discovered the shivering, unconscious form of James Lawson. After reviving him, Tatton half-led and half-carried Lawson to the nearest residence, the home of Mr. and Mrs. Horace Bennett, where Lawson was given treatment.

He sent others to discover if anyone else from the wreck might still be alive, and after several hours they found six men clustered at the foot of the towering cliff. Since the tide had gone down, the men were carried along the base of the cliff to safety.

After rescuing these six survivors, the island volunteers returned to look for more victims of the shipwreck. Rounding another headland as they made their way along the rocky beach, they came across a long row of men evidently sitting down to rest. The leader of the rescuers stepped up to the first man and spoke to him. There was no answer—and the islanders soon discovered that every man in that long row was dead, either by freezing or drowning. Later that day the twenty-two lifeless bodies were carried up to the graveyard, where they were buried together in a single plot. The brother of Owen Crerar arrived from Pictou later that year to claim the captain's body, but the twenty-one other sailors still lie in the cemetery on Grand Manan. Little is known about them, except that one sailor named Sweeney came from Portland, Maine, and that the chief mate was a native of Brighton, England.

Early the next month the seven survivors were taken ashore to the Marine Hospital at St. John. As a result of his climb up the face of the cliff, James Lawson lost all his toes and part of both feet. It is said that his stay in the St. John Hospital lasted more than five years. When he finally recovered, Law-

son returned to Grand Manan Island and set himself up as a
shoemaker there.

James Lawson was living on the island in 1872 when the
Sarah Sloane was wrecked near the spot where he himself had
been cast against the cliff in 1857. On this occasion only one
man lived to tell the story, a young Baltimore Negro named
Charles Turner. The other seven crew members were
drowned. It is said that at the time of the *Sloane* shipwreck
Lawson was extremely solicitous on Turner's behalf and
assisted in getting him to Captain Eben Gaskill's residence.
Turner's feet were badly frozen and later they had to be
amputated.

The remains of the other members of the crew were eventually found on the shore, horribly mutilated by the pounding
on the rocks, and were buried in the cemetery beside those
lost from the *Ashburton*. Two of the bodies were removed
afterward to the mainland.

In 1874 the Canadian government erected a fog signal near
Ashburton Head at Long Eddy Point, around the headland
northwest of the location of the two shipwrecks. James Tatton, the man who found Lawson near death in the barn, was
appointed as the new fog-signal keeper.

Lawson remained at his chosen vocation, shoemaker of
Grand Manan Island, and eventually became a good workman. He was always troubled by his feet, of course, and
walking was difficult for him. But he led a long and full life,
during which he married and had two children. He died at a
good old age on February 22, 1918.

My first contact with Lawson's story had come one day in
1940 when I was doing research work for my book *Storms and
Shipwrecks*. Captain Ernest Delesdernier Sproul, Curator of
the Marine Museum at Boston's Old State House, was telling
me of shipwrecks around Quoddy Head, and he mentioned

James Lawson and the *Ashburton*. He said that the sailor dropped a mitten halfway up the cliff and that when the others later doubted his climbing the cliff, he challenged them to lower a man over the edge to verify the story. When the mitten was discovered, the doubting Thomases were forced to believe that Lawson had climbed the cliff.

Captain Sproul had been told that a Negro was saved with Lawson, but obviously the story of the young Negro's survival was confused with the *Sloane* disaster fifteen years later.

Many other wrecks have occurred on the island, including a French ship more than two centuries ago, the bark *Mavourneen* in 1866, the *Humber* in 1872, and the two-master *Nelson Y. McFarland,* lost with all hands during the winter of 1936–37. But for sheer drama and spectacular bravery, none of them can approach the *Lord Ashburton* disaster when James Lawson climbed a three-hundred-foot cliff and saved himself from death.

2

Walled Up Alive

One afternoon many generations ago a Massachusetts stone mason named Michael Abrantes, an expert in his field, was having dinner in a reputable dining establishment in the vicinity of Scollay Square, Boston.

Abrantes finished his meal, paid his bill, and walked out. Three men who had been awaiting him then blocked his path. When he attempted to step around them, the gray-haired leader of the group spoke to him by name.

"Mr. Abrantes," he began, "I have a special task for you in your business which has to be completed before tomorrow. I realize that you may have other plans for the next dozen hours or so, but if you accept I will pay you far in excess of what you normally could make. In this bag I have twenty-five twenty-dollar gold pieces, and I promise you all of them if you agree to place yourself entirely at my disposal until dawn tomorrow morning."

The gray-haired stranger emptied the gold into his hands and clinked the coins significantly as he put them back in the pouch one by one. "We already have the mortar and the granite blocks for this particular task, and all we need is your ability."

At once Abrantes sensed that there was indeed something unusual about the entire proposition. As he later explained, he knew even then that he should refuse. However, his curiosity and the five hundred dollars decided him to go ahead and accept.

"I agree," he answered, "but I'll have to go over to my shop, get my bag and working clothes, and then I'll be ready."

The men escorted him to a waiting carriage. They all climbed in, and the curtains were drawn at once. In ten minutes the carriage drew up at Abrantes' business establishment. Twenty minutes later the mason was back in the carriage, dressed in his working clothes. The leader gave directions to the driver, and soon the vehicle halted in a deserted part of Boston Neck.

"What I must do is quite necessary for the success of my plans," he explained. "Some part of what is going to take place I know will confuse you, but all I ask is that you do what you are told and keep your mouth shut. Now, off with your cap!"

Abrantes began a protest, but the gray-haired leader pulled out an enormous white handkerchief and blindfolded the mason securely. Abrantes was willing to give up the entire project then and there, but the others held him tightly.

Then followed a trip in the carriage of more than an hour's duration. Abrantes' blindfold was extremely efficient, for he found that he couldn't see anything. In any case, he knew that the carriage curtains were all tightly drawn.

He began listening to the sounds of the carriage wheels as they passed over surfaces of different types. The cobblestones of Boston he easily recognized, then the wooden bridges, and finally a dirt road. He knew most of the varying sounds carriage wheels made, and he heard them all before the end of the journey. Finally, not too long after going over another wooden bridge, the carriage stopped. The handkerchief, however, remained in place. Two strong arms guided him out of the carriage and down a flight of steps. Reaching a level surface with a wooden floor, he was taken to the right and through what was apparently an entrance. Then he heard a door shut close at hand. The next move of his escorts was to walk him down a passageway, judging from the echo, and into a second room, after which another door closed.

After being led through several other passageways and up and down two flights of stairs, probably to confuse him even more, Abrantes found himself seated at a table. The blindfold was then removed. The mason discovered that he was in a fairly large room, which was lighted on all four sides by a series of wax candles, arranged in tiers, in back of which hung black drapes. He guessed that there must have been 180 candles in the room, creating a funereal appearance. The floors themselves, the ceiling, and the furniture were all covered with the black drapery.

Across the room from the place where he had entered was a series of white cords. The gray-haired man now stood close to them.

"This will be your task," he told Abrantes, and pulled the cords to reveal a waist-high niche in the granite wall of the room. Below the niche was a heap of granite stones piled in disorder. Although terrified and confused, the Bostonian noted mentally that an attempt had been made by inexperienced workmen to tear out a section of the granite wall, and a mess had resulted.

There were several freshly mixed buckets of mortar standing close to the rubble of granite on the floor, and Abrantes realized that he had been brought to the room because those who had torn the wall down could never have put it back properly.

Studying the niche-like opening in the wall, he estimated that the aperture was six feet long, three feet high, and about four feet deep. Evidently behind the wall was nothing but dirt. The area in the niche was approximately seventy-five cubic feet.

The gray-haired leader now closed the curtains. Abrantes, nevertheless, was an expert and had already memorized certain details of the masonry, and he knew that he would never forget that particular wall. Closing his eyes to make sure that he had the wall area properly identified in his memory, he sat there for several minutes.

When he opened his eyes again he realized that the others had gone, and he was alone. Standing up, he started to walk across to the granite wall again, but then he heard the others coming.

A moment later the draperies were pulled aside and several men he had never seen before entered the room. Wearing black masks and cloaks, they presented a weird, ghastly appearance as they lined up across the room from him.

The next thing Abrantes heard was a scuffling sound in the corridor. The same men who had been in the carriage with him entered the room dragging with them a beautiful young woman. Her disheveled hair, tear-stained eyes, and torn dress proved that she had been forcibly brought to the room where the mason waited. When they had pulled her to the center of the room, the guards released her. Sinking down on her knees before her captors, the girl implored them to have pity.

In particular she addressed herself to the gray-haired man.

"By the Holy Name of the Father, please be merciful," she cried. Wrapping her arms around his knees, she begged for her life, sobbing and crying. The leader's only answer was to raise his hand as a signal. At once the other men dragged her toward the niche. The gray-haired man then told Abrantes to earn his money and begin his work. The poor mason, horror-stricken at what was going on, looked first at the niche and next at the struggling woman, and then back to the granite and mortar.

The woman appealed to Michael Abrantes. "Do not do this," she begged. "Please, I implore you. I wish to live!"

Immediately the men pulled their daggers and went to the mason. "We will cut you in pieces," said the ringleader, "unless you carry out that which you agreed to do. They bound and gagged the woman, after which they forced her into the niche. Her eyes, however, still focused on Abrantes.

Trembling, the poor man explained that he did not wish to be a party to a murder, but the gray-haired individual spoke at once.

"It's too late now. You had your chance to back out. It's either you and her or her alone. Make no mistake, we will kill you now if we have to. I order you to go on. Incidentally, to help your conscience, I've decided that your reward will be doubled.

"Besides, you cannot possibly know what you are talking about. This woman has committed an act which affects her family in such a way that she must be eliminated forever.

"She is not of New England, and what she has done cannot be undone. This does not concern you except that your talent as a mason is vital to our success.

"If you wish to stay alive, carry out your promise! Our time is short, as we must sail at dawn. Make up your mind. I'll give you one minute!"

Apparently with no alternative, the unwilling Abrantes picked up his trowel, dipped it into the bucket, and started his horrible task. Furtively he glanced into the niche at the woman, whose eyes still followed every move he made. Suddenly he realized the full significance of his act and he threw down the trowel.

"Nothing can make me continue. It's inhuman."

The others rushed at him. As soon as he was held firmly, the gray-haired leader confronted Abrantes.

"Do you really wish to die, Mr. Abrantes?"

The mason kept up his struggle only a few moments more, and then gave in. He realized the inevitability of doing what he had agreed to do. Now resigned to his fate, he picked up the trowel again and resumed his work.

Abrantes soon arranged the mortar to receive the first granite block. All the others assisted him as he guided the heavy stone into place. Then followed one stone after another, until two hours later the mason had almost completed his gruesome task. Again and again muffled shrieks came from behind the newly walled-up area. Finally the awesome act was completed, with the niche hermetically sealed with solid masonry. By this time the mason had memorized every contour of each granite block he had put back into the niche-like crypt.

Almost as in a dream Abrantes threw down his trowel, turning away from the location where he had walled up a live human being. The gray-haired man handed the mason his bag of gold and his aides quickly adjusted the bandage over Abrantes' face. Strong arms seized him and he was escorted from the room where the tragedy had taken place. Up and down through many passages, again to confuse him, he was hurried. Finally taken to the door of the building, Abrantes was led up the steps to the waiting carriage.

Again he was taken on a long trip of more than an hour. Then the vehicle stopped. Stepping out on a sidewalk, he heard a sharp command from inside the carriage, and the horses galloped away into the night. He still had his eyes covered, but he pulled the handkerchief off as fast as he could, just in time to see the carriage turning a corner a few streets away.

The night was far advanced; in fact morning was almost at hand. Stunned and bewildered by what he had witnessed and carried out, the mason went into his home, where he opened the money bag and found that it contained one thousand dollars in gold pieces.

He now sat down and drew from memory the side of the wall he had filled in with granite in sealing up the woman.

A very religious man, Abrantes decided to go to the pastor of the Old South Church, the Reverend Dr. Joseph Eckley, who was a man of culture and bearing. Since it was only seven o'clock in the morning, he had to wait a few hours before the day was advanced enough for calling on his religious adviser. At nine o'clock he presented himself at Dr. Eckley's parsonage, where he told the Doctor the entire story. Although Doctor Eckley did not show it, Abrantes had the feeling that the preacher was reluctant to accept what he heard. It is true that Abrantes occasionally was known to indulge in a drink or two, but he assured the minister it had been several days since he had taken even a drop.

"I know this sounds incredible, Dr. Eckley," said the mason, "but in addition to being cold sober I have the money at home to prove my tale and I don't know what to do. A woman is probably dying in a sealed-up room within a few miles of where we are. What can I do? What should I do?"

Dr. Eckley agreed that he and Abrantes should go to the authorities. That very afternoon the two men were closeted with a police inspector, who listened respectfully but also appeared to be skeptical of the account as the mason told it.

As a result of their conversation, the mason realized that his story was so improbable that few people would ever believe him. The official, although courteous in his attitude, asked so many questions that both the Reverend Dr. Eckley and Abrantes were convinced the policeman regarded what Abrantes told him as a dream and not a fact.

Nevertheless, in the next few hours a thorough investigation was carried out. Michael Abrantes knew that the woman could only live a relatively short time, walled up as she was, and that each hour brought nearer the moment of her death either by terror or suffocation.

However, the days became weeks, the weeks months, and the months years, but no further results developed. A generation later, when the certainty of the woman's death had long been realized by Abrantes, he still thought that the perpetrator of the crime should be punished. He would often walk around the streets of Boston, wondering if he might be in the vicinity of the body of the woman he had walled up in such a terrible manner. He had memorized the pattern of the granite wall he had worked on, and had drawn a sketch which he could use for comparison, but he never did find the wall.

The wall, incidentally, has recently been identified, but unfortunately for those who might like to break down the granite tiers and investigate the crypt, the owner of the property has asked me never to reveal where it is. He has, however, consented to my inclusion of Abrantes' sketch among the illustrations of this book.

3

The Wreck and Escape of
Dr. Johnson

New England has often sent missionaries into the far north. I have in my possession a copy of a manuscript written by Dr. William Johnson, a chaplain, who had a terrible experience in the year 1648, while on his way to impart Christianity to those who lived in Eskimo country. The following painfully interesting narrative of the perils and disasters attending a polar voyage is from Dr. Johnson's pen, and comes to us through the kindness of his New England collateral descendant—a Bostonian—who has chosen anonymity.

The chaplain embarked at Harwich on board an Ipswich vessel, the *William and John,* under the command of Daniel Morgan. Dr. Johnson does not explain in detail the purpose of his voyage, nor his exact destination, save that he went as a missionary in "the cause of religion."

From this we are led to believe that he was anxious to convert the natives who lived in the far North American area. I believe that we can all learn something from his amazing

story, written in the quaint language of three centuries ago.
Following is Dr. Johnson's journal:

"We embarked at Harwich on Michaelmas-day, the twenty-
ninth day of September, 1648. A dull kind of sadness op-
pressed my spirits, so that I could not look cheerfully on my
friends at parting, but I took leave of them as if I had been
going out of the world. This seemed unaccountable to me, for
I went on a good message—the cause of religion.

"I had embarked in a stout ship, with a fair wind and a
skillful pilot, so that I could not suspect danger. Yet no sooner
was I at sea, than I suffered the extreme of shipwreck, the
pain of sickness was so great and grievous, combining all
human evils, as it seemed, together, that to have been
drowned would have been no punishment.

"One afternoon, about four o'clock, the master of the ship
came into our cabin with more than ordinary haste; though
he concealed from me the cause, I saw plainly fear and amazement on his countenance. I asked him whether all was well;
to which he, like a tender-hearted man loth to tell his friend
he was near his end, answered 'All is well.'

"His clothes I saw him shift and hasten out again with
great speed; I then rose from my bed, and crawling upon deck,
beheld a melancholy spectacle; the ship having sprung a leak,
was ready to sink.

"How every man's face was changed with terror! We could
hardly know each other! One was at prayers, another wringing
his hands, and a third shedding tears; but, after this fit they
fell to work, though, as sometimes happens in such extremities, all were busy doing nothing. They began with one thing,
then went to another, but perfected nothing to accomplish
their safety.

"The master's mate, and a man who had been down to
search out the leak, returned with sad countenances, and pale

with fear. In faltering accounts, they signified that the leak was incurable, that it could not be stopped, and the water was rushing in so fast, we must instantly perish. They said nothing, however, that we did not read in their visages, where our fate was pictured.

"There was no time for consultation; the longboat was hoisted out, and guns discharged as a signal of distress to Bartholomew Cook, the master of a ship in company, only a little ahead. Trusting to relief, we leaped into the boat; but unfortunately I fell short, and with difficulty got out of the sea. No sooner had I secured myself, than a mariner leapt from the ship upon me, and crushed me down with his weight.

"This I did not regret, as I should willingly have borne them all to have saved their lives. There was only one person remaining on board, who made such grievous lamentations, that although the ship's sails now lay on the water, and her sinking would have drawn down the boat along with her, we approached and took him in.

"We now rowed clear of the ship, when not seeing Bartholomew Cook come to our relief, we began to talk reproachfully of them, as if he were negligent of our welfare; unhappily this honest master drank a deeper draught of affliction, for in that hour he and all his men had perished.

"Our hopes of safety were small. We were in the North Seas, which are seldom smooth, and at this time a storm raised the waves into mountains. How could we hope to escape in a small and open shallop, when a large ship had not been able to resist them? We were many leagues from shore, wanting a compass and provisions, and night was approaching, nothing was in the boat except a small kettle, which was used in baling out the water, and three bags of pieces of eight, to the value of 300 pounds sterling.

"Money was then truly proved to be only a burden of no worth. We betook ourselves to prayers, our complaints were louder than our invocations; but God had compassion on us, and we descried a vessel making towards the boat. Unfortunately having only two oars, we could make little effect on the boat, and the sea ran high. We sat with our backs to receive it, but it broke so much over us, that we had difficulty in clearing it out with the kettle.

"Notwithstanding all our endeavours, we could not reach the ship. She got before the wind and drove much faster than our little vessel could follow. Thus having death before our eyes, and at the same time the possibility of relief increased our distress.

"A dark night came on, which made us more desperate to reach the ship. The master of her hung out a light, and redoubling our energy, we began to get nearer. Lest he should think we were lost, as the darkness precluded him from seeing us, and therefore make sail, we gave a loud shout whenever we rose on top of a wave.

"At length by God's assistance, we drew very near the vessel, and not to endanger our safety from too much haste, resolved to go up the side regularly, and in the same order in which we sat. However, we had no sooner arrived, than all strove to run up at once, and the seamen being more dexterous in the art of climbing, accomplished it in a moment, leaving me alone in the boat.

"I was now in the greatest danger, for besides a natural weakness in my hands, they were so benumbed with cold and set, that I was incapable of climbing up a rope, though my existence depended upon it. Nevertheless, I held fast by one which they threw out, with both my hands, to prevent the boat from staving off; and, while doing so, the boat struck three times against the ship's side, owing to the heavy sea, and as often the shock threw me down to the bottom, which was half full of water.

"Fortunately, the boat did not give way, and two seamen

at length came down to assist me up the ship's side, which the weight of my clothes, and weakness, had prevented; a rope with a noose was handed down by one of them, who directed me to put it about my middle; but he began to pull when I had got it over one shoulder, and nearly drew me overboard.

"Having secured myself, and the boat casting off, I was drawn through the sea, where I had the narrowest escape; for the seaman having neglected to tie the rope, as he afterwards told me in England, it was prevented from slipping by a knot, which was by chance at the end, otherwise I must have gone down. I may truly say there was not an inch between me and death. The next pull stunned me against the side of the ship.

"When I came to myself the following morning, I found the master's own cabin had been devoted to my service. Though severely bruised, I rose from my bed to make inquiries concerning my fellow-sufferers, and found them, contrary to my expectation, overcome with sorrow. Their looks were dejected, and every man brooding over his misfortunes. The truth is, that, having saved their lives, they now had leisure to think of the loss of their goods, though it bore differently on different individuals.

"For my own part, the losses I then suffered involved me in debt, from which I have not yet extricated myself. But what grieved me most, was being deprived of my library, and all my sermons, as also my notes and observations, during my travels abroad, the fruits of many years' labor and study. But it was impious to grieve for such losses, when God had so miraculously preserved our lives.

"Next day, which was Tuesday, the wind was fair for Norway, whither our ship, which was a Howzoner, was bound. About twelve o'clock we came in sight of the coast, rugged and full of rocks; and as we could not reach it during daylight, we designed to stand off and on till morning.

"We then sat down to a repast. Some of us had taken no

sustenance since being at sea, and I myself, having ate nothing for five days, now made a hearty meal.

"About ten at night, when we had set our watch and prayed, and then laid ourselves down to rest, the ship, in full sail, struck on a rock with a shock so great that it awakened the soundest sleeper. Though I was ignorant of what had happened, the mariners better aware of the danger, loudly cried, 'Mercy! Mercy! Mercy!'

"I hastened out of my cabin, and, coming on deck, met the master of our own vessel, who, while tears streamed down his cheeks, desired me to pray for them, for we should all perish. I could not but believe the truth of what he said; so falling on my knees, like a condemned person awaiting the stroke of the executioner, I began to pray.

"But, after having prayed some time, under perfect resignation to death, I wondered that the waves did not overwhelm us. It had pleased God that the ship ran herself so fast between two ledges of rock with her over another, that she stood fixed as firm as the rock itself.

"I immediately rose and pulled off my coat, designing to throw myself into the sea and swim ashore; but the height of the waves breaking against the rocks deterred me. The stern of the vessel was soon beat in by the sea, which compelled us to retreat towards the bow, when Matthew Bird, the same seaman who had formerly drawn me on board, leapt ashore with a rope in his hand, and held it so securely, one end being tied to the mast, that another seaman got down by it. In this manner, the whole of our company, and some of the Danes who were eight and twenty in number, reached the rock in safety.

"All this time I was ignorant of the means used for our deliverance; but perceiving the people crowd toward the head of the ship, I also repaired thither, and discovered what had taken place. A Dane was then trying to slide down the rope and carry a small leather trunk along with him, but he presently removed his trunk, and desired me to descend. I repaid his kindness by requesting him to do so first, not so much out of compliment, but that I might know how to slide down, as I had seen none go before me. However, I got on the rope, from which I was almost beat by the waves, and came safely to the side of the rock, whence I crawled on hands and feet to the rest who were ashore.

"I was the last who accomplished this manner of escaping. The ship at this moment began to give way, which the master, who was still on board, perceiving, earnestly implored us to assist him with our utmost endeavours; but she broke up immediately and went down. Thus was that good man, and four of the mariners drowned. I observed the master, who had a light in his hand, fall into the sea. It was the saddest sight I ever beheld, to see him who had saved our lives, lose his own. I cannot even now look back upon it without regret. Perhaps, had he not delayed on our account, he might have reached the haven in safety.

"We did not know where the rock which had received us was situated. Some of the people before my arrival had ascertained it to be an island, but uninhabited. We waited the rising of the sun in hopes of discovering land in the neighborhood. It was a long and melancholy night, for stones make but a hard pillow, besides having thrown off my coat when intending to swim, I was thinly clad.

"Wandering up and down the rock, I often fell owing to it slipperiness; and without shoes, my feet were cut with the sharp stones. This being winter time, the cold was extremely piercing.

"At length we found a hole in the rock, which sheltered us from the wind, and then morning broke. During the twilight we flattered ourselves that every black cloud was land; but when the sun rose, we saw nothing except a glimpse of the coast of Norway at a distance. When I viewed the sea and the place, the sight of so many hundred of rocks surrounding us, struck me with amazement.

"It was only from God's providence that we had not gone among the breakers during the night, and under full sail, instead of running between the two ledges, which proved asylum. Had we touched in any other part, we must have instantly perished.

"Our sole hope of relief was the approach of some ship, from which we might be seen; but of this I thought there was little prospect; for should one accidentally come by day, she would be deterred by the surrounding dangers, from giving us succour; and if she came in the night, she would certainly be wrecked like our own vessel. Having seen nothing in the course of the whole day, we began to despair; and wanting sustenance to support us, and hardly having clothes to keep us warm, we crept into a hole of the rock, and there rested during the second night.

"Next morning we arose before the sun, and some of our company searching with their arms in the sea, drew out small muscles, which they ate heartily; and one of the boys brought me a leaf of scurvy-grass: but I began to be sick with a feverish complaint, and became so parched with thirst, that I would have given all I had for a draught of fresh water.

"Trusting that the water which stood in holes would be freshest in the highest part of the rock, I sought for it, but it proved salt; I drank it, however, until my thirst was quenched, though vomiting followed, which I am persuaded preserved my life.

"Between ten and eleven we saw a ship in full sail standing towards us, which lifted up our hearts with joy. She came nearer and nearer, and we all ascended to the top of the rock, and waved our hats to show ourselves to the men on board.

But they neither approached nor sent their boat to learn our condition, for what reason we knew not.

"The captain was a Dane, of the same country with our former kind master. As the ship receded our hearts began to fail, and our countenances changed to their former paleness. We conceived ourselves utterly abandoned. We could not suppose, even should another ship by chance come in sight, that the mariners would venture their own lives to save ours. Therefore we betook ourselves to our old devotions, and as long as I was able to speak, I prayed with the company.

"After some exhortation to my fellow-sufferers I lay down on the rock, thinking I should rise no more in this world; but I overheard one of the seamen, he who had first leaped on the rock, say 'Let us make a raft and venture to sea, I had rather be drowned than lie here and be starved.' The rest coincided with him, and though the design was full of danger, everything conspired to favor it.

"The water had at this time fallen, and left the bottom of the ship on the rock, the anchors, mast, and sails, lying there also, like linen on a hedge. The seamen soon broke up the mast, and untwisted a cable for small cords. Next they tied four or five boards to the broken mast, got up the mizen-top-mast, and made a slight stern. Then having cut out a small sail, two Danes and two Englishmen embarked on the raft.

"A moderate breeze carried the adventurers safely through the breakers, and towards that part, where according to supposition, the coast lay. We followed them as far as our eyes could reach, with great anxiety, for the hope of our deliverance rested on their safety. But we did not long remain in suspense, for before night their security was announced by several yawls rowing toward us.

"They brought provisions likewise, which we little regarded, from our eagerness to get on shore. The rock where we were now situated was called Arnscare; and by God's goodness, having embarked we reached an island in Norway, named Waller Island by its inhabitants. This island is so inconsiderable, that Ortelius overlooks it in his maps, but, although unworthy to be remembered by him, it ought not to be forgotten by us. There was but one house where we landed, belonging to the parson, an honest Lutheran, whose family consisted of many individuals all of whom showed us no little kindness. They spoke the Norse language, which I think resembles the Dutch, for those of us who spoke Dutch could partly understand them, and make ourselves understood.

"When we made a shift to explain our misfortunes to the people of the house, the relation drew tears from their eyes; and whatever provisions they had being now set before us, the seamen soon repaired their long fasting.

"The ordinary bread of the inhabitants was rye pancakes, and they had beer which was very strong. This reminded me of the English proverb, 'A cup of good beer is meat, drink, and clothing,' and surely these people thought so, for though at such a cold season, while they had neither stockings nor shoes, they kept themselves warm with beer.

"Next morning, we began to examine each other's finances, to discover what money had been saved from the shipwreck. Suspecting concealment in one of our number, we searched him, and found no less than four-and-twenty pieces of eight, which he undoubtedly stole from our bags in the boat, after our first shipwreck; when every moment we looked for destruction. It was well for us he had done so, for in the second all our money was lost.

"We remained in the island until Sunday, and in the morning heard our landlord preach, after which he gave us a meal, full of variety in one dish, as beef, mutton, goat and roots, mixed together, according to the custom here.

"We then parted with the good old priest, having returned him many thanks, accompanied with a little money; and travelled to Fredericstadt, a city in Norway on the coast. There we were kindly entertained by the burgomaster, whose chief discourse was in praise of the late Archbishop of Canterbury, though I wonder how he came to know him.

"Truly we were much indebted to this person, for he not only commanded several persons of the city to entertain us civilly, but gave us some provision at his own charge. Everywhere we experienced great civility, and the people ran after us in the streets to bestow what we needed, without asking.

"Having left Fredericstadt, we repaired to Oster Sound, three or four miles distant, where shipping lay, and laid in as much provision as our stock could afford, into one bound for England. We embarked in the evening. In the morning before making sail, a ship from Lynn, in Norfolk, coming in, was wrecked on the rocks near the harbor. We had not been at sea more than three or two hours when great alarm arose from the ship very nearly striking on a half-sunken rock, unseen until almost touching it. But about noon we cleared all the rocks on the Norwegian coast.

"A fair wind brought us in view of the English coast, near Winterton, after four or five days' sail. There we saw the remains of a shipwreck and the country people enriching themselves with the spoils. At length having reached Yarmouth Roads we came to an anchor. It began to blow hard, and the ship in driving, nearly ran foul of a Scotchman. But we brought up again, and rode securely through the night. On a signal next morning for a pilot, four men came off from Yarmouth.

"They demanded no less than thirty shilling to carry me, a single person, on shore, while our whole stock was only two pieces of eight, and although I did long for land, I could not purchase it at such a rate, therefore they were content to take less.

"But no sooner had I got into the boat, than they rowed up and down to weigh anchors, for the storm during the preceeding night, had occasioned many ships to part with their cables. Nevertheless they were unsuccessful, and then made for the shore.

"The landing-place was so bad, that four other men awaiting the arrival of the boat, ran up to their middle in the sea, and dragged it on the beach.

"I thence got into the town of Yarmouth, with a company of people at my heels, wondering at my sad and ragged condition. The host of an inn, with a sign, the arms of Yarmouth, treated me with uncommon kindness, and I hope God will reward him for it."

4

Three Pirates of Marblehead

In previous books I have mentioned the careers of two of the three sailors included in this chapter. Now for the first time, as no one living can possibly be embarrassed, I will give the complete stories of all three men of eighteenth-century Marblehead, Massachusetts, Joseph Libbey, Nicholas Merritt, and Philip Ashton. Never before in any book have I given Libbey's sad life history. Actually, Libbey was a pirate, but in my opinion both Merritt and Ashton were honest men, although British law in 1722 would classify them technically in the piratical category.

During the late spring of the year 1722, Merritt, Ashton, and Libbey, all from Marblehead, were aboard fishing vessels off the shores of Cape Sable, Nova Scotia. On Friday, June 15, without warning, pirate Captain Edward Low's brigantine descended on the Marblehead fishermen and captured twelve of their vessels. The three sailors mentioned above were among those asked to sign articles with the pirate chieftain.

When Ashton refused, he was thrown below. Two days later, on Sunday, June 17, Ashton was brought up on deck.

With five others, Nicholas Merritt, Laurence Fabens, Joseph Libbey, and two men whose names are not known, Ashton was taken across in a small boat to Low's brigantine, where they all were lined up on the quarter deck. All six were under twenty-one years of age.

Captain Ned Low approached them, pistol in hand.

"Are any of you married men?" asked Low. The question, unexpected as it was, struck the listeners dumb at the moment. The silence infuriated the great pirate, and he cocked his pistol, shoving it against Philip Ashton's head.

"You dog," cried Low. "Why don't you answer me? I shall shoot you through the head unless you . . . tell me now if you are married or not."

Ashton, greatly frightened, stammered that he was not married, and the rest of the group also answered that they were still single. Low then walked away from them. Ashton later learned that the pirate's concern was due to Low's wife having died, leaving a small child who even then was living at Boston.

Later in the day Low again interview the six men, asking them to sign papers, and all six refused. Still later he had each man sent for, singly, whereupon he asked again. Each fisherman again refused. Then Philip Ashton was taken below into the steerage, where Quartermaster Russel tried to tempt him with stories of great riches and wealth. Other pirates gathered about Ashton and tried to be friendly, to win his confidence, and asked him to

> Drink with them, not doubting but that this wile would sufficiently entangle me, and so they should prevail with me to do that in my Cups, which they perceived they could not bring me to do while I was Sober; but . . . I had no Inclination to drown my Sorrows with my Senses in their Inebriating Bowls, and so refused their Drink, as well as their Proposals.

After his final refusal Ashton was taken up on deck again, where Captain Low threatened him with death unless he changed his mind. Ashton said that whatever happened he could not join the pirate band, but finally Low signed him on anyway as a pirate, but as a forced man, and added the names of all his companions to the list.

The following Tuesday the buccaneers chose a schooner * belonging to Joseph Dolliber of Marblehead as the new flagship, and all the pirates went aboard her. With the exception of the six forced men and four others who had joined from the Isles of Shoals, the prisoners were sent over to the brigantine and allowed to proceed to Boston. This was discouraging to Philip Ashton, who made one final attempt to appeal for freedom. Together with Nicholas Merritt he went to Low, and the two young men fell on their knees before the pirate captain, asking for release. Low scornfully refused, telling them if they attempted to break away they would be shot. The brigantine soon sailed off, and the forced sailors were alone with the highwaymen of the sea.

Just as Ashton had given up all thought of deliverance, an accident occurred that gave him hope. One of the pirates had come back to the ship after leaving a dog on the beach, and the dog began to howl dismally. Low, hearing the disturbance, ordered that the dog be brought out. Two Marblehead boys volunteered to row in and get him, and nineteen-year-old Philip Ashton decided this was a good chance to escape. He rushed to the side of the ship and was about to jump into the

---

* In this chapter I have reason to mention several types of sailing vessels with which the average reader may not be familiar. For example, a brigantine is a sailing craft of two masts having its foremast square-rigged and its mainmast rigged fore and aft. In contrast a brig has both masts square-rigged.

A schooner is a fore and aft rigged vessel of more than one mast, and a sloop is a craft of one mast rigged fore and aft with one jib.

A pinkie is a vessel with a narrow stern, and a shallop is any small, open boat propelled by sails and oars. A frigate of the period was a ship-rigged war vessel intermediate between a corvette and a ship-of-the-line.

boat, when the quartermaster caught hold of his shoulder, saying that two men were sufficient to bring out one dog.

Surely enough, the pirates watched the boat land on the shore and the Marblehead men walk inland away from it. They never returned, and the pirates lost their boat as well, while the dog soon wandered off and was not seen again. Of course, the quartermaster now believed that Ashton had tried to join the two, knowing that they had planned to escape, but the truth was that while Ashton had planned to escape himself, he did not know the other two had the same objective. Nevertheless, the quartermaster was so infuriated that he attempted to kill Ashton then and there.

Seizing Ashton by the shoulder, he clapped his great pistol against the boy's skull and pulled the trigger, but the gun missed fire. Again and again the quartermaster snapped the pistol, but each time it failed to go off. Disgusted with his firearm, the quartermaster went over to the side of the ship. Standing by the rail, he reset the pistol, pulled the trigger, and aimed the gun into the ocean. It fired successfully. The exasperated pirate now drew his cutlass and lunged for the boy. Terrified, Ashton ran down into the hold, where he cowered in the midst of a group of the other pirates, and thus escaped the quartermaster's wrath.

It was a hard lot that lay ahead for the Marblehead lad, and he soon learned to hide in the hold most of the time. Once a week, however, he was brought up under examination and asked to sign articles, and every time he refused. Thrashed and beaten with sword and cane after each refusal, Ashton would escape to the hold as soon as he could to nurse his cuts and bruises for another week. Probably some of the kinderhearted rogues took care of this poor lad in their crude way, so that he was able to get something to eat every day.

But as the weeks went by despair made Ashton utterly miserable. In the book he wrote later, Ashton speaks of Low's narrow escape from an encounter with a British man-of-war in the harbor of St. John's, Newfoundland, telling of the seizure of seven or eight vessels the next day. Later a captured sloop manned by impressed pirates ran away from Low and was never seen again. Nicholas Merritt, mentioned above, was aboard this vessel. The schooner and a captured pinkie were careened at the island of Bonavista, after which seven or eight forced men from the pinkie went ashore to hunt. They never returned to the ship. Ashton felt that with so many escaping from Low, his chance would eventually come, and in this he was not mistaken.

A terrible storm caught the pirates shortly afterward, and for five days and nights Ashton feared that they would all go to the bottom. Even the most foul of the buccaneers was afraid during the fearful tempest, as Ashton recorded one of the bloodthirsty ruffian's exclaiming in his particular moment of spiritual anguish, "Oh! I wish I were at Home."

At last the storm went down, and the pirates headed for the three islands called the Triangles, located in the West Indies about forty leagues from Surinam. Captain Low decided that another careening was necessary. In heaving down the pinkie, so many hands climbed into the shrouds that it threw her open ports under water. Low and the doctor, then below in the cabin, almost drowned but managed to get out in time. The vessel went over on her beam ends in forty feet of water, throwing the men into the sea. As the vessel righted itself, the men climbed back into the shrouds. The entire hull remained far under water. It had been a narrow escape for the notorious Captain Low.

In the excitement two men drowned, and Ashton, who was a poor swimmer, almost perished before he was rescued. The pinkie had carried most of the provisions and the drinking water, both of which were lost, so every sailor transferred to the schooner, which at once put out to sea.

Reaching the island of Grand Grenada, eighteen leagues westward of Tobago, they went ashore for water. The French on the island suspected them of being in the smuggling trade, so sailed out to capture Low and his men. When Low saw them coming, he ordered all the pirates to their stations, and the French sloop was quickly seized and made one of the pirate fleet. The buccaneers captured seven or eight vessels in short order, after which they took two sloops off Santa Cruz.

Saturday, March 9, 1723, was an eventful and thrilling day for Philip Ashton of Marblehead. Noticing the cooper with six men getting ready to row ashore, he asked to be taken with them, for he had not been on land since his capture almost nine months before. Since the island was desolate and uninhabited, the cooper finally gave in to the desperate pleadings of the lad from Marblehead, and into the long boat jumped young Philip. As it happened, Ashton had asked the cooper on the impulse of the moment, and was dressed

> with only an Ozenbrigs Frock and Trousers on, and a Mill'd Cap upon my Head, having neither Shirt, Shoes, not Stockings, nor any thing else about me; whereas, had I been aware of such an Opportunity, but one quarter of an Hour before, I could have provided my self something better. However, thought I, if I can but once get footing on Terra-Firma, tho' in never so bad Circumstances, I shall call it a happy Deliverance; for I was resolved, come what would, never to come on board again.

When the long boat landed, Ashton was the most active worker of all in moving the heavy casks up on the beach, so when the task was over he naturally went off by himself as if to rest, strolling along the beach, picking up stones and shells as we all do along the seashore, until he was quite a distance from the others. Then he walked toward the edge of the

woods, whereupon the cooper called out to him, asking where
he was going.

"I'm going to get some coconuts," was Ashton's reply, and
he soon reached the forest. Once out of sight of the pirates, he
broke out in a keen run, possibly resembling Stevenson's hero
in *Treasure Island*, for whom he may have served as a model.

In the meantime the pirates had filled the water casks and
were ready to return to the ship. Ashton huddled in the dense
forest, burrowing into a thicket, while the cries sounded out
around him, calling him back to the long boat. Ashton kept
a discreet silence. After a long time, the pirates gave up and
rowed out to their ship.

Philip Ashton was thus left alone on a desolate and uninhabited island. When he was sure the pirates had left him, he
ventured forth from his hiding place, appearing down on the
beach about a mile from the watering place, where he could
observe what went on aboard the pirate vessels. Five days later
they sailed away, leaving him alone. His thoughts follow:

> I began to reflect upon myself, and my present Condi-
> tion; I was upon an island from whence I could not get off;
> I knew of no Humane Creature within many scores of Miles
> of me; I had but a Scanty Cloathing, and no possibility of
> getting more; I was destitute of all Provision for my Sup-
> port, and knew not how I should come at any. . . .

Philip Ashton was destined to remain on the island alone
until one day in June 1724, when he was overjoyed to sight
two large canoes approaching the shore. When they landed,
the men seemed friendly, and Ashton went down to greet
them.

The visitors found a "Poor, Ragged, Lean, Wan, Forlorn,
Wild, Miscrable" man, who explained that he had been on
the island alone for sixteen months!

The men gave Ashton a small drink of rum, whereupon the islander fell down insensible. Later he revived to tell them of his unfortunate adventures, beginning with his trials and tribulations at the time of his capture by pirate Low.

The men decided to move in with Ashton, and they built a substantial dwelling on the island. After it was finished, they named it the Castle of Comfort. Several families joined them soon afterward. Six months later the pirates appeared. The islanders fled into the woods, but not before the pirates killed one man, burned him, and then captured several other people whom they took aboard their ship.

One day at the height of the season for the Jamaica traders, Ashton noticed a large fleet of vessels offshore. Three Englishmen came in from a brigantine in a longboat and he told them he was "an Englishman run away from pirates." Amazingly, the brigantine from which the men had landed was from Salem, Massachusetts, less than three miles from Ashton's home. The men invited Ashton to join the crew and sail back to Salem.

Weeks later the brigantine came abeam of Half Way Rock, Massachusetts Bay, and soon landed in Salem. Ashton had been away for two years, ten months, and fifteen days. Journeying at once to his home in Marblehead, he found that his family had given him up for lost. The homecoming was a joyful one.

Although I knew of the existence of the manuscript of Philip Ashton's fellow townsman Nicholas Merritt, the pages of this chapter are the first in which I have been able to include Merritt's full account of his own escape from the pirates:

"I was taken by the Pirate Low, at Port-Rossaway, at the same time my Kinsman Philip Ashton was; and while I continued under Low's Custody was used much as he was; and all my entreaties of him to free me were but in vain; I shall not enlarge in telling how it fared with me under the Pirates hands, but only give some short Account of the manner of my Escape from them, and what I met with afterwards till I Arrived at Marblehead, where I belong.

"Low had with him the Rose Pink, the Scooner, and a Sloop taken from one Pier of Bristol, and was standing away for Bonavista. I who was on board the Scooner had been greatly abused by an old Pirate, whom they called Jacob, but what his Sirname was I know not: I desired some that were upon occasion going on board Low, to acquaint him how much I was beat and abused by old Jacob; they did so; and Low ordered me to be put aboard the Sloop. Thus the Foundation of my Escape was lay'd, and my Sufferings proved the means of my deliverance.

"On board the Sloop there were Nine hands, (one of them a Portugue) whom Low had no Suspicion of, but thought he could trust them as much as any Men he had; and when I came on board I made the Tenth Man. We perceived that the Sloop greatly wronged both the Pink and Scooner, and there Six of us (as we found by sounding one another at a distance) that wanted to get away. When we understood one anothers minds pretty fully, we resolved upon an Escape. Accordingly the Fifth of September, 1722, a little after break of Day, all hands being upon Deck, three of us Six went forward, and three aft, and one John Rhodes, who was a Stout hand, step'd into the Cabbin and took a couple of Pistols in his hands, and stood in the Cabin Door, and said, If there were any that would go along with him, they should be welcome, for he designed to carry the Sloop home, and Surrender himself; but if any Man attempted to make resistance, he Swore he would shoot down the first Man that stirred.

"There being five of us that wanted to gain our Liberty, he was sure of us; and as for the other four they saw plainly it was in vain for them to attempt to oppose us. So we haled close upon a Wind, and stood away.

"When we parted with Low, we had but a very little Water aboard, and but two or three pieces of Meat among us all; but we had Bread eno'. We designed for England; but our want of Water was so great, being put to half a Pint a Man, and that very muddy and foul, from the time we parted with Low, and meeting with no Vessel of whom we could beg a Supply, that it made us come to a Resolution, to put in at the first Port: so we Steered for St. Michales, where we arrived September 26.

"So soon as we got in, we sent a Man or two ashoar, to inform who we were, and to get us some Provisions and Water. The Consul who was a French Protestant, with a Magistrate, and some other Officers came on board us, to whom we gave an Account of our selves, and our Circumstances.

"The Consul told us, there should not a Hair of our Heads be hurt. Upon which we were all carried ashoar, and examined before the Governor; but we understood nothing of their Language, and could make him no Answer, till one Mr. Gould a Linguistor was brought to us; and upon understanding our Case, the Governor cleared us. But the Crusidore, a sort of superintendent over the Islands, whose power was Superiour to the Governours refused to clear us, and put us in Jayl, where we lay 24 Hours.

"The next Day we were brought under Examination again, and then we had for our Linguistor one Mr. John Curre, who had formerly been in New-England. We gave them as full and distinct Account as we could, where, and when, we were severally taken and how we had made our Escape from the Pirates. They brought several Witnesses Portuguese against us, as that we had taken them, and had Personally been Active in the Caption and Abuse of them, which yet they agreed not in; only they generally agreed that they heard some of us Curse the Virgin Mary, upon which the Curisdore would have condemned us all for Pirates.

"But the Governour, who thought we had acted the honest part, interposed on our behalf, and said, that it was very plain, that if these Men had been Pirates, they had no need to have left Low, and under such Circumstances, and come in here, and resign themselves as they did; they could have stayed with their Old Companions, and have been easily eno' supplied with what they wanted; whereas their taking the first opportunity to get away from their Commander, and so poorly accommodated, was a proof to him, that we had no Piratical designs; and if he (the Crusidore) treated us at this rate, it was the way to make us, and all that had the unhappiness to fall into Pirates hands, turn Pirates with them.

"Yet all he could say would not wholly save us from the Angry Resentments of the Crusidore, who we thought was inflamed by the Portague that was among us. So he committed us all to Prison again: me with three others to the Castle, the rest to another Prison at some considerable distance off; and so much pains was taken to Swear us out of our Lives, that I altogether despaired of Escaping the Death of a Pirate; till a Gentleman, Capt. Littleton (if I mistake not) told me it was not in their power to hang us, and this comforted me a little.

"In this Prison we lay for about four Months, where, at first we had tolerable allowance, of such as it was, for our Subsistance; but after three Months time they gave us only one Meal a Day, of Cabbage, Bread, and Water boiled together which they called Soop. This very scanty allowance put us out of Temper, and made us resolve rather than Starve, to break Prison, and make head against the Portuguese, and get some Victuals; for Hunger will break thro' Stone Walls.

"The Governour understanding how we fared, told the Crusidor that we should stay in his Prison no longer, as the

Castle peculiarly was; and greatly asserted our Cause, and urged we might be set at Liberty; but the Crusidore would not hearken as yet to the clearing us, tho' he was forced to remove us from the Castle, to the Prison in which our Comrades were, where they put us down into close Confinement; tho' our allowance was a small matter better than it had been.

"Under all this Difficulty of Imprisonment, short allowance, and hard fare, false Witnesses, and fear lest I should still have my Life taken from me, (when I had flattered myself, that if I could but once set Foot upon a Christian shoar, I should be out of the reach of Danger) I had a great many uneasy Reflections.

"I thought no bodies case was so hard as mine; first to be taken by the Pirates, and threatened with Death for not Joyning with them; to be forced away, and suffer many a drubbing Bout among them for not doing as they would have me; to be in fears of Death for being among them, if we should be taken by any Superiour force; and now that I had designedly, and with Joy, made my Escape from them, to be Imprisoned and threatened with the Halter.

"Thought I, When can a Man be safe? He must look for Death to be found among Pirates; and Death seems as threatening, if he Escapes from them; where is the Justice of this! It seemed an exceeding hardship to me. Yet it made me Reflect, with Humility I hope, on the Justice of GOD in so Punishing of me for my Transgressions; for tho' the tender Mercies of Man seemed to be Cruelty, yet I could not but see the Mercy and Goodness of GOD to me, not only in Punishing me less than I deserved, but in preserving me under many and sore Temptations, and at length delivering me out of the Pirates hands; and I had some hope that GOD would yet appear for me, and bring me out of my distress, and set my Feet in a large place.

"I thought my Case was exceedingly like that of the Psalmist; and the Meditation on some Verses in the XXV. Psalm was a peculiar support to me: I thought I might say with him, False Witnesses did rise up, they laid to my charge things that I knew not; they rewarded me evil for good.

"But as for me, when they were taken (tho' I don't remember I had ever seen the Faces of any of them then) I humbled my self, and my Prayer returned into my own bosom; I behaved my self as tho' they had been my friends, I bowed down heavily, as one that mourneth for his mother; but in my adversity they rejoyced, and gathered themselves together against me; yea, they opened their mouth wide against me,—they gnashed upon me with their teeth, and said Aba, Aba, our eye hath seen it,—so would we have it.

"But Lord how long wilt thou look on? preserve my Soul from their Destruction, let not them that are mine Enemies wrongfully rejoyce over me,—cause, my God and my Lord, and let them not rejoyce over me—and I will give thee thanks in the great Congregation; my tongue shall speak of thy Righteousness, and thy Praise all the day long.

"In the midst of all my other Calamities, after I had been in this Prison about two Months, I was taken down with the Small-Pox, and this to be sure was a very great addition to my Misery. I knew well how we dreaded this Distemper in my own Country; and thought I, how can I possibly escape with Life?

"To be seised with it in a Prison, where I had no Help, no Physician, nor any Provision suitable therefore; only upon my first being taken I sent word of it to the Consul, who was so kind as to send some Bundles of Straw for me to lye upon, instead of the hard Stones which as yet had been my Lodging; and the Portuguese gave me some Brandy, and Wine & Water to drive out the Pock.

"I was exceedingly dejected, and had nothing to do but to commit my self to the Mercy of GOD, and prepare my self for Death, which seemed to have laid hold upon me; for which way soever I looked, I could see nothing but Death in such a Distemper, under such Circumstances; and I could see the Portuguese how they stared upon me, looked sad, and shook their heads; which told me their apprehensions, that I was a Dead Man. Yet I had this comfort, that it was better to Die thus by the hand of GOD, than to Die a vile Death by the hand of Man, as if I had been one of the worst of Male-factors.

"But after all it pleased GOD in His Wonderful Goodness so to order it, that the Pock came out well, and filled kindly and then I had the comfort of seeing the Portuguese look more pleasant, and hearing them say, in their Language, that it was a good sort. In about five or six Days the Pock began to turn upon me, and then it made me very Sick, and at times I was something out of my Head; and having no Tender or Watcher, I got up in the Night to the Pail of Water to drink, which at another time, and in another place, would have been thought fatal to me; but GOD in infinite Mercy prevented my receiving any hurt thereby, and raised me up from this Sickness.

"After I recovered of this Illness, I was but in a weak Con-dition for a long time, having no other Nourishment and Comfort, than what a Jayl afforded, where I still lay for near three Months longer. At length, sometime in June, 1723, I was taken out of jayl, and had the Liberty of the Consul's House given me, who treated me kindly and did not suffer me to want any thing that was necessary for my Support.

"While I was at Liberty, I understood there was one John Welch, an Irishman, bound to Lisbon, whom I desired to carry me thither. And in the latter end of June I set Sail in him for Lisbon, where we Arrived about the middle of July, after we have been 21 Days upon the Passage. When I had got to Lisbon, being almost Naked, I apply'd my self to the Envoy, told him my Condition and desired him to bestow some old Cloaths upon me.

"But he, (Good Man!) said to me, that as I had Run away from the Pirates, I might go to Work for my Support, and provide my self with Cloaths as well as I could. And I found I must do so, for none would he give me. I had nothing against Working, but I should have been glad to have been put into a Working Garb; for I was sensible it would be a considerable while before I could purchase me any Cloaths, because Welch play'd me such a Irish trick, that he would not release me, unless I promised to give him the first Moidore I got by my Labour; tho' I had wroght for him all however when I came to Sail for New-England, Welch was better than his Word, and forgave me the Moidore, after I had been at the Labour of unloading his Vessel.

"I spent some time in Lisbon; at length heard there was one Capt. Skillegorne bound to New-England, in whom I took my Passage home; who Clothed me for my Labour in my Passage. We touched in at Madara, and Arrived at Boston upon Wednesday, September 25, 1723. And I at my Father's House in Marblehead the Saturday after.

"So had GOD been with me in six troubles, and in seven. He has suffered no evil to come nigh me. He has drawn me out of the Pit, Redeemed my Life from Destruction, and Crowned me with Loving Kindness and Tender Mercies; until Him be the Glory for ever. Amen."

Lest the good citizens of Marblehead rush to their defense, I repeat that both Ashton and Merritt can only technically be classified as pirates. However, another Marbleheader captured with them by Low, Joseph Libbey, evidently made no effort to escape "the brethren" and eventually was won over to becoming a dyed-in-the-wool pirate. As a favor to a collateral descendant, I have refrained from telling of his unfortunate career until now, as the descendant only recently died.

Joseph Libbey at first served the pirates unwillingly. Having been with Low in the *Rose* frigate, Libbey had saved Ashton's life by pulling the youth from the water when the frigate had been careened in the spring of 1723. Libbey then served with Low's consort, Captain Charles Harris, in the sloop *Ranger*.

By this time he was an out-and-out pirate.

On the morning of June 10, 1723, Libbey was still aboard the *Ranger* when a large ship was sighted off Block Island. Captain Low, in company with the *Ranger* aboard the *Fortune,* signaled for Harris to join him and chase the strange craft. All that day and early into the next morning the chase continued.

What happened next can best be quoted from the Boston *News Letter* for June 20, 1723:

"Rhode Island, June 12. On the 11th Instant arrived here His Majesty's Ship *Grayhound,* Capt. Peter Solgard Commander, from his Cruize at Sea and brought in a Pirate Sloop of 8 Guns, Barmudas built, 42 White Men and 6 Blacks, of which number eight were wounded in the Engagement and four killed; the Sloop was commanded by one Harris, very well fitted, and loaded with all sorts of Provisions: One of the wounded Pirates died, on board of the Man of War, with an Oath on his Departure; thirty lusty bold young Fellows, were brought on shore, and received by one of the Town Companys under Arms guarding them to the Goal, and all are now in Irons under a strong Guard. The Man of War had but two Men wounded, who are in a brave way of Recovery.

"Here follows an Account (from on board of the Man of War) of the Engagement between Capt. Solgard and the two Pirates Sloops: Capt. Solgard being informed by a Vessel, that Low the Pirate, in a Sloop of 10 Guns and 70 Men, with his

Consort of 8 Guns and 48 Men, had sailed off the East End
of Long-Island; The Capt. thereupon steered his Course after
them; and on the 10th Currant, half an hour past 4 in the
Morning we saw two Sloops N.2 Leagues distance, the Wind
W.N.W.

"At 5 we tack'd and stood Southward, and clear'd the Ship,
the Sloops giving us Chase, at half an hour past 7 we tack'd
to the Northward, with little Wind, and stood down to them;
at 8 a Clock they each fired a Gun, and hoisted a Black
Flag; at half an hour past 8 on the near approach of the Man
of War, they haul'd it down, (fearing a Tartar) and put up a
Bloody Flag, stemming with us distant 3 quarters of a Mile:

"We hoisted up our Main-Sail and made easy Sail to the
Windward, received their Fire several times; but when a
breast we gave them ours with round & grape Shot, upon
which the head Sloop edg'd Away, as did the other soon after,
and we with them.

"The Fire continued on both sides for about an hour; but
when they hall'd from us with the help of their Oars, we left
off Firing, and turned to Rowing with 86 Hands and half an
Hour past Two in the Afternoon we came up with them;
when they clapt on a Wind to receive us; we again kept close
to Windward, and ply'd them warmly with small and grape
shot; and during the Action we fell between them, and having shot down one of the Main Sails we kept close to him, and
at 4 a Clock he call'd for Quarters; at 5 having got the Prisoners on board, we continued to Chase the other Sloop, when
at 8 a Clock in the evening he bore from us N.W. by W. two
Leagues, when we lost sight of him near Block Island. One
Desperado was for blowing up this Sloop rather than surren-
dering, and being hindered, he went forward, and with his
Pistol shot out his own Brains.

"Capt. Solgard designing to make sure of one of the Pirate
Sloops, if not both, took this, seeming to be the Chief, but

proved otherwise, and if we had more Day-light the other of Low's had also been taken, she being very much batter'd; and 'tis tho't he was slain,* with his cutlas in his hand, encouraging his Men in the Engagement to Fight, and that a great many more Men were kill'd and wounded in her, than the other we took.

"The Two Pirate Sloops Commanded by the said Low and Harris intended to have boarded the Man of War, but he plying them so successfully they were discouraged, and endeavoured all they could to escape, notwithstanding they had sworn Damnation to themselves, if they should give over Fighting, tho' the Ship should even prove to be a Man of War. They also intended to have hoisted their Standard upon Block-Island, but we suppose now, there will be a more suitable Standard hoisted for those that are taken, according to their Desarts.

"On the 12th Currant Capt. Solgard was fitting out again to go in the Quest of the said Low the other Pirate Sloop, (having the Master of this with him, he knowing what Course they intended by Agreement to Steer, in order to meet with a third Consort) which we hope he'll overtake and bring in."

The New England Courant of Boston printed an account of the fight and capture, and mentioned the fact that Joseph Sweetser of Charlestown was one of the men taken, and that both he and Charles Harris "who was the master or navigator" had previously been advertised in the "public prints" as forced men.

A week later the *Courant* published a list of the names of the men who had been taken by "HMS *Grayhound* in the pirate sloop *Ranger*" and were then confined in "his Majesty's Gaol in Rhode-Island." There were thirty in all. They included every pirate captured except seven still aboard the

---

* Actually Low was not slain, and did not die until the spring of 1724, when he was abandoned at sea, captured, and executed.

Grayhound. Captain Solgard hoped the pirates on the government ship would guide them to Captain Low, but when this plan failed they joined the others in prison.

The seven pirates included Captain Harris himself, Thomas Hazell, John Bright, Patrick Cunningham, John Fletcher, fifteen-year-old Thomas Child, and Joseph Libbey, the Marblehead sailor turned pirate.

When the news of this greatest capture of pirates in all New England history was made known, a tremendous number of citizens decided to journey to Newport so that they could be there in time for the expected hangings. Thus a large gathering of people was assured for the executions soon to come. Three weeks later, on Wednesday, July 10, the Honorable William Dummer, Esq., Lieutenant Governor of Massachusetts, Governor Cranston of Rhode Island, and other judges arrived at the Newport Town House.

At eight o'clock the next morning twenty-eight desperadoes of the sea were put on trial for piracy and robbery. Although every pirate pleaded not guilty, all but two were sentenced to be hanged.

The gallows were set up between high and low water at Gravelly Point, Newport, where on July 19, 1723, between twelve and one o'clock, twenty-six pirates were hanged by the neck until dead. This greatest pirate execution in New England history included Joseph Libbey, from Marblehead, Massachusetts.

5

A Sea Horror

There are more than three-score tales that I have been hoarding, some of which cannot be accepted because a vital, important link in the story is still missing, while others still seem so improbable that I often wonder if the incidents could have taken place at all. In the present account, however, additional information has recently been made available by a resident of Hingham, Massachusetts, which allows me to reveal the story although much of it can never be explained.

This tale of terror took place near the yacht *Dolphin* eighty-six years ago far out in the Atlantic, off the shores of the Lesser Antilles. After the evening meal several of the *Dolphin*'s passengers were enjoying a stroll on the deck. A brilliant moon lighted the sky and the sea, and the stars were beginning to come out. There was just enough wind filling the sails to keep the *Dolphin* moving at a steady rate.

On the hurricane deck, a short distance away from the others, stood two lovers—William Prescott and Vivian Warren. Looking out upon the quiet ocean, they were deep in conversation.

"How different this sky is from what we see in the United States," remarked Vivian. "I can scarcely recognize my favorite constellation. Of course, the Southern Cross is beautiful, but I miss the others."

As the *Dolphin* took a different tack, one of the passengers thought he heard the tolling of a bell from across the water. Conversation stopped when he asked if the others could hear it too. Several of the men agreed that it was definitely a bell and began asking each other where it could be.

After an interval, again there came across the sea, faint but distinct, the soft sound of a bell.

Captain Ephraim Liscomb walked over to the group and Prescott questioned him.

"Are we approaching land, sir?"

"No," responded the captain, "the nearest island is a good hundred miles away, and that sound we hear doesn't even come from that direction."

"Perhaps it is on board a ship," William suggested.

"I don't think it is," replied the captain, shaking his head. "At least, not on any craft which has a crew aboard, for there is neither rhyme nor reason in the way that bell is sounding."

"What can it be then?" Vivian asked.

To this no one ventured a reply.

In the meantime, the tolling of the bell became louder.

"It's the bell of doom!" exclaimed a tall scarred sailor from his helmsman's position at the wheel.

The bell was now heard clearer than ever, coming from the south. As the moments passed, the peals became louder. Everyone on deck now realized that the course of the *Dolphin* was bringing the yacht and all on board closer and closer to the mysterious tolling.

A short time later, the captain, using his night-glass, gazed long and intently in the direction of the sound of the bell. Lowering it, he announced:

"I can just see a dark body rising and falling on the waves, but nothing more. Bob, take a look."

Sailor Bob Batchelder came forward. Picking up the telescope, he walked over to the rail. There he braced the spy glass, held it to his eye for several minutes without speaking and, to all appearances, without breathing. Everyone waited. Finally he heaved a great sigh and lowered the glass.

"How does it look?" one of them asked.

"I'll be hanged if I can tell! There's no bowsprit, no sail, no nothing, just a shape in the sea. But there is one mast."

Bob leveled the glass again, and shortly afterward continued his observations.

"I've got her in range now. She doesn't have the least mite of a boom, yard, or anything. She looks like some old hulk. Hold on again. Now I see the bell! They've rigged it up at the masthead, so that it swings back and forward every time the thing gives a lurch."

"Can you see anything aboard?"

"Not a creature, living or dead."

"Keep her away two points," cried the captain to the man at the wheel.

"Aye, aye, sir!" The *Dolphin's* course was altered.

Several of the company were now frightened. They openly stated that there must be something supernatural connected with the hulk and its tolling bell. The captain, however, told the others that they were too superstitious.

"Wait just a few minutes," said the master. "I'll get aboard that old lumbering craft and find out what really is going on, and don't you think I won't. Even if it is the Flying Dutchman himself, or the Davy Jones flagship, I'll search that craft from stem to stern. Heave to!"

A boat was put over. Then, as the captain and his men rowed toward the hulk, Vivian told William that she could now actually see the tolling bell hanging from the masthead.

Those aboard the *Dolphin* watched with great interest as the longboat reached the hulk. Following every movement Captain Liscomb made in the moonlight as he clambered aboard with his gun and a lantern, they saw him disappear below.

Suddenly there was a terrible roar, followed instantaneously by a pistol shot.

A few minutes later the longboat started back from the hulk, the brilliant moonlight showing the men desperately rowing with all their strength to return to the yacht.

As the oarsmen approached the *Dolphin,* the passengers discovered that the master was missing!

"You cowardly dogs! Where is Captain Liscomb?" shouted the mate.

"Please, Chief, let us explain!"

The sailors then told the mate that the moment they came alongside the derelict they all heard a low, hollow, growling sound, which caused them to hesitate about going aboard. Captain Liscomb, however, climbed over the rail, started down the companion hatchway, and was soon out of sight.

The sailors explained that when they had reached the hulk the master had hardly gone below when a terrible bellowlike roar came. It was then repeated, louder and fiercer, the same roar that had been heard across on the ship by the passengers. The next moment came the report of the captain's pistol. Then echoing across the sea came the shriek of a human being in great pain, after which there was complete silence.

Afraid to go below without a light, the sailors shouted for their captain. When no answer came, the men, panic-stricken, rowed back to the yacht.

Realizing that he would have to organize another trip, the mate chose a new crew for which passenger Prescott volunteered. Several lanterns were taken along for the second journey.

"I'll not desert Captain Liscomb," shouted the mate on leaving for the derelict.

Prescott, the passenger volunteer, had taken his revolver and a small dagger. He handled the dagger constantly as if to assure himself that it was a satisfactory weapon for whatever lay ahead. The small boat drew closer and closer, with the moon still brilliantly illuminating the area.

Alongside the derelict, the men agreed that six of the eight should stay in the boat, with Prescott and Batchelder going aboard.

Prescott leaped over the rail, his pistol in his belt and swinging a lantern in his left hand. Bob followed with a cutlass. They descended the hatchway. All was still for an instant, and then those in the boat heard Prescott shout, "Oh, my God!"

His words were followed an instant later by a terrible roar. Next there came a quick succession of pistol shots. Five minutes went by, and then Prescott and Batchelder appeared, covered with blood.

"Come aboard," said Prescott. "The danger is over, but be prepared!"

The others climbed up over the side and went down into the hold. By the light of the lantern they saw a mangled body that they finally identified as Captain Liscomb. The head and one arm were gone. Near him was the gigantic lifeless form of what had been a ferocious Bengal tiger, with lumber and boards piled helter-skelter near the tiger's remains.

Prescott explained what had occurred. When they first entered the cabin they had seen the body of Captain Liscomb, but before they could approach the captain's remains, they heard a strange purring sound. Prescott turned in the direction of the noise. There to his startled gaze, was revealed a crouching tiger, in the very act of springing. Dropping his lantern, Prescott fired the revolver several times before the beast crushed him to the deck. One arm was still free, and with it he drew his dagger to stab the tiger again and again. By this time Batchelder had come to his aid, slashing and knifing with the cutlass. Between the efforts of the two men, the tiger finally collapsed. A moment later the animal's death throes ended, and the fight was over.

After resting for a few minutes, for the battle had been a fierce, terrible affair, the mate ordered the captain's body taken back to the yacht. Later the remains were sewn into a blanket and given Christian burial at sea.

After the excitement had quieted down, the men decided to explore the craft. One sailor, more inquisitive than the others, located what must have been the tiger's den, especially built for the animal on the ship. Nearby were fragments of two human skeletons, several articles of wearing apparel, shoes of both a man and a woman, and a leather wallet. The den was ten feet long, and at each end was a massive iron chain attached to a heavy ringbolt in a wooden beam.

Ordering the men to scuttle the hulk, with all its gruesome memories, the mate stood off in the longboat until it disappeared from view.

When the men returned to the yacht, the mate and Prescott told the passengers the details of their almost unbelievable experience.

Prescott explained that he had spent some time examining the dead tiger. The brute had an expensive collar around his neck, with a chain that had evidently been fastened to an iron ring. The ring had been bolted to a timber in such a way that the lightest strain would have pulled out the bolt. Over the center of the room, burned into the beam, was inscribed a number of words in one of the many languages of India. A free translation follows:

"I have sought—I have found that which I have sought—vengeance."

The original message appears below:

Mai NE KHÒNJĀ — WO MEELĀ JO
Mai NE KHÒNJĀ — PRATEEDANDITĀ

6

———————❧———————

Ghosts of Newport

Never before have I discussed in detail the many stories of ghosts which are associated with Newport's fascinating past. Last winter when we visited Newport and dined at Christie's with York, Pennsylvania, historian Walter Ehrenfeld, I thought of the many other times I had been in this old capital of Rhode Island. That night after returning home, I decided to review some of the countless incidents of the past connected with what many believe is Rhode Island's most fascinating city.

In 1767 when the brig *Dolphyn* went down in flames off Point Judith, Rhode Island, those lost included the wife and daughter of a Mr. Roland Henry who was said to be the father of the American stage. The disastrous holocaust, blamed on the cabin boy, is said to have occurred when the lad's lighted candle dropped against the rum-soaked side of a rum barrel. It is said that the ghost of the actor's wife often appeared in the Point Judith area on misty nights, but the keeper of the lighthouse there assures me that he has never seen it.

Of course, there are said to be many reappearances of the

ghosts of twenty-six pirates hanged on Gravelly Point, Newport, and later buried on Goat Island. Newport also has the ghost of the limping druggist, who hobbles out into the light of the moon wearing an old white, rusty beaver hat. Actually a cabinetmaker, he was known as Abiel Spencer, and in his store he sold drugs. There were those in Newport who called him "Doc" or "Doctor."

Captain Kidd's treasure is said to be buried in the basement of the home where Solomon Southwick, the editor of the *Newport Mercury,* lived on the corner of Walnut and Washington Streets. However, since the house was built around 1760 and William Kidd was executed in 1701, the tale could not possibly be authentic. Kidd actually buried his treasure on Gardiners Island in 1699, and it was dug out of the ground there and brought to Boston the same year!

There are those who claim that the ghost of Stephen Decatur, who lived in Newport for some time, is seen on occasion at Newport. Decatur was the famous captain of the *Constitution.* It was my privilege one night to attend a Boston banquet in honor of Decatur. Those with me at the table were all captains or former captains of the *Constitution.* Decatur's presence was acknowledged by a vacant chair, and we drank a toast to him. His ghost, however, did not appear! Decatur fought a fatal duel with Commodore Baron, losing his life on March 22, 1820.

The importance of all the ghosts mentioned above pales into insignificance when we discuss the famous Captain Samuel Cranston, who sailed away from Newport in 1755 in command of a fine ship. Some readers may object to the story of a ghost who came back to life, but nevertheless I include it in this chapter. His wife thought that he had died at sea and actually believed that his ghost appeared to her on several occasions in Newport. Eventually, according to her story, his alleged ghost influenced her in making a very important decision, that of marrying a young man from Boston.

Actually, Captain Cranston was still alive, having been captured by pirates at the mouth of what is now the St. Johns River in Florida. The pirates mistakenly believed there were several thousand dollars aboard the Cranston vessel.

They smeared the windlass of the ship with the blood of chickens, after which the sea robbers led the members of the crew out from the forecastle one by one and threatened each man that if he didn't tell the truth regarding the captain's assertion that there was no money hidden aboard, he would die in the sea.

Each man, on noticing the blood covering the capstan, realized the seriousness of the occasion and told the truth, but it did not save him. One by one every sailor was made to walk the plank to his death in the ocean.

Finally only the captain remained alive. Having witnessed the execution of the others, he expected to be similarly dealt with. To his surprise, Cranston was told that because of his truthfulness he would be given a chance to join the piratical brethren. Otherwise he would follow the others and be thrown over the side to die. Choosing to stay alive, Cranston signed papers with the pirates.

A large, strong man, more than six feet three in height, he was informed by the pirates that they had saved him to work as a regular sailor.

For the next seven years he labored as a pirate, watching for a possible opportunity to escape and return to Newport, but the others were too clever, watching him at all times. Cranston's chance finally came in 1763, during a particularly boisterous celebration after the capture of a vessel loaded with Jamaica rum. The pirates and their female companions became so exuberant that for the moment the officers relaxed their guard, and by midnight almost every man was hopelessly drunk.

Picking an ideal moment, Cranston let himself down the side of the pirate craft into a small boat which had been tied alongside. Two hours later he was far out at sea, his sail hoisted and pushed along by a fair wind. Three days afterward he ran out of food and water, but the following morning he was picked up in an exhausted condition by an English vessel that eventually landed him in Halifax. There he signed as a sailor on a Boston-bound ship.

On his arrival in Boston he went to the home of a friend who thought at first that he was seeing a ghost and then greeted him as if he were returning from the dead. Here Cranston learned that he had arrived at a vital time in his wife's life. He discovered that she either had just been married or was about to be married in Newport to a Mr. Russell of Boston!

Astounded at the news, Samuel Cranston spent half an hour alone trying to decide whether or not he should be the Enoch Arden of Newport. Should he give his wife a chance to take him back, or was it his duty to stay away and never reveal that he was still alive? His deep love for his wife won out. He made up his mind that he owed it to her to go to Newport, and then if she had not remarried he would give her a chance to make her own decision, after which he would step back into her life or go away forever.

Taking the next stagecoach out of Boston, he wondered all the way down to Providence whether he was too late. Had the marriage already taken place, or would he have a chance to see her before the ceremony?

Transferring to the Newport-bound omnibus at Providence, he arrived in three hours at the capital.

At Newport he found with relief that the wedding was not to occur until the following Sunday.

When he reached his estate, Cranston knocked at the door of his residence. Without revealing his identity he asked the servant for an audience with Mrs. Cranston, but the haughty butler soon returned with the message that Mrs. Cranston would not receive him.

Walking away from his own home, Cranston wondered what he should do. The following morning he made his decision and went back with the news that he was a bearer of tidings, for he had recently seen her husband. Actually Mrs. Cranston at the moment was being fitted for her wedding dress. When she was told it was a sailor waiting in the vestibule with word of her husband, she stopped the fitting of the dress and hastened to find out what the strange seaman might tell her.

Captain Cranston was then allowed to go into his own parlor, where he saw his wife again for the first time in seven years. She failed to recognize him because of his uncouth hair, his full beard, and his generally sailorlike appearance. As he began talking to her, he suddenly uttered a word that had meaning only to the two of them. Startled, then incredulous, she recognized her loved one and rushed into his arms.

"My darling!" she cried.

An hour later Mr. Russell and the preacher arrived at the house for a dress rehearsal of the wedding. Unfortunately, in her great joy and happiness, Mrs. Cranston was hardly civil to the Bostonian when he greeted her. Giving Mr. Russell no explanation at all, she walked away from the confused bridegroom-to-be, and he and the minister went to the parlor, bewildered by the turn of events.

When she calmed down somewhat, Mrs. Cranston realized that she should explain the situation and went into the parlor where she told Mr. Russell of her husband's return.

After the captain had bathed and shaved and dressed in the best finery which his wardrobe afforded, he presented himself to his wife. Arm in arm they walked into the parlor, where the prospective bridegroom and the minister were still waiting.

Mr. Russell, who had never seen Cranston before, offered congratulations to the missing husband on his return. Consolation for Russell followed, and then the Bostonian made a strange suggestion.

"I know that this will be an unusual thought, but why not let me give the bride away and thus let the two of you have a second marriage."

This was agreed on. Not only did he give the bride away on the scheduled date of his own wedding, but Mr. Russell actually presented her with a dower, the amount he had intended to settle upon her when she became Mrs. Russell.

7

Man Overboard

On several occasions I have been dangerously close to death in the sea. Because of this, stories concerning those who have been lucky or unlucky in their own awesome marine encounters with the grim reaper have always impressed me. Of all manners of death, to fall overboard far out on the ocean and sink down into the depths is indeed one of the most terrible ways to die.

My grandfather, Captain Joshua N. Rowe, often told my mother, Alice Rowe Snow, the story of his brother Adelbert, who fell overboard one day far at sea.

After his career on the clipper ship *Crystal Palace* (during which time the clipper broke all records between Boston and Melbourne *), Captain Rowe took his brother Adelbert aboard the lumber schooner *Village Belle* as mate. One day, during a terrific storm, Adelbert was lost overboard.

Frantic with fear, Adelbert tried to grab a line thrown to him as the *Village Belle* sailed by, but it was no use. Let Grandfather Rowe tell what happened in his own words:

* Leaving Boston May 22, 1854, she arrived at Melbourne eighty-four days later.

"No sooner was he in the ocean than I ripped out a plank from the deckload we were carrying, and flung it to him!

"I gave orders to heave to, but of course the *Village Belle* was moving all this time and Del was soon far astern. We lowered the boat, and with two men rowing, started off in the almost hopeless hunt for my brother.

"Where was he? How far had the ship gone before we hove to? Had he already drowned? Could we possibly find him in all that tumult of wind and water? These questions were rushing through my mind and they could not be answered. We went on and on, rowing and hoping and praying that we would soon find him.

"The men at the oars rowed harder and harder. Soon we lost sight of the schooner, then caught a view of her again, from the top of a wave. As time passed we began to lose hope of ever catching sight of my brother again, and I feared that he must have gone down. Should we stay away from the schooner any longer?

"I looked dejectedly at the men pulling on the oars and decided we had lost our fight. I told them that it wasn't any use hunting any longer for we had better head back for the schooner. But, oh, how I hated to go back home and have to tell his wife, Clara.

"Suddenly, as I stood there in the stern sheets, an idea struck me. 'Men,' I yelled, 'we haven't found the plank and that plank couldn't sink. I saw him reach for it after I threw it to him! Then a big wave got in the way and I didn't see him again. Come on, men, pull for the plank!'

" 'Aye, aye, sir,' the sailors roared out at me. And the men with raw, blistered hands went at it again, pulling their strongest stroke, making the boat go faster and even faster, throwing the spray over us all.

"On and on we went. Then I saw something far in the distance. Could it be the plank? Probably not. But wait—yes, now I am sure, now, it *is* the plank! Yes, thank the Lord, I'm sure of it now. I hope Del is holding on to it. We'll soon find out.

"Nearer and nearer we came to the plank, and then we saw the poor fellow's body lying across it! Were we too late? He did look as though he were dead.

"We dragged him into the boat. I found his heart was beating, but weakly. I rubbed and rubbed him, while the men pulled for the ship. Then, wonder of wonders, his eyes opened and he looked at me.

" 'Del, oh, Del, old boy, you *are* alive.' I just roared at him.

" 'You bet I am, Josh.'

" 'Pull away men, as fast as you can.'

"It didn't take long to get him into a warm bunk with some nice hot coffee in his stomach heating him up and taking the chill out of his half-drowned body."

One of the most historic "man overboard" instances in recorded history occurred during the voyage of the *Mayflower* to the New World in 1620. While far at sea, during a great storm, passenger John Howland, called by William Bradford a "lustie yonge man," was unable to stay below in the stuffy hold any longer. Coming up on deck, almost at once he was caught by a great wave that roared along the deck and swept him overboard.

Luckily, there were several of "ye top-saile halliards" trailing in the sea, and John Howland made a frantic but successful attempt to grab one. He hung on for dear life, although, according to William Bradford, Howland was "sundrie fadomes under water." Finally, he was rescued by a "boat hooke & other means" and was carried below.

Bradford states that Howland was "something ill with it, yet he lived many years after, and became a profitable member both in church & comone wealthe." During the same gale the great main beam of the *Mayflower* buckled, but emergency repairs were carried out successfully.

In the year 1842 the steamer *Independence* took Washington Irving to Europe in his new post as minister to Spain. Also sailing on the same craft was a writer named Richard Burleigh Kimball.*

As the voyage progressed, both Irving and Kimball became concerned in watching almost every person and event on the ship, observing with deep interest each individual sailor until the two writers had familiarized themselves with every peculiarity of look, gesture, or habit.

The second day out Kimball's attention was drawn to a young sailor named Frank Chisholm, who had shipped as cabin boy on his first voyage. Fifteen years old, he was an only son and his mother was a widow. She had, at much sacrifice, managed to buy his sea clothes, an all-new sailor outfit, but had knitted his woolen stockings herself. In addition to giving him many items for his sea chest, she had taken pains to meet and talk to the first mate, who promised to look after the young fellow and bring him back safe and sound.

On the third day out a squall developed, and for the first time young Frank was told by Second Mate Whitfield to go aloft. It was blowing moderately hard, and to test him the mate told Frank to carry out some relatively unimportant task in the main top. Frank hesitated only long enough to give a glance upward. Then, springing forward, he began to climb the shrouds vigorously. Richard Kimball told about it years later:

"We looked with keen interest to see if he would reach the main top sailor fashion (rather a nervous affair on the first occasion), or creep through the 'lubber's hole.' To our de-

---

* Born in 1816, Kimball died in 1892. His best-known novel was *St. Leger*. He founded Kimball, Texas, and built the first railroad in the state.

light, he went up in the accepted manner, carried out his work, and came down."

The second mate was a perfect old "salt" but he did not disguise a grim satisfaction at the way Frank handled himself, which was manifested by growling at him, in a good-natured tone, about his shoes, which were too new and stiff to please the mate.

Frank was proud and happy as he jumped down to the deck safely. From that moment on, Frank advanced rapidly in sailor craft. Four days later he volunteered to go aloft and help reef topsails. Soon he was treated as a regular seaman and the crew stopped playing the usual tricks veteran sailors play on new hands. In fact, at the end of ten days Frank was accepted as the ship's favorite.

One morning later in the voyage the ship was logging eleven knots under full sail, with a heavy sea following. Nearly all the passengers had come out on deck. Just as he stepped into his stateroom, Richard Kimball heard a confused shout that for some reason filled him with uneasiness and apprehension.

There are some sounds that are charged with terror. Kimball realized that this was one of them, and hurried on deck. He noticed a gathering on the larboard * side and heard a hoarse order from the mate to "bring the ship to."

At the same time he heard another command: "Lower away."

"What is it?" he asked the steward, who stood next to him.

"Poor Frank, sir," was all the steward could say, as he pointed astern. Kimball looked and saw something floating in the distance. It was Frank, the sailor boy, lost overboard. It seemed he had stepped over the rail to cast off a rope that was foul. Suddenly he slipped, lost his footing, and was gone.

Second Mate Whitfield, rushing from the forecastle, took

* Now known as port, as opposed to starboard side.

command of the longboat. He wore nothing but his woolen shirt and pantaloons. Barefooted, his hair streaming in the wind, Whitfield looked neither right nor left. A split second later he leaped into the longboat.

"Easy now—careful!" was heard from the captain, who had come to take over the delicate work of launching. Would the boat strike the water in safety? Despite the excitement of the scene, one could not but admire the gallant conduct of the able-bodied seamen, who never gave a thought to their own danger in attempting to save a shipmate.

The longboat was soon rolling dangerously in the heavy seas. All eyes were now focused on the little craft, which moved rapidly toward the area where Frank had plunged into the waves. Every so often the seas would seem to bury the longboat, but time and again it reappeared from the hollow gulf.

Watching and waiting, those on the *Independence* prayed that they would see from the boat some sign that the lad was found, but it was all in vain.

After pulling in several directions for more than an hour, long after any hope remained, the sailors rowed back to the ship. The watch on deck went to duty; the watch below turned in; the ship was put on her course. The search for Frank Chisholm was over.

A few days later the chief mate was talking with Henry Kimball.

"How can I ever look his mother in the face? I ordered Frank over the ship's side."

"That was not it at all!" said Whitfield. " 'Twas them new stiff, slippery, landlubber shoes the boy had on."

In 1852 the steamer *Pacific* was crossing to Liverpool. Writer Kimball, mentioned earlier, was a passenger. It was the height of glory for the Collins Line, for they were beating the Cunarders on almost every trip. The voyages across were completed with such regularity that people counted almost to the hour when they would receive their friends at the dock.

On this particular 1852 voyage there was a mixed company of passengers from England, France, Germany, and the United States. One of the Englishmen was from Liverpool. Frank and genial, he distinguished himself by never being seasick.

"I wrote my wife," he said to several of the other passengers one day, "that I should be home on Saturday to dinner, and I asked her to invite a few friends to meet me, and have the carriage waiting for me at the Prince's Dock."

This would make a ten days' passage for the *Pacific,* her usual time when the weather was average. Because of his prediction, all the others became interested in the moment when the *Pacific* would actually dock, for often trifling things achieve a great importance at sea. When the *Pacific* was but a day off the Irish coast, it was evident that with good luck the Englishman would make his date for dinner on shore.

Late that afternoon the passengers finished their final meal aboard, and all came out on deck just as the sun was setting. Kimball went forward with the others to see if land might be in sight. As he stood near the galley the Englishman passed him. The two men exchanged greetings, and then the Englishman began to climb to the small forecastle deck.

For the past few hours the wind had been rising, and by now the ocean was in turmoil, with the ship rolling considerably in the rough sea. Reaching the deck, the Englishman grabbed one of the ropes with his left hand, but a sudden lurch broke his grasp, slid him across over the side of the ship and down into the sea.

Almost everyone topside heard the Englishman's cry of terror. The helmsman had not noticed the man as he fell overboard, but now saw the unfortunate in the water. The engines slowed to a stop.

By this time the Englishman had struck out to clear the paddle wheels. As the steamer swept past him, still going at twelve knots, the helmsman looked down into the sea.

"My eyes met his. I can never forget the agonizing look of despair. The next moment he was far astern."

Then, with the engines stopped, the ship's boat was manned, but Captain Ephraim Nye soon realized the waves were too rough for launching.

"Avast!" shouted Captain Nye. "Stand by for orders."

Deliberately he climbed up the shrouds and stood in them, looking carefully westward. He remained there motionless for ten minutes. Descending to the deck, the captain pulled the bell for the engines to turn forward, and said one word to the quartermaster: "Course!"

In this way the captain made it clear that no further search could be made for the unfortunate Englishman. Of course, there were several passengers who objected to what they regarded as the indifference of Captain Nye.

"Even if there was no chance of finding the poor man, a decent regard to a fellow creature was lacking. The boat should have been lowered and they should have tried to save him," one passenger claimed.

Nevertheless, as Captain Nye explained later, the man was dead less than three minutes after he fell overboard. "I saw a 'comber' strike him," explained the captain. "He never breathed after that. As to launching a boat, there is not one chance in ten it could have lived, if not swamped instantly, and there was no possible chance of saving him. I could not peril five lives at such a hazard."

Eventually, sailors and passengers settled down to the usual life of people at sea. The *Pacific* reached dock at five o'clock Saturday afternoon. A neat brougham, with servant in livery, was waiting. A lady sat in the carriage, in eager expectation, while a footman came on board to find the Englishman and tell him that "dinner was ready."

It was a sad task that confronted Captain Nye of the *Pacific*. First he asked the footman to escort him to the lady in the carriage, after which the captain told the Englishman's wife with as gentle and kind an explanation as he could give that her husband had been lost overboard at sea.

We now discuss the adventure of James William English, whose terrible experience occurred in the Mediterranean in September 1965.

Sailor English, who came from Blackpool on the coast of England, was never an expert swimmer. One dark night his tanker, the 36,000-ton *Esso Durham*, steamed along off the southern tip of Sicily. English had worked without letup all the previous day and half that night, but he was accustomed to such a schedule. Twenty-nine years of age, he had been at sea since he was fourteen.

His duties included inspection of the starboard tanks, which at times carried him out where he was almost balancing over the side of the craft. Suddenly he turned, missed his footing, and plunged down into the Mediterranean. Later he remembered his sensations.

'As I hit the water, I knew I was in for it and waited for the propeller to chew me to bits."

Nevertheless, a few seconds later Bill English surfaced, unharmed, gasping for breath. Watching the lights of his *Esso Durham* grow smaller and smaller, he shouted at the top of his voice. No one heard him, and soon the tanker's lights disappeared in the distance.

Twisting off his clothes, Bill decided that all he could do was to swim in the general direction of the nearest land, which he knew was Sicily, with the North Star giving him his course. He swam steadily until tired, after which he turned over on his back and floated. After resting, he started to swim again. Time after time he continued this plan.

On three different occasions ships went by fairly close to the swimmer. "I waved and yelled," says Bill, "but they never stopped."

For some reason, Bill did not worry about sharks but was terrified that porpoises might find him. He had been told that they were so very playful they often drowned their victims without realizing what they were doing. All the time he was in the water English never did see a porpoise or a shark.

Finally the huge waves began to overwhelm him, and he wondered how long he could last.

Why should he die so young, he asked himself. By late afternoon, he was ready to give up, for his strength was almost gone.

Suddenly, while he was on his back attempting to rest, he saw several seagulls dive at him, trying to peck at his face and eyes, but he fought them off. He then attempted to take a cat nap. Half asleep, his mind went to Enid, the girl he planned to marry. She had chosen January as the month for their wedding, but he now began to wonder if the marriage would ever take place.

He was brought back to full consciousness by another flock of seagulls that evidently considered him too far gone to survive. One by one they began to dive at him, and he rolled over and began to swim.

Finding that their supposed victim was alive, the gulls stopped their attacks and dropped down into the water to serve as escort for the man they had found in the sea.

For several hours more Bill continued swimming through the dusk and then the darkness of the Mediterranean night. After another period of drowsiness, he opened his eyes and saw a light far ahead. There was no way he could tell what sort of light it was or how far away it might be. As he explained later, all he wanted then was a drink of milk. He wondered if he was able to reach the light, how his request for a glass of milk could be translated.

Finally, his joy knew no bounds, for he touched bottom! Gathering his strength, he stumbled ashore on the southern coast of Sicily. By then, however, Bill English was not interested in milk.

It was ascertained later that he had been floating and swimming in the water for a total distance of thirty-three miles. Stumbling up on a rocky shore, he reached a sandy beach and collapsed.

Watching the shore from a vantage point above the beach, two men had seen Bill wade out of the water and then collapse. Running down to him, they pulled him up above the high-water mark and soon had him dressed in a shirt and a pair of corduroy pants. After giving him a shot of brandy, they drove him to the nearest hospital.

When Bill was interviewed concerning his unbelievable swim, he was asked if he had finished with the sea.

"I should say not," was his reply. "Of course I'll go back to sea—it is my life, nice and secure!"

8

Frozen People

Incredible tales of people who have frozen to death after which they were brought back to life are fascinating to almost everyone, but I am still bewildered as to how this can possibly happen. Alton Hall Blackington, the radio personality whose "Yankee Yarns" interested millions, was the first one to tell me of the aging Vermont folk who were put out of doors in the late fall to freeze and were brought back to life in the spring. Of course, few people believe the Vermont tale, but concerning other accounts, can we really tell?

Years ago, an old-time whaler named Charles H. Smith had a truly bizarre experience in the frozen north when he discovered a sailing vessel with three dead men aboard who had been transformed into solid blocks of ice. I'll tell this weird story later on in this chapter.

Then, down in Rockland, Maine, I learned the story of the frozen couple of Owl's Head Light, which I now relate.

The lighthouses of Maine have long attracted those who love the seacoast. I have always enjoyed my Flying Santa flight each year from Boston to Maine for this reason. Portland Head, Pemaquid Point, Petit Manan, West Quoddy with its unusual red and white stripes, and Owl's Head lighthouses are all impressive, both from the air and from the water. Owl's Head Light is a particularly beautiful picture. There is a delightful contrast between the green pine trees, the red and white government buildings, and the brown, rocky cliffs surrounded by dark blue water. The white lighthouse itself, only twenty feet high, is perched in the midst of the trees at the highest point of the rugged headland, and the steady beam it shows at night is one hundred feet above the waters of Penobscot Bay. After a wintertime snowstorm it is indeed a fairyland.

In the year 1850, one of the strangest events in the entire history of Maine occurred near Owl's Head Light. A gale hit the coast on December 22, and no less than five staunch vessels were wrecked along the rocky shores between Owl's Head Light and Spruce Head. That night the temperature went far below zero, and the wrecks and the shoreline were heavily encased in ice by morning.

Before the storm began, a coasting schooner had been anchored in the vicinity of Jameson's Point across the bay. The schooner was without its captain, who had either fled from the vessel because of a premonition or had decided not to make the trip for personal reasons. There were those who claimed that he had been relieved of his command by the owner of the schooner. For whatever reason, the captain was absent when the storm broke, and the only persons on board the schooner were the two members of the crew—Richard B. Ingraham and Rôger Elliott—and Ingraham's fiancée, Miss Lydia Dyer, whom the owner had allowed to go aboard for the journey to Boston. As soon as the storm struck, Lydia Dyer went below and retired for the evening.

The gale increased hour by hour. By eleven o'clock the schooner was in great difficulty. Suddenly, a few moments before midnight, the cables snapped and the helpless schooner began her journey across the bay toward Owl's Head. Although clearing Owl's Head itself, she piled up on the cruel ledges to the south, where the rocks soon pierced her hull in several places. The craft filled and settled in a rocky cradle just a short distance offshore.

When the schooner hit, Lydia Dyer rushed up on deck, carrying a comforter and a large blanket. Ingraham quickly wrapped them around her as protection from the driving snow and icy surf. Then he and Elliott tried to decide what to do before high tide should arrive in something more than an hour. Locating a sheltered part of the deck against the taffrail, the survivors crouched there to get some protection from the wind and waves. But with the tide coming in, the spray and surf dashed with increasing fury against the helpless trio, drenching them thoroughly. Their clothing began to stiffen, freezing to their bodies. Richard Ingraham, standing by the taffrail, realized that there was little chance of their living through the night unless he could arrange some better shelter at once. The wind was still rising, and the tide was almost high.

"Lydia," Dick said to his sweetheart, "I don't have to tell you that we're in great danger, but I've thought of a plan that may save our lives."

"I'll do whatever you say," Lydia answered.

Dick continued: "Put the blanket down as close as you can get it to the taffrail and then lie down on it and pull it around yourself."

Lydia did as directed, and when she had pulled the blanket around her back, Dick placed himself beside her. Wrapping a blanket from his bunk around both of them, he placed his arms firmly around her wet, icy body. Then Elliott crawled in beside Dick, forced himself as close as he could and pulled an old comforter he brought up from below around him.

Although he believed that Ingraham was right in suggesting that they all huddle together for the night to keep alive, Elliott took the precaution of making sure his sheath knife was handy to chip the ice away so that he could breathe.

By this time it was dead high tide, and the wind was stronger than before. Each wave was now breaking over the entire hull of the vessel, and the icy covering was inches thick. Finally the two lovers lost consciousness. The ice jacket kept the air away from them.

Nevertheless Elliott, a cautious but determined man, kept picking away at a small opening in the ice near his face. In this way he was able to breathe. Then, although the three prisoners under the icecap did not know it, the tide began to turn and go out, and, as is so often the case, the storm went down with the tide. The sun rose a few hours later and Elliott, seeing the glow, began to hack and chop in earnest.

Soon he had punched his knife through enough of the ice to break off a large section six inches thick. By squeezing, clubbing with his hands, and pushing against the edges, he squirmed his way through the narrow opening in the ice and found himself on the slippery deck. With his hands cut and bleeding, Elliott rested a few moments against the taffrail to plan his next move.

Elliott glanced at his two companions frozen under the shelter of the taffrail. The ice was at least six inches thick over their bodies. There was no movement at all. It appeared that they had frozen to death. This panicked him into action. Stumbling over to the side of the ship, he looked down upon the rocks below. It was dead low tide and, to his amazement, he suddenly realized that he could walk ashore.

By this time the schooner had broken in two. Elliott climbed down through the break to reach the rocks and begin his journey toward civilization. But the ledges were icy and extremely slippery, and his stiffened clothing was an enormous hindrance. He stumbled and staggered over the rocks, falling down at almost every step. Finally it became too much of a temptation to remain where he fell and rest before he went on.

Elliott relaxed against a giant boulder and fell into a deep sleep, a sleep from which he might never have awakened, if luck had not been with him. The tide was turning. Soon it began to come in and a giant wave splashed over the sleeping man. The icy wave revived him—and saved his life.

Elliott tried to scramble to his feet, but the effort was too sudden and he toppled over backward, hitting his head as he fell. The shock helped to bring him to his senses, and he got up again, this time more slowly and deliberately. Eventually, after agonizing minutes of tortured walking, he reached the high-tide mark, where giant snowdrifts blocked his way.

Foot by foot, yard by yard, Elliott broke a path through the drifts until he finally reached a road. Of course he had no way of knowing where the nearest house was located or in what direction he should turn. The tracks of a pung with the hoofmarks of a horse decided his course. He would follow the tracks until he reached help. Turning to the right, he started along the road, which actually led to Owl's Head Light.

Now upright, now falling, Elliott made slow but steady progress. He did not know how much longer he could continue in his weakened condition. Then, through the cold morning air he heard the sound of bells. He looked up and thought he saw a sleigh coming toward him along the road. A minute later he realized that it was a pung. With a half-cry Elliott collapsed in the road.

The driver of the pung was Keeper William Masters of Owl's Head Light. Masters soon lifted Elliott onto the pung and drove toward the lighthouse, where he took the freezing man inside and cut the stiffened clothing from his body. A

Looking up the three-hundred-foot cliff at Grand Manan, climbed by Lawson after the shipwreck of the *Lord Ashburton* in 1857.

Granite wall in back of which a girl was sealed up alive by stone-mason Abrantes. The heavy outline is from Abrantes' sketch.

Adelbert Rowe falling overboard at sea.

Charles Smith's vessel arrives near the iceberg where the mystery craft frozen high in the ice was sighted.

The *Norseman* the day before she was towed to Boston. Two tugs and two lighters can be seen in the picture.

Mermaid seen by Munro in
Scotland.

Captain John Henry Latham Giles sighting a Hunt gun.

Terrible struggle between boa constrictor and soldier in the Enchanted Silo in Oran, North Africa.

The *Veronica* pirates being tried in court. A model of the *Veronica* is shown in the foreground. The pirates are in the partially glassed-in dock. Left to right: Otto Monsson, the youth; Gustav Rau, the ringleader; and Willem Smith.

Alfred Willis, able-bodied seaman on the ill-fated *Erne*, showing a picture of the bowsprit where the mate lost his life.

Quincy Yacht Club floats where pirate Franz Palow sailed away to meet his doom off the coast of Holland.

Photo by R. L. Graham

Ill-fated *Yarmouth Castle,* formerly the *Evangeline,* as she appeared shortly before the disaster.

Grave of Solomon P. Rich, who mysteriously drowned in Cape Cod
Bay on September 15, 1844.

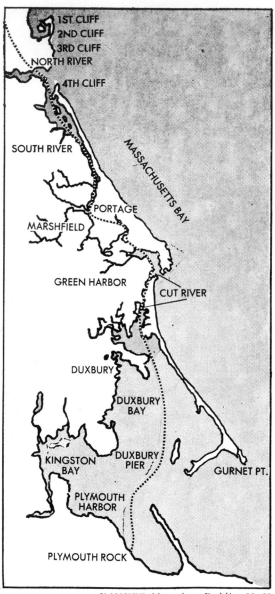

YANKEE Magazine, Dublin, N. H.

Route of author and family in canoe is indicated by dotted line. The trip through America's first canal began in upper left of the map and ended at Plymouth Rock in lower center.

Statue of Andrea Doria brought up from the Italian liner of the same name by divers from the *Top Cat*.

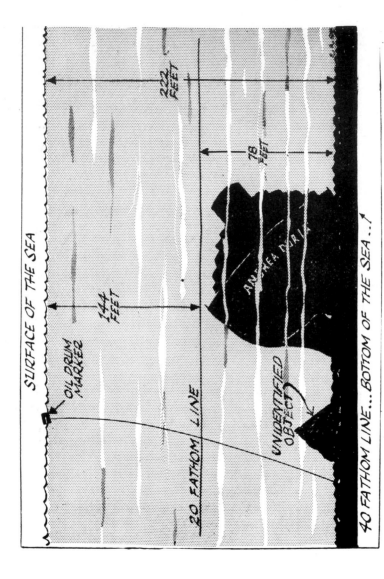

Cross-section view of how the *Andrea Doria* looks today at the bottom of the sea.

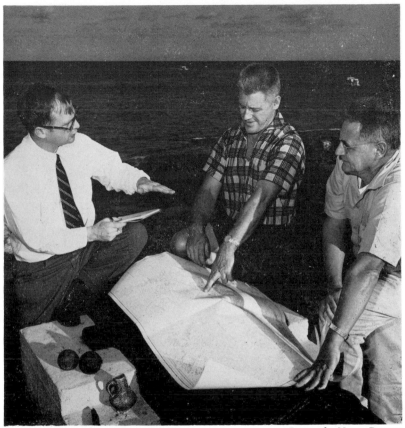

Bermuda News Bureau

Diver Edmund Downing, center, pointing out the exact location of the timbers of the famed *Sea Venture* wrecked off Bermuda in 1609. At the left is Henry Baker of the Bermuda News Bureau. On the right is Downing's associate, Floyd Heird.

Anna-Myrle Snow examining a treasure hoard gathered from the beaches and water of Bermuda. Several of the coins are believed to be from the *Sea Venture*.

drink of hot rum was forced down his throat, and he was put to bed and covered with heavy blankets, comforters, and quilts. But even in his semiconscious condition, Elliott remembered that there was an urgent message he should give to the lighthouse keeper at once. With a tremendous effort he opened his eyes and tried to get up.

"Take it easy there," admonished Masters. "You've had a hard time of it. Just lie back and go to sleep." Elliott was not to be denied, however, and opened his mouth to speak.

"Others are on the wreck," he gasped faintly. "Please get them."

"All right," Masters assured him. "We'll leave at once. Now you go to sleep."

A moment later Elliott was so deeply asleep that he didn't her the lighthouse bell signaling every able-bodied man in the surrounding countryside to leave his home and aid in rescue work. Soon Masters' pung with a dozen men aboard was following Elliott's tracks back to the shore. The wreck out on the rocks was quickly sighted.

By now the tide was well on the way in. It was quite a task to reach the broken vessel, but the men waded out and clambered aboard. They began to hack away at the two bodies frozen in the ice by the taffrail and soon had them free of the deck. The tide was rising quickly, and they had to work fast. Ten strong men moved the heavy ice cake containing the two lovers over to the break in the deck and handed it down to others waiting below in waist-deep surf. Then men of Owl's Head then carried their icy burden ashore in the bitter cold and loaded it onto the pung.

"They're both dead, all right," exclaimed one of the men.

"I'm afraid so," answered Masters, "but we've got to try to bring them back to life."

The huge ice cake was carried into the kitchen of the nearest house, and by careful thawing and chipping, the ice was completely removed from the blankets that covered the bodies. Cold-water applications were then administered, with the water as near freezing as possible. The temperature of the water was slowly raised, until eventually it was about fifty-five degrees. The next step was to move the hands and feet of the victims, slowly at first, and then at a more rapid rate. Their bodies were massaged slowly, carefully, and then vigorously for half an hour.

Lydia was the first to show signs of life, stirring slightly after having two hours of constant attention. Ingraham took almost a full hour longer to respond to the treatment, but finally he moved uneasily and opened his eyes.

"What is all this? Where are we?" he asked, and they told him the whole story. He looked across at Lydia, and she smiled at him faintly.

Then after Lydia and Ingraham were covered with extra blankets and fed hot drinks, they fell asleep. The following day they were well enough to eat, but it was many, many weeks before they could get up and walk about. Spring came before their complete recovery.

The state of Dick's finances prevented his marrying Lydia at once, but eventually they married and had four children. One of their descendants, Mrs. Louise Thompson Squires, was living in Whitestone, New York, when I last communicated with her in 1951. It is to Mrs. Squires that I am deeply indebted for the background of this truly unusual story.

Roger Elliott, incidentally, never fully recovered from the effects of his terrible experience. He did not go to sea again, but frequently he visited the Rockland waterfront, where he told and retold his incredible story.

Declared a miracle, the story of the frozen couple was discussed for years afterward around the fireplaces up and down the Maine coast. Whether or not the lovers actually froze to

death and were thawed back to life is a question that is still
hotly debated.

I have never really dared in my previous books to write of
Charlie Smith and his adventures—without question one of
the weirdest stories of all. The manuscript of the story came
to me after the death of my aunt, Annabel Snow, in 1952.

Now with the discovery of burial records proving certain
statements correct, I am revealing the entire account for the
first time.

When I was a child, Charlie Smith, former deep-sea sailor,
often took me to the movies. Once we visited the Boston
Arena, probably half a century ago, to watch Buffalo Bill and
his great "101 Wild West Show." On other days Charlie
would climb to the top of Winthrop's Great Head with me,
where he would explain the workings of the sextant he had
brought along, and take the sun, a feat he had learned during
his youth on whalers.

I never realized that Charlie Smith had literary ambitions
at the time, for his strong or rather weak point was rum. My
Aunt Annabel Snow was probably the kindest soul who ever
lived, always feeling sorry for some unfortunate and giving
him odd jobs as handyman. Charlie Smith, the drinking ex-
sailor, could almost always be depended on for three or four
good bottle excursions a year. I recall Charlie more than the
others Aunt Annabel befriended, because I was at that im-
pressionable age, enjoying movies and shows to the utmost.
Aunt Annabel saw to it that Charlie would take me to many
of those entertainments.

Some years after the Buffalo Bill days, matters in Charlie's
life came to a crisis when his leg began to bother him. During
a thrilling chase while whaling forty years earlier, Charlie had
suffered a terribly lacerated leg. The longboat he was in had
been crunched to pieces by the jaws of an enraged whale. The

limb never properly healed and eventually had to be taken off.

Charlie did not live too long after the amputation. At his death his sea chest, stored away for years, was brought out and examined. Among other things, including the metal end of Charlie's favorite harpoon, were scores of pages of manuscript, written both in pen and pencil, with a few pages of badly typed material, telling of important moments in the last thirty years of his existence.*

None of us ever paid too much attention to the stories, but when Annabel died in 1952 I was given the task of arranging and disposing of everything to do with Charlie Smith and several others who either preceded or came after him.

The following story, most of it written by Charles Smith, concerns his trip on a sealing voyage to arctic climes almost a century ago.

"We sailed out of Dartmouth, Nova Scotia, aboard the *Marion* in the spring of 1869. Several weeks later we came across an amazing scene, an ancient brig high in an iceberg. Evidently it had been frozen in the ice some years before, and pressure from below had pushed it higher and higher. Indeed, it was an extraordinary sight. I was very anxious to climb up the giant iceberg to visit the craft, but the captain would have none of it."

Strangely enough two weeks later the *Marion* herself encountered a gale and went down, but not before Smith and two others had launched the longboat. They rowed to the nearest Eskimo village, where they obtained supplies and warm clothing. Then they tramped overland to the nearest civilized settlement, eventually reaching Ontario.

Charlie, however, often dreamed of the unusual craft high on the iceberg. In fact he became so interested that he made careful plans to return to the berg, whose longitude and lati-

* According to Long Island Hospital records, Charles Smith died there in 1921.

tude he had carefully noted. Strangely attracted to the little kayaks the Eskimo men operated with their tandem paddles, Charlie vowed that he would return to the settlement, borrow a kayak, and start out for the last known location of the mysterious craft he had seen at least seventy feet up on the iceberg. Realizing that he might never find the brig, Charlie decided that no matter how long it took him, he would make another journey to the frozen north and somehow do everything he could to get aboard the vessel.

For the next ten months he worked ashore at various jobs, and—even to his own surprise—abstained from drinking. Finally, he had amassed $780. He bought the necessary equipment for his strange journey and two months later, ashore in the Eskimo village, sought out the chief, who remembered him well.

He explained to the chief that he wished to exchange trinkets and ironware, such as hatchets, knives, and axes, for the best kayak in the village. He planned a voyage of exploration along the coast, after which he would return and give the kayak back to the Eskimo leader.

Although the chief realized that Smith was not going to tell him the actual reason for the journey, it didn't really matter. When he examined the high standard of hardware Charlie had brought along, he announced that he was ready to trade. Picking out a kayak with a good beam, one which was so substantially built that it could carry several hundred pounds in food and skins, Charlie took lessons in kayak handling for two solid weeks, morning and afternoon. Finally came the day when Charlie was accepted as a kayak paddler of ability.

Loading his supplies of blubber, water, and tinned articles of food, he bade farewell to the Eskimo village and was soon out of sight.

A kayak in skillful hands can travel rapidly through the water. For the next eleven days, as he plotted on his chart,

Charlie paddled between forty and sixty miles each twenty-four hours, stopping at night only to sleep. The Arctic summer gave him daylight as long as he cared to paddle. Not really accustomed to journeys such as he was engaged in, when he went ashore and put up his tent for the night, Charlie slept the sleep of the exhausted. Luckily he had good weather.

On the twelfth day he reached the latitude and longitude he had recorded on his previous journey, but the berg was not in sight, nor did he really expect it to be. Now began the ambitious search for the enormous mass of ice that he hoped still held the brig.

It was not until four days later that he sighted a gigantic berg which could have been the one. At the moment of his discovery he was west of the berg, not to the east of it as the *Marion* had been. He paddled directly toward his goal.

It took many hours to circle the great mass. Just before he approached a lofty spire of ice, he sensed he was in the right area. Then, rounding the berg slowly, he caught sight of what might have been a topmast. Half an hour later the entire upper works of the craft were revealed. He went ashore almost under the vessel.

In the intervening time since he had last sighted the berg, the general position of the brig on the wall of ice had changed, and it appeared at least twenty feet lower than before. Although the berg was now in a frozen field of ice, the entire mass, possibly ten miles in area, had pivoted as it attained its new position, which was roughly fifteen miles southeast of where Charlie had last seen it. Actually, as he estimated later, the brig had slid down about thirty feet toward the level of the sea, and a large crack was forming immediately under the hull. Pulling his kayak far above the surface of the sea, Charlie let out a line to a small anchor which he drove into the ice, and hiked over to a point immediately under the brig.

After adjusting to his boots the crampons he had brought

along, Charlie started up the side of the berg, testing the ice
every so often with his pick. An hour later he was alongside
the craft. Climbing into the frozen forechains, he went aboard.

In his manuscript Charlie tells the details of his adventure:

"I climbed off the bulwark down onto the deck, which was
canted with a list to larboard of about fifteen degrees. Thus
the brig sort of leaned against the mountain of ice.

"Then I saw something which at first terribly frightened
me. There at the larboard rail, clinging to the rigging, was a
man covered with ice and snow. He seemed like a statue,
heroic in size, for the frozen ice had built up all over his body,
substantially enlarging his size.

"The sun now came out from behind the clouds for the first
time that day, and the vessel presented a gleaming fairyland
of whiteness.

"Everything was covered by frozen snow and ice, just as it
is in New England after a severe ice storm. The entire brig
glistened and shined. The spars, tattered sails, and the masts
appeared as if carved from ice.

"I stared at the ice-covered sentinel. To tell the truth,
his horrible appearance made me hesitate about going below.
But, mustering my courage, I searched through the snow to
locate the afterhatch.

"After scraping away, I found the hatchway. As I had
feared, the door was frozen solid. I recalled seeing a sword
hanging from under the cloak of the figure on deck, and went
up to get it.

"It was quite a struggle, but I finally freed the dagger from
the scabbard. Ten minutes later I had chopped the ice away
with the sword. Then I pushed open the door.

"The wind had been coming up, and as I entered the cabin
I could hear it moan.

"Crossing the threshold, I was met by a strange cold smell
in which I detected an odor of wood and leather. Also, I was

temporarily blinded by the sudden change from brilliant sunlight to the blackness of the cabin.

"Stumbling forward, my hand outstretched, I walked a few steps, and then received a terrible shock. I had encountered the unmistakable marblelike projection of a human nose, with frozen bristles of hair below. After that I lost my nerve completely.

"Backing away, I almost ran up the companionway in my anxiety to reach the deck again.

"After a few minutes in the sunshine, I recovered enough to decide to return, but realized I'd have to carry a lantern or candle on my second trip.

"Going below, I scratched one of the matches I'd brought along. I crossed the cabin with the match held high and stepped gingerly around the body of the man whose nose I'd run into. I came across several candles still in their sticks, and lit one at once. Picking up the candle, I resumed my journey around the cabin.

"Suddenly, off in the area near the frames or ribs, I detected the crouched-over body of another human. It was a huge man, partly in and partly out of the lazarette,* the cover of which was turned over nearby.

"I went over to him, and found that like the other two, he was a cake of ice.

"I felt uneasy with the bodies aboard the brig with me. I couldn't leave the frozen man half in and half out of the lazarette, and his twisted body would have to be thawed out before I could get his remains out of the cabin.

"Finding the furnace, I lit a fire. Within an hour I had fed it enough coal to bring the temperature of the cabin up to a point where the arctic cold gave way to a warmth which was slowly approaching body heat.

"I then carried and pulled the frozen victim to a point not

* The area below deck where supplies are kept.

too far from the red-hot furnace, and placed his terribly twisted remains on his left side close to the heat of the furnace. In this way, I hoped, he would eventually thaw out so that I could bend his limbs enough to get him up the companionway. Then I replenished the wood and decided to make myself comfortable for the night.

"I do not know how long I slept, but something awakened me. The heat from the furnace had diminished, but when I looked at the frozen body near the heat, I received a shock, for I had left the man on his side, and he was now lying on his back!

"Jumping to my feet, I started over to him. As I did so, his right leg, which had been frozen at a terrible angle, suddenly slumped down and assumed a more relaxed position.

"Then I heard a deep sigh. A moment later, a miracle occurred, for he opened his eyes. Overwhelmed, I managed to get some brandy from the cabinet and force it down his throat.

"It was a good hour later before he began to talk. Although I conversed with him in English, I shall always wonder what his nationality really was. He claimed to be Chief Mate Edward Finch.

"As I had been examining the frozen stores, I was able to give him a meal shortly afterwards consisting of oatmeal, broth, and wine biscuit. He ate everything with relish, after which I swung him into the nearest bunk and he fell asleep at once.

"The next morning I awakened him. He began to wonder just what I was doing aboard. In return, I had many questions to ask him.

"Our first difference came when he asked what day of the month it was. I told him the seventeenth. He gasped at once, claiming it was March 10, but when I told him it was June 17th, Finch became belligerent and asked me where the others were and what I was doing aboard. I told him how months before I had sighted the brig on the iceberg, and had come back to visit it. He didn't believe that either.

"I explained that the only other men I saw were just as frozen as he had been. He would not rest until he had seen and identified the other two victims.

"Two minutes later we were both standing by the side of the other frozen officer, whom Finch identified as Captain Montressor.

" 'Why didn't you also bring him back to life?' Finch asked me.

" 'You were all I could manage, and your captain is much heavier than you. If you wish, we'll move him together.'

" 'I am far too tired. We'll make the effort in the morning.'

"But when I awakened in the morning Finch had left the cabin. I finally located him on deck.

" 'I have had to throw Captain Montressor over the side,' explained Finch. 'I also got rid of the cook. I found him frozen on the deck. It was the easy way out.' "

Although Charlie remonstrated with the mate, he knew there had been bad blood between all three, and the frozen deck of a vessel high on the side of an iceberg was no place to discuss the ethics of the situation.

Charlie, still amazed at bringing Finch back to life, now studied the sailor's face carefully and seemed to detect an aging taking place.

By this time he and Finch had discovered that each had a different idea as to what year it really was. Finch insisted that the year was 1793, while Smith knew the date was 1876.

Two days later Chief Mate Finch revealed a secret of importance. Down in the hold, according to Finch was the sum of $70,000 in gold, which had been put aboard the brig for the purpose of trading in furs.

Finch had been puzzling over what probably had happened after the brig was trapped in the ice. Evidently one by one those aboard had frozen to death. Finch realized the fact that he was alive again only because of Smith, but he was quite confused as to what incident led to his freezing. Finch told Smith he recalled falling asleep on the deck in the cabin across from the furnace, but had awakened at least twice. The other crew members had hiked away from the brig several days before and had not come back.

Finch decided that probably he and the captain may have been overcome by gases from the furnace. Then, as they were unconscious, the furnace went out, and gradually the eternal below-zero atmosphere seeped into the cabin, eventually freezing the interior and all its contents. Of course, in this Finch could only conjecture.

What really did upset Finch, however, was the statement by Smith that the year was 1876 and not 1793, when Finch and Captain Montressor had fallen asleep in the cabin.

No matter how Smith tried, Finch was adamant. He simply would not accept what Smith knew was the truth, that the mate had been in a sort of deep freeze for more than eighty years.

Finch, who in 1793 had left a family waiting for him back in Europe, could not admit the possibility that all of his loved ones might have died of old age.

His mind was simply unable to comprehend what had happened to him, and he believed that for some reason Charlie Smith was not telling the truth.

The very next morning, when the two men awakened, Charlie Smith realized that Finch's body was continuing to deteriorate. The lines around his eyes and his mouth were much more prominent than they had been twenty-four hours before, and he realized with a shock that the frozen man who had been thawed back to life would probably show his full age in a relatively short time.

Indeed he was right. The next day and the day after that,

Finch looked older almost by the hour. It was not long before the old man began to totter and eventually he was unable to get out of his bunk. Then came the morning when the ancient denizen of the frozen craft could no longer respond to repeated urgings. However, Charlie Smith stayed with the man, who by then was showing his 140 years, until the sailor's heart stopped beating.

Charlie Smith now had to make a decision. Would he load his kayak with as much gold as he could carry or would he make an attempt to get back to civilization as he had come— still poor but with a wonderful story to tell, which few would ever believe?

He decided to compromise. Entering the hold, he began packing some of the gold. First he filled small wooden containers with cotton, then he inserted about $500 worth of gold into each container. Soon he had $18,500 worth of gold stored away in the kayak.

He took the kayak down to the water's edge at a point a quarter of a mile from the brigantine. Then, after getting enough food from the stores to last him three or four weeks, he arranged a bonfire in the ship and set it ablaze. In the general fashion of Robert Service's *Cremation of Sam McGee,** the ancient sailor was cremated.

The heat of the burning ship melted the ice around it, and it slowly slid down into the sea. By the next morning, only a few embers were floating in the water.

Charlie packed his kayak and started back for the Eskimo headquarters. After many days of travel, during which time he encountered a storm, he reached his destination.

Charlie delivered his kayak to the Eskimo leader, and gave the native an account of his adventures.

The problem of the gold was a serious one, and Charlie

---

* The flame just soared, and the furnace roared—such a blaze you seldom see
And I burrowed a hole in the glowing coal, and stuffed in Sam McGee.

carefully considered the situation. Then, on the final night before he was to depart, he transferred the gold to two knapsacks, and told the chief that he needed a man to help him reach the nearest outpost of Canadian civilization. He said he would reward all concerned. This was agreed upon, and Smith made a final gift of a much valued knife to the chief. Charlie was given an Eskimo to make the trip with him.

Three weeks later the two men walked into a Canadian village, where Charlie presented his companion with a suitable gift. The two then said their farewells. Two months later, after transportation by dog sled, Charlie Smith arrived in a large village, and was able to take a train to Toronto.

Three days later he reached Boston. Smith set up headquarters in a modest rooming house bordering on Copley Square, where he lived in comfort for the next few years. At first he did not dip too much into what was a substantial principal, but later he developed a taste for ladies and liquor that began to reduce his wealth more rapidly than he had planned.

By 1907 his gold was almost all spent, and Charlie realized that he would again need money to live. He obtained a position in a shoe store and worked there for six months, but after several vacations of his own choosing, he was fired. He then began to take odd jobs, which gave him enough money for his immediate needs.

When he met my Aunt Annabel shortly after this, he had developed such a taste for the "cup that cheers" that he was reduced to a schedule that allowed him to work for about twenty-two days each month.

The amputation of his leg and subsequent death at Long Island Hospital ended the career of this man who in his lifetime had seen another human brought back to life after being frozen for more than eighty years—if we are to believe his story.

9

The *Norseman* at Marblehead

During the early morning hours of Wednesday, March 29, 1899, in foggy, stormy weather, the Warren Line freighter *Norseman* drove aground on the iron ledges near Tom Moore Rocks off Marblehead Neck, Massachusetts, where she remained hard and fast within a thousand feet of the Marblehead shore. Helpless, the *Norseman* was in danger of pounding to pieces if the northeaster then lashing the coast increased in intensity.

The wreck was the one subject of interest in the town the week she was aground. As the stranding of the *Etrusco* * did more than half a century later on the South Shore, the *Norseman* attracted visitors from the surrounding towns and cities. On the Wednesday of the stranding a vast crowd gathered on the rocky ledges across from the *Norseman* in time to witness the lifesavers as they finished taking off the 102 men aboard. It was the chance of a lifetime to see a real wreck and watch the breeches buoy in operation without any of the loss of life,

---

* See my *Legends of the New England Coast,* page 136.

suffering, or other harrowing incidents that ordinarily attend a wreck of this magnitude.

The townspeople gradually awakened that foggy morning around three o'clock when repeated shrieks of a siren whistle, penetrating to all but the farthest parts of the town, aroused even the soundest of sleepers. The fog was thick and the storm at that hour was at its height.

There was one man, however, who was always on the alert for such signals, and whose life as a seafaring man had taught him to know instinctively when such signals require the promptest kind of response. This man was John H. L. Giles, captain of the Massachusetts Humane Society's Elbridge Goodwin Life-Saving Station and night patrolman on the police force.

Giles was on State Street in Marblehead when the siren whistle first sounded. "It's a steamer, and she's back of the Neck, close in, too," said Captain Giles to himself. He hurried to the police station and asked James F. Frost to go with him out to Front Street, where others in the Humane Society life-saving group were soon reached by telephone. Every man responded at the first call, and in less time than seemed possible, a lifeboat was dragged to Fort Beach and launched on the Little Harbor side by the willing hands of as enthusiastic a crew as ever manned the oars.*

The wind was at its height, and the fog was so thick that it was impossible to distinguish any landmarks. The life-savers were more than halfway across the mouth of the harbor before the lighthouse on Marblehead Point Neck gleamed as a distant star.

The freighter's whistle had been sounding at intervals, but at the moment of launching the lifeboat, the boom of a signal

---

* The members of the crew of the lifeboat were all Marbleheaders born and bred: Captain John H. L. Giles, James F. Frost, Edward H. Curtis, John E. Biles, Joseph F. Snow, James W. Mullett, William H. Sweet, Joseph Phillips, J. Augustus Perkins, and Edward O. Perkins.

gun hurried the men even more. When near Marblehead Point Neck, the lifesavers waited until another gun boomed out so they could judge the location of the wrecked vessel, but since this did not help them, they decided to lay to briefly under the lee of Marblehead Rock. As daylight came on, they strained to catch a glimpse of the steamer. Lowell Island first appeared in outline to the eastward and then the shoreline to the southward took shape. Next they detected the unmistakable shape of a steamer apparently on Tom Moore's Rocks.

Now sure of their direction, they began a hard pull in the gale, and succeeded in getting alongside within hailing distance. The high seas made it impossible to approach closely enough to do effective work, and so upon learning that the craft was in no immediate danger of sinking, Captain Giles shouted that he would return to shore and attempt to reach the wreck by breeches buoy from Marblehead Neck.

The lifeboat started back and suddenly almost pitchpoled, the stern settling in the sea's trough and the bow rising high on a wave's crest. The long steering oar touched bottom and snapped in two. Fortunately the men were able to pull out of the trough and continue. By this time the wind began to go down, and a short time later the lifeboat landed without further incident. With the help of additional volunteers, Giles pulled the Humane Society wagon with the lifesaving apparatus across to Marblehead Neck and soon set it up opposite the *Norseman.*

With great care Captain Giles now trained the Hunt gun on the steamer and made certain that the direction was correct. Many were fearful the line would not carry out that far; also, success at the first attempt was not to be expected. Nevertheless, Captain Giles took careful aim and fired. The twelve-pound projectile shot straight out over the topmast rigging. When the men aboard had grabbed the line and secured it,

Giles sent out a cable, which the sailors fastened at the fore topmasthead. Next the lifesavers sent the breeches buoy out on the cable to the steamer.

Exactly nine minutes from the time Captain Giles fired the projectile the breeches buoy safely landed the first man from the *Norseman* on the rocks of Marblehead. He proved to be Alfred Adams, a cattle foreman employed by the Morris Beef Company of Boston.* Others of the crew followed rapidly, many of them being pulled across two at a time. It is said that more men were taken off from the *Norseman* than were ever before rescued in that manner. Captain Giles had proved his exceptional skill as a lifesaver.

Captain John Rees of the *Norseman* later explained that up to the time of the stranding the voyage had been without incident. The *Norseman* had carried across to Europe a load of about a thousand head of cattle, and brought back a general cargo of 996 tons. Forty-four of the men aboard were cattlemen, a group of them being from the steamer *Cambroman*. Officers and crew numbered fifty-eight more, making 102 aboard.

Captain Rees and his second officer had been on the bridge at the time the *Norseman* struck. The captain realized the dangerous position he was in, but he could do nothing to save the ship. He telegraphed the engine room to reverse at full speed just as the shock of grounding came. The steamer rose forward, with a grinding, crunching noise as the iron hull slipped up and onto the ledge. Stopping when her length was on the ledge, the *Norseman* apparently balanced upon a pivot that bore about midship.

There she hung. All attempts to back her off did not move

* The *Norseman* was owned by another company and leased to the Warren Line as a cattle steamer. Her officers were John Rees, captain; T. James, chief officer; J. Davis, second officer; T. Hatton, third officer; H. Rees, chief engineer; J. Hughes, second engineer; David Rowbottom, third engineer; A. J. Cunningham, fourth engineer; and E. J. Stewart, fifth engineer.

her an inch. Not only was she stove in forward, but water began pouring into her two forward compartments. Then Captain Rees ordered the signals sounded, which alerted the residents of Marblehead.

To those aboard the *Norseman* waiting in the darkness, it seemed a terribly long time before the lifeboat reached them with the message of assurance. By this time all aboard had donned life preservers and were prepared for the uncertain future.

Captain Rees was not to leave the *Norseman* until the middle of the afternoon. True to the traditions of the sea, he waited until all others were ashore before he left his ship.

"My last sight of land," he explained later, "was when the lights of Sable Island flashed out. Up to the time the *Norseman* went ashore, the trip across the ocean had been without incident. The sea on Tuesday, March 28, was as smooth as a billiard table until well after dark. Last night I turned in about nine o'clock. I had an idea then that I would reach Boston Light about seven o'clock. A little after midnight I was awakened by the first officer. He shouted out to me that storm and fog had come up and he had lost his bearings. The first officer was in charge of the wheel at the time.

"I hurriedly donned my oilskins and ran on deck. The rain was coming down in torrents, and I noticed that the night was foggy and extremely dark. On shore I saw a faint glimmer from a dull small light, probably Marblehead Light. It was the only inkling of my position. I fired off rockets, gave the whistle full steam, and kept the small cannon on board constantly booming. My first impression was that I had struck a sunken ledge or a derelict. There was about fifteen feet of water at the time.

"I gave orders to the chief engineer to back water. Our engines, however, although taxed to their utmost, could not budge the boat an inch. I made up my mind that our condition was serious and that we were on a jagged rock.

"A hasty examination below showed that the forward part of the boat was rapidly filling. A hole had been stoved in, and a good size breach was made in the vessel. Compartments No. 1 and No. 2 rapidly filled with water. The water was finally held in the bulkheads; not, however, until the coal bunkers got wet some. For fear of the boat completely filling with water, I ordered all the fires drawn."

The work of taking off the men proceeded all that Wednesday morning. At about nine o'clock Captain Giles rigged another hawser on which a second breeches buoy was operated. Leaving one in charge of William H. Frost and the second with Edward Perkins, he picked another crew for the lifeboat and went out to the steamer. The waves had gone down some, but great seas still broke against the port or ocean side. Comparatively smooth water was found on the starboard or shore side.

As the men came ashore in the breeches buoy, they were taken to a cottage nearby owned by Isaac C. Wyman, where they warmed themselves. Later in the day, hot coffee and lunch were served in the Wyman cottage at the town's expense. There were no accidents, and with two exceptions every man pulled ashore was landed without even a spray wetting.

The exceptions were Chief Steward John Phillips and James Barry, a crewman. They started in on the breeches buoy without signaling and at a time when the rescuers on shore had loosened the line to make a new hitch. Buried in the water, the two men were pulled out safely after getting a ducking.

No regulars in the life-saving service on government pay could have done better than Captain Giles' volunteers, while the scores of willing helpers who pulled on the rope as the hours went by should not be forgotten. Everything moved like clockwork. There were no unnecessary orders, no hysterical shouts, no unwillingness on the part of anybody to lend a hand when needed.

The forty-four cattlemen were sent to Boston Wednesday afternoon. Charles Ballem, through whom they shipped, addressed on their behalf a letter of thanks to Captain Giles and his crew, and also to the townspeople who helped them when they reached shore. Captain Rees retained his ship's crew for service, about twenty-five being put up at the Atlantic House, and twenty more finding temporary lodging at the almshouse.

Across in Boston, at the first news of the Wednesday-morning shipwreck, the agents of the Warren Line began the task of saving vessel and cargo. On Thursday morning at daylight a working force of lighters, tugs, and longshoremen arrived. All day and part of that night the men continued removing the cargo. Indeed, the scene viewed from the shore was a busy one, as the steamer was fairly alive with workers, machinery, and booms for hoisting out the heavy cases and crates.

Soundings at low tide around the *Norseman* gave twelve feet of water, which was sufficient depth for the largest of the lighters to get close alongside. As the *Norseman* drew twenty-six feet, the salvage men realized the tremendous force of wind and waves the night of the stranding to push the steamer so far up on the rocky ledge.*

On Friday there was considerably more water in the ship than the day before, and it was evident that some of the com-

---

* The *Norseman* was built by Laird Brothers at Birkenhead in 1882. She was a vessel of 2834 tons net, 4450 tons gross, and her dimensions were as follows: length, 392 feet; breadth of beam, 44 feet; depth of hold, 25 feet 3 inches. She was owned by the British and North Atlantic Steamship Company, Ltd., of which Richards, Mills & Company, the owners of the Dominion Lines, were the managers.

partment bulwarks were leaking. The lower hold was full with the exception of the after compartments. The plan was to unload the forward part first to lift the bow and permit the pumps to free the ship from water. The first freight removed was consigned to New York parties and showed serious water damage.

Divers Michael Sullivan and Martin Cook went down under water to check hull damage. They reported that although the ledge had cut jagged holes forward, the craft could be pontooned and towed to Boston when the cargo was removed.

The Boston Towboat Company was in charge of the unloading, with wrecking-master Edwin Burgess superintending the activity and Captain Barton Humphrey, treasurer of the towboat company, lending a hand. Captain Rees and his chief officers had gone back on the *Norseman*. Although the ship's engineer got up steam to run donkey engines for the winches, the main boilers could not be used, for the engine room was flooded. Lighter after lighter was loaded and taken in tow for Boston.

By Friday noon the unloading was practically completed and only a small part of the cargo was still aboard. Customs Collector Walter Gateman was aboard during the discharge of cargo, checking each piece as it was hoisted out. Marblehead thus became the *Norseman*'s port of entry, and she discharged the largest cargo ever entered in the long marine history of that famous Massachusetts town.

Incidentally, there was one young fellow aboard the steamer who was too frightened even to think about being saved. Refusing point-blank to try to use the breeches buoy, he was later lowered into the lifeboat and then put aboard the pilot boat, evidently powerless to help himself by one motion.

A boon to carriage owners, the wreck was responsible for many a dollar made carrying passengers to and from the Neck.

It is estimated that not less than two thousand people visited the scene on March 29 and 30.

The causeway to the shore, which was in damaged condition, made driving perilous, and in many places there was not room for two carriages. Drivers had to watch for chances to pass each other.

With most of the cargo ashore, the salvagers decided to attempt pulling the *Norseman* off the ledge stern first at the next good high tide. Pontoons were secured at low water, and the Boston tugs *Juno, Pallas, Mercury,* and *Confidence,* their hawsers ready, stood by. Then, half an hour before high water, they started pulling on the stranded *Norseman*'s stern. For ninety minutes the strain was kept up, but the *Norseman* did not move an inch.

Predictions for the next high tide ran almost a foot higher, and two more pontoons were brought down from Boston and secured amidships as additional insurance for getting the *Norseman* off.

This time efforts began a full hour before predicted high water, when all four towboats began straining at their hawsers. Then, suddenly, ten minutes before high tide, the *Norseman* jarred loose. Scraping and sliding, she moved off the ledge foot by foot, and twenty minutes after high tide she floated free.

Those who watched from the Marblehead shore that spring day never forgot the *Norseman* for the remainder of their lives. Soon the little fleet of tugs and the steamer started out for Boston, and half an hour later they were far in the distance. The *Norseman* eventually disappeared around Nahant, on her way to the Port of the Puritans.

10

—————❦—————

Mermaids and Mermen

I have always been more than interested in stories of sea serpents, mermaids, and ghosts. Of the three, however, I believe only in the existence of sea serpents. In this I am in good company, for sea serpents alone are accepted by scientists. Incidentally, there are skeletons of sea serpents at both Harvard and the University of California in Berkeley. It should not surprise most of my readers to know that sea serpents are acknowledged today by far more people than those who believe in the existence of mermaids. However, it was not always so.

Incidentally, the intense interest in mermaids which rose almost to fever pitch several generations ago might be compared by some to today's excitement concerning UFO's or unidentified flying objects.

In gathering information on mermaids and mermen, I have collected more than one hundred stories that have been told down through the centuries, each sincerely believed by the person who first related it. From the hundred, I have chosen to tell here those stories which have interested me the most.

Mermaids and mermen, it seems, have frequented the waters of the Atlantic more than any other area. On November 16, 1822, a British publication, *The Mirror,* had a special edition on mermaids, listing in all a total of ten different appearances of these unusual denizens of the sea.

Across the ocean, on the eastern seaboard of the Western Hemisphere, the first mention of a North American mermaid came in 1610. In that year a mariner named Captain Whitbourne reported sighting one in the harbor of St. John's, Newfoundland. He described the creature carefully.

Four years later, in 1614, during the same voyage on which he discovered Maine and Monhegan Island off the coast, Captain John Smith saw a mermaid "swimming about with all possible grace." He pictured her as having large eyes, a finely shaped nose that was "somewhat short," and "well-formed ears" that were rather too long. Smith goes on to say that her "long green hair imparted to her an original character by no means unattractive." He states that he had already begun "to experience the first effect of love" toward the creature until the moment when she revealed that from the waist down she was in reality a fish.

In 1673 John Jocelyn was visiting America. Jocelyn reported that a friend of his, a Mr. Miller, had sighted a merman, the male counterpart of the mermaid species, in Maine's Casco Bay. Miller was out in his canoe one day when the monster put a hand up over the side of the canoe, threatening to capsize it. To save himself, the terrified canoeist seized a hatchet and chopped off the hand, whereupon the dweller of the deep sank to the bottom, dyeing the water purple with its blood. The creature was seen no more.

Benoît de Maillet in his *Teliamede* refers to a merman that was seen by the entire company of a French ship's crew "off Newfoundland, in 1730, for some hours." The account was signed by "all the crew who could write," and was sent to the Compte de Maurepas.

Some years later a Gloucester, Massachusetts, fisherman told of a mermaid who boarded his fishing craft during a calm spell. Overcome with panic, the sailors grabbed hatchets and attacked the creature. The mermaid managed to clamber over the side and into the water, clinging to the taffrail with one hand. Then, just as Miller had done to the merman in 1673, the terrified fisherman amputated the hand. The mermaid sank immediately. She came to the surface once more and gave a deep "human" sigh, as though she felt great pain, and then she disappeared for good. Later when the men examined the hand they found it had five fingers with fingernails exactly like those of a woman.

Early in the eighteenth century, another mermaid was said to have been sighted off Nantucket Island from a passing vessel. It is unfortunate that the details of this encounter are lacking, for the creature is reported to have gone ashore and disappeared into the strange forest at Great Point. Over two centuries later a Great Point lighthouse keeper found evidence that some "marine being" had lived in the forest. Several Nantucket residents at the time believed that a mermaid might have taken up her abode there.

Although mermen and mermaids were said to exist in many quarters of the globe, until the year 1700 there were very few claims that they had actually been seen. Nevertheless, great interest was shown in the mermaid family not only by men of science, but by the average person.

Poetry of the ancients, which includes references to the tritons, half men and half fish, was often recited in the seventeenth and eighteenth centuries. The so-called tritons were said to have power "to calm the stormy surge." Nor should we forget the sirens, the marine nymphs whose melody charmed the entranced sailors and led them to their ultimate doom.

Beneath the depths of the ocean an atmosphere existed, according to one writer, which was adapted to the respiratory organs of a general class of life including the human race. According to some, these beings were possessed of surpassing beauty but of limited supernatural powers. We are told that they lived in a wide territory of the globe, and there they possessed habitations constructed of the "pearly and coralline productions of the ocean."

One theory is that these beings had lungs not adapted to a watery medium, but only to the nature of atmospheric air. It would have been impossible for them to pass through the volume of waters that intervened between the submarine and the supramarine world, if it were not for the extraordinary power of entering the skin of some animal capable of existing in the sea.

The shape they were said to assume was that of a creature which was human above the waist yet terminated below in the tail of a fish. Possessing an amphibious nature, they were enabled not only to exist in the ocean but to land on the shores, where they frequently lighten themselves of their sea dress, resume their proper shape, and with much curiosity examine the nature of the upper world.*

Is there any substantial background to what at first glance seems preposterous? My answer is yes, if we are to believe the records, for many years ago the Wernerian Natural History Society of Scotland publicly offered a prize of considerable pecuniary value to the individual who would first present them with one of these mermen or mermaids.

This offer was regarded in many seacoast towns as proof of "weakness and credulity." Not long afterward, however, the following statements, accepted by many readers as general truth, appeared in an Edinburgh magazine:

"A short while ago it was reported that a fishing boat, off

---

* Samuel Hibbert's *Shetland Islands,* 1822, page 566.

the island of Yell, one of the Shetland group, had captured a
mermaid by its getting entangled in the lines! The statement
is that the animal was about three feet long, the upper part of
the body resembling the human, with protuberant mammae
like a woman; the face, forehead and neck, were short, and
resembling those of a monkey; the arms, which were small,
were kept folded across the breast; the fingers were distinct,
not webbed; a few stiff long bristles were on top of the head,
extending down to the shoulders, and them it could erect and
depress at pleasure, something like a crest.

"The inferior part of the body was like a fish. The skin was
smooth, and of a grey colour. It offered no resistance, nor
attempted to bite, but uttered a low plaintive sound. The
crew, six in number, took it within their boat, but supersti-
tion getting the better of curiosity, they carefully disen-
tangled it from the lines, and a hook which had accidentally
fastened in its body, and returned it to its native element. It
instantly dived, descending in a perpendicular direction."

After writing the above, the narrator had an interview with
the skipper of the boat and one of the crew, from whom he
learned additional particulars. The animal had been aboard
for three hours. Without scales or hair, it was a silvery gray
color above, with a whiteness below resembling the human
skin. No gills were observed, nor were there fins on the back
or belly. The tail was like that of a dogfish. The breasts were
about as large as those of an average-sized woman, while the
mouth and lips were very distinct, resembling human features.

Mr. Edmondston, a well-known, intelligent writer, recorded his observations:

"That a very peculiar animal has been taken, no one can
doubt. It was seen and handled by six men, on one occasion,
and for some time, not one of whom dreams of a doubt of its
being a mermaid. If it were supposed that their fears magni-
fied its supposed resemblance to the human form, it must at

all events be admitted that there was some ground for exciting these fears.

"But no such fears were likely to be entertained; for the mermaid is not an object of terror to the fisherman; it is rather a welcome guest, and danger is apprehended only from its experiencing bad treatment. The usual resources of scepticism, that the Seals and other Sea-Animals, appearing under certain circumstances, operating upon an excited imagination, and so producing ocular illusion, cannot avail here. It is quite impossible that, under the circumstances, six Shetland fishermen could commit such a mistake."

Having supplied a so-called personal interview with a mermaid, we shall next do as much for a merman.

Eric Pontopildon, in his *Natural History of Norway*, tells us of a merman of the North Sea. About a mile from the coast of Denmark, near Landscrone, three sailors, observing something like a dead body floating in the water, rowed toward it. When they came within seven or eight fathoms, it still appeared as at first, for it had not stirred; but at that instant it went down, and came up almost immediately in the same place.

"Upon this, out of fear, they lay still, and let the boat float, that they might the better examine this monster, which, by the help of the current, came nearer and nearer to them. He turned his face and stared at them, which gave them a good opportunity of examining him narrowly; he stood in the same place for seven or eight minutes, and was seen above the water breast high.

"At last they grew apprehensive of some danger, and began to retire; upon which the monster blew up his cheeks, and made a kind of roaring noise, and then dived from their view."

"In regard to his form, they declare in their affidavits, which were regularly taken and recorded, that he appeared like an old man, strong-limbed, with broad shoulders, but his arms they could not see. His head was small in proportion to his body, and had short curled black hair, which did not reach below his ears; his eyes lay deep in his head, and he had a meagre face, with a black beard; about the body and downwards this Merman was quite pointed like a fish."

On May 1, 1714, a traveler and writer named François Valentyn, while on a long voyage, sighted a creature of the mermaid variety. I quote:

"I, the captain, purser and mate of the watch, and a great many of the ship's company, saw at about the distance of thrice the length of the ship from us, very distinctly, on the surface of the water seemingly sitting with his back to us and half the body above the water, a creature of a grizzlish, or gray color, like that of a codfish skin.

"It appeared like a sailor, or a man sitting on something; and more like a sailor, as on its head there appeared to be something like an English cap of the same color.

"We all agreed that he must be some shipwrecked person. After some time I begged the captain to steer the ship more directly toward it, being somewhat on the starboard side, and we had got within a ship's length of him, when the people on the forecastle made such a noise that he plunged down, head foremost, and got presently out of sight.

"But the man who was on the watch at the masthead declared that he saw him for the space of two hundred yards, and that he had a monstrous long tail."

Evidently bothered by scoffers, in later years Valentyn made a statement to the effect that if "there shall be found those who disbelieve the existence of such creatures as mermen, or mermaids, of which we have given great reason to believe that there are, let them please themselves: I shall give myself no more trouble about them."

In the year 1822, a vessel sailed into Boston Harbor commanded by a Captain Dodge who announced that he had captured a mermaid. He declared that he had put her ashore on an island where he planned to educate her in human ways. After studying his drawing of the mermaid, several told the captain to his face that the sketch had been made from imagination.

Leaving Boston, Captain Dodge promised to have the mermaid aboard his vessel when he returned. When he did come back without her, he announced sadly that the mermaid had died. He seemed genuinely remorseful, refusing to discuss the matter further.

The captain was later approached by several scientists who had heard about the mermaid, and they asked him to bring her remains back on his next voyage. Captain Dodge listened to them with respectful attention.

After he sailed, the scientists decided to investigate the history of mermaids. They were surprised to discover from their research that mermaids had been reported all over the world almost from the earliest days of antiquity. Omitting the obvious hoaxes and inaccurate legends, they found more than a hundred accounts of mermaids. They learned that both Pliny and Pausanias recorded instances in which mermaids were sighted, especially around the island of Taprobane and on the nearby mainland.

Alexander ab Alexandro said that Theodore Gaza once saw a mermaid cast ashore in the Morea immediately after a heavy gale had swept the area. Gaza described this mermaid as having a "human and charming countenance," but with a scaly body and tail. Gaza went on to say that as a crowd gathered on the shore the mermaid became embarrassed and then burst into tears of fright when people crowded around her. Finally, when an opening in the ring of spectators appeared, the mermaid flipped down toward the beach like an inchworm, and disappeared into the surf then raging.

In 1403, during a series of great storms, the Holland dikes collapsed. A "sea woman" was driven through the breach into the Parmer Sea, where she was caught by the Dutch people. They brought the captive to Edam, where the natives dried her, cleaned "marine impurities" from her, and dressed her in clothes. The people at Haarlem heard about the mermaid and she was taken there, where she was taught to eat civilized food and spin yarns. Finally she accepted religion and on her death received a Christian burial.

In 1554, Fondelet told of a Polish mermaid clothed by nature "with the garb of a bishop." Then we have the devil mermaid, *monstrum marinum daemoniforme,* captured at Illyria and taken to Antwerp.

It was also found that when King Roger reigned over Sicily in the eleventh century a young man bathing on shore met a mermaid of "great beauty," who remained with him for some time but never spoke. Finally she returned to the sea and vanished forever.

In 1712 a sea woman fifty-nine inches tall was taken alive near the island of Boeroe, Dutch East Indies. She refused to associate with the natives on the island and slowly wasted away. After four days and seven hours without uttering a sound, she died. Her remains were preserved by Samuel Flavers in the neighboring island of Ceram at Amboina and were on exhibition for many years. The head was as perfectly proportioned as any female human head could be. The eyes were very light blue, just a little too light to be human. The hair was sea-green. She had arms, hands, and breasts, and her upper body was almost as white as that of a woman. The lower part of her body was like the "hinder part of a fish."

In dignified Boston these stories soon became well known since they were reported from person to person. The arguments for and against the existence of mermaids were thoroughly discussed.

Finally Captain Dodge returned from another long voyage, and when his ship appeared in Boston Harbor a pilot went aboard. Captain Dodge informed him he had the mermaid aboard.

"Are you serious?" asked the pilot.

"That I am, sir, for I have her encased in a transparent coffin."

Within a week the lifeless remains of the creature in a glass case were on public exhibition and attracted widespread attention. Many scientists and laymen alike wished to remove the glass and examine the remains more closely, but Captain Dodge was firm. He would not allow it. He had brought the mermaid to Boston to prove he had not exaggerated, but all must view her at a respectful distance.

Those who saw this exhibit were frequently called upon during the remainder of their lives to recount how a mermaid had appeared in Boston.

When Captain Dodge concluded his exhibition and took his attraction away, he returned to his first love, the sea, but nobody knows what happened to the girl-fish in the glass coffin.

The greatest showman of them all, Phineas T. Barnum, naturally had to produce the mummified remains of another mermaid to satisfy his audiences, but there are those who said that this particular exhibit was presented with tongue in cheek.

The following incident occurred in the Southern Hemisphere late in the eighteenth century. "A very singular circumstance happened," wrote Captain Richard Colnett, "off the coast of Chili, in lat. 24 S., which, as it spread some alarm among my people, and awakened their superstitious apprehension, I shall mention.

"About eight o'clock in the evening an animal rose alongside the ship, and uttered such shrieks and tones of lamentation, so much like those produced by the female human voice when expressing the deepest distress, as to occasion no small degree of alarm among those who first heard it. These cries continued for upwards of three hours, and seemed to increase as the ship sailed from it. I never heard any noise whatever that approached so near those sounds which proceed from the organs of utterance in the human species."

Captain Colnett subsequently mentioned that one man was so panic-stricken that had he been much longer before reaching port he would certainly have died.*

Our next mermaid story takes us to the Antarctic.

"A boat's crew," according to Antarctic explorer James Weddell,** "were employed on Hall's Island, when one of the crew, left ashore to take care of some produce, saw an animal whose voice was distinctly musical. The sailor had gone to sleep. About ten o'clock he heard a noise resembling human cries. As daylight in these latitudes never disappears at this season, he rose and looked round; but, on seeing no person, returned to bed; presently he heard the noise again; rose a second time, but still saw nothing.

"Conceiving, however, the possibility of a boat being upset, and that some of the crew might be clinging to detached rocks, he walked along the beach a few steps, and heard the noise more distinctly, but in a musical strain. Upon searching round he saw an object lying on a rock a dozen yards from the shore, at which he was somewhat frightened. The face and shoulders appeared of human form, and of a reddish colour; over the shoulders hung long green hair; the tail resembled that of the Seal, but the extremities of the arms he could not see distinctly.

"The creature continued to make a musical noise while he gazed about two minutes, and on perceiving him it disap-

* *Voyage to the South Atlantic,* London, 1793.
** *A Voyage Toward the South Pole,* 1825, page 143.

peared in an instant. Immediately when the man saw his officer, he told this wild tale, and to add to the weight of his
testimony, (being a Romanist,) he made a cross on the sand
which he kissed, so making oath to the truth of his statement.
When I saw him, he told the story in so clear and positive a
manner, making oath to its truth, that I concluded he must
really have seen the animal he described, or that it must have
been the effects of a disturbed imagination."

In many northern regions it is generally believed that mermen and mermaids are actually some species of seal, very frequently the *Barbata,* which from its solitary habits has given
rise to these legends.

It is also possible that young whales, from the striking
fashion of raising their heads perpendicularly above the waves,
and so taking a deliberate survey of surrounding objects, may
occasionally have led to the same result.

The mermaid is known in Gaelic as the *ceasg, maighdean
na tuinne* ("maid of the wave") and *maighdean mhara* ("maid
of the sea"). A *ceasg* is a half-woman, half-grilse, who haunts
rivers and streams and is said to be very beautiful but dangerous. The "maid of the wave," if caught, can be prevailed
upon to grant three wishes.

There are stories of men marrying mermaids who had left
off their skin coverings. Like the swan maidens, they recover
their hidden skins and escape, but they always take an interest
in their human descendants, shielding them in storms or
guiding them to the best fishing grounds. Families of pilots
are reputed to be descended from mermaids.

One must have a dedicated belief in mermaids to accept
the so-called giant maid-of-the-wave tale as truth. According
to legend, one of these fierce demons swallows a hero, who
remains alive in her stomach. The hero's wife plays her harp,
charming the mermaid until she is so entranced that she
opens her mouth, gapes, and the hero escapes. Then the

mermaid turns on the wife and swallows her. The hero consults a wizard who informs him that the mermaid's life can be ended by finding her life-egg and crushing it. With the death of the mermaid the hero's bride is freed from the dead body, returns to her husband, and they live happily ever after.

The unusual story of the mermaid of Cromarty was well known in that region of Scotland until a hundred years ago. Many had seen her sitting on a rock on a lonely promontory where she combed her golden locks, while others had listened to her sweet voice singing. Usually, she was seen in solitary places. If approached by a human, she would escape into the sea.

There were those who claimed that she possessed the power either to harm or to help man, and that she preferred to use the power to harm. If a man succeeded in seizing and overpowering her, she always bought her escape by granting three wishes. However, if she was victorious in the struggle, she would carry the unfortunate assailant with her into the sea.

Writing in 1834, Hugh Miller stated that John Reid, a Cromarty shipmaster, was shrewd, sensible, calculating, good-humored, and fortunate. His early life had been spent in ships sailing to the ends of the earth. He returned to Cromarty with sufficient funds to purchase a fine large sloop for the lucrative Holland trade.

In spite of all this, Reid was an unhappy man. While on a solitary walk in Cromarty shortly after his return from the Indies, he had seen and fallen in love with the lovely village heiress, Helen Stuart, and she never left his thoughts. However, the young lady was not impressed.

Weeks and months passed, and John returned from a voyage in late April. On May Day he arose early, hoping to catch a glimpse of the fair Helen with her friends gathering May-dew on the green slopes of Drieminory.

The shipmaster, with thoughts only of the lovely Helen,

had no fear as he approached the notorious Dropping Cave, a huge pile of rock covered with moss and lichen, which stands out of the beach like an old ruined castle. Surmounted by hanging battlements and broken turrets, it conceals the cave itself and the skerries or ledges abreast of it from the travelers who approach them from the west.

John thought he heard a song and looked for the reason. He saw nothing but a seal that appeared to be listening to the music.

Rounding the cliff, he suddenly noticed a young mermaid who was sitting half on the rock, half in the water, on one of the outer ledges. Her long yellow hair fell in luxuriant profusion on her shoulders. Her face was turned toward the cave, and at times her song seemed to be answered from within the cavern by a faint, low chorus.

Reid, well acquainted with the beliefs of the age, realized that a great opportunity lay ahead of him. If only he could gain power over this creature, he might win the hand of his beloved Helen. He silently stole toward the shelf on which the creature was seated using every possible cover on the way. Once he reached the shelf, she turned and saw him. Her song changed to a shriek as she tried to fling herself into the sea, but the shipmaster was too quick. Although her strength was almost equal to his as she tried to drag him into the waves, he succeeded in overpowering her, forcing her against the cliff.

"Man, what with me?" she said in a tone of voice at once sweet and chilling.

"Wishes three," he answered, and then proceeded to state them. His first wish was that neither he nor any of his friends should perish by the sea as his father had; his second was that he should be fortunate in all his undertakings; and the third was that he should marry the fair Helen.

"Quit, and have," replied the creature.

Reid slackened his hold, and she sprang into the sea. He

wiped his brow and started up the hill in search of Helen, whom he found with a companion. It seemed to him the charm had already begun to work.

Helen had been unhappy because she could get no May-dew, but then she heard a tinkling of drops against the bottom of the pitcher and found that John had shaken May-dew of pure gold from the bushes so recently dry, filling the pitcher to the brim.

Reid explained to Helen that he had heard the mermaid's song and actually talked with the mermaid herself. Helen was troubled, for she recalled that the last time anyone had talked with the mermaid had been just before the storm in which Reid's father was drowned.

"But I am the creature's master," said the sailor, "and need not be so wary."

He told his story, and Helen listened with feelings of wonder, admiration, and terror. While returning home, she leaned for support and protection on the arm of the man who loved her. By the following May Day, he had become her husband.

In the *Contemporary Review* for 1881 Dr. Karl Blind tells of the mermen and merwomen of the British Isles.

"In Shetland, and elsewhere in the North, the sometimes animal-shaped creatures of this myth, but who in reality are human in a higher sense, are called Finns. Their transfiguration into seals seems to be more a kind of deception they practise. For the males are described as most daring boatmen, with powerful sweep of the oar, who chase foreign vessels on the sea. At the same time they are held to be deeply versed in magic spells and in the healing art, as well as in soothsaying. By means of a 'skin' which they possess, the men and the women among them are able to change themselves into seals.

"But on shore, after having taken off their wrappage, they are, and behave like, real human beings. Anyone who gets hold of their protecting garment has the Finns in his power. Only by means of the skin can they go back to the water. Many a Finn woman has got into the power of a Shetlander and borne children to him; but if a Finn woman succeeded in reobtaining her sea-skin, or seal-skin, she escaped across the water.

"Among the older generation in the Northern isles persons are still sometimes heard of who boast of hailing from Finns; and they attribute to themselves a peculiar luckiness on account of that higher descent."

The story of the brig *Yankee Doodle,* which in 1834 came across a party of mermen and mermaids off the Riding Rocks in the West Indies, is not too well known. However, if we are to believe the records, one of the crew became interested in visiting the mermaid haunts on the sea bottom, which he was able to do by attaching something resembling scuba-diving apparatus to his body.

The manatee of Florida and the West Indies, the dugong of eastern seas, and the stellerus, which is an inhabitant of the polar regions, all may often have been confused with mermaids. Their heads are scarcely distinguished from the body by a neck; they have no blowholes on the summit of the head, but nostrils on their snouts. The shape of the body is fishlike, but they have no dorsal fin.

Writing of the three groups in 1839, Dr. Robert Hamilton stated that they have not even the rudiments of the posterior extremity, while their pectoral fins are actually swimming paws. "Their mammae are pectoral; their skin is nearly destitute of hair, and their teeth are not those of carnivorous but of herbivorous animals."

In the *Histoire de la Compaigne de Jesus,* No. 276, we are told that during the sixteenth century mermaids and mermen were said to be off the coasts of Ceylon; for some fishermen there caught, at one draught, no less than seven. "They were dissected, and found made exactly like human beings." Authenticity is given to this extraordinary story by an account of the dissections.

A merman caught in the Baltic in 1531 was presented to King Sigismund of Poland. This merman was described as "a huge animal of the human form, but very much resembling a bishop in his pontificals."

In Epirus, Greece, a merman came on the shore and hid near a spring of water, endeavoring to catch young women who came there. He was captured while lying in wait for his human quarry. In captivity he could not be induced to eat, and he died in the course of a few days.

In the eighteenth century there were six so-called authentic records of these unusual denizens of the deep, listed as occurring in 1714, 1730, 1758, 1775, 1794, and 1797.

A fair at St. Germains, France, featured a mermaid, a picture of which was drawn from life by the famous French artist Gautier Villiers in the year 1758.

In 1775, while the American Revolution was beginning, a mermaid was exhibited in London. It was claimed that she was captured by a merchantman during the preceding year. Incidentally, she had three sets of fins.

Nineteen years later another mermaid was put on exhibition at Covent Garden. This female had been captured in the North Sea by a Captain Foriter.

In 1797 a mermaid was seen by William Munro, a schoolmaster of Thurso, Scotland, "in the act of combing its hair." Twelve years later Munroe wrote a letter to the London *Times,* which was published on September 8, 1809. An excerpt follows:

"I can say of a truth, that it was only by seeing the phenomenon, I was perfectly convinced of its existence."

There were five sightings between 1801 and 1819. In 1801

several mermaids were sighted in the West Indies. The natives called them *méné mamma* or mother of waters.

In 1809 the mermaid formerly seen in 1797 in the parish of Reay in Caithness, Scotland, was again sighted. She was observed by several persons less than twenty yards away.

Two years later when John McIsaac saw a mermaid in Corphine, Scotland, he made oath before the sheriff-substitute at Campbelltown, in the presence of the minister of Campbelltown, that he was telling the truth.

On August 11, 1812, a Mr. Toupin of Exmouth, Scotland, sighted a singing mermaid a mile from Exmouth bar. Her neck, back, and loins were covered with "broad feathers."

In 1819 a mermaid appeared on the coast of Ireland, the size of a girl of ten, but with a bosom as prominent as a girl of sixteen. She had long dark hair, and full dark eyes. When a man tried to shoot her, she plunged into the sea with a loud scream.

Another mermaid appeared in Buchan, Scotland. "In the village," said H. G. Reid, writing in 1870, "lived a man who had seen and conversed with the mermaid under a great cliff off the Bullers of Buchan."

Belief in the mermaid prevailed among many seafaring men who thought the creatures lived along the coast in caves. One incident concerns a mermaid climbing up on the bowsprit of a small vessel belonging to a resident of Peterhead, in Aberdeen, Scotland. The craft was driven among the rocks near Slains Castle, and all hands perished save one man who reached shore to tell of the disaster. This story indicated to the residents there that the appearance of the mermaid usually meant trouble.

In the beginning of the nineteenth century a mermaid was often seen on the Cromarty Firth shores in the moonlight, sitting on a stone and braiding her long yellow tresses.

There was widespread belief in the mermaid among the

fishing populations. A merman was seen off Portgordon, Banff-shire, Scotland, April 15, 1814.

George McKenzie, the schoolmaster of Rathven stated in the Aberdeen *Chronicle* the next day that two fishermen were near Portgordon, "when about a quarter of a mile from the shore, the sea being perfectly calm, they observed, at a small distance from their boat, with its back towards them, and half its body above the water, a creature of a tawny colour, appearing like a man sitting, with his body half-bent.

"Surprised at this, they approached towards him, till they came within a few yards, when the noise made by the boat occasioned the creature to turn about, which gave the men a better opportunity of observing him. His countenance was swarthy, his hair short and curled, of a colour between a green and a grey: he had small eyes, a flat nose, his mouth was large, and his arms were of an extraordinary length.

"Above the waist, he was shaped like a man, but as the water was clear, my informants could perceive that from the waist downwards, his body tapered considerably or, as they expressed it, like a large fish without scales, but could not see the extremity."

There was little time left to observe the creature. Looking at them steadily for a moment, the animal suddenly dived, rising again at some distance from the boat. This time he had a mermaid with him. She had breasts and her hair was not curled, but reached a little below the shoulders. The men were much alarmed at the apparitions, and made for the shore with all haste, where they gave the above account to the schoolmaster without any variation.

There are many who believe, consciously or unconsciously, that the mermaid is the ultimate in feminine perfection. We are told that many men have dedicated themselves to pursuing the mermaid, at the same time realizing that they will never catch up with her.

In closing this chapter, I can do no better than to quote from the pen of Oliver Wendell Holmes. In writing his poem "Chambered Nautilus" he tells of

> gulfs enchanted, where the siren sings,
> And coral reefs lie bare,
> Where the cold sea-maids rise to sun their
> streaming hair.

11

──────❦──────

The Frigate *Erfprins*

I am often asked, during or at the conclusion of a lecture, what shipwreck off the New England coast caused the greatest loss of life.

Actually, the worst disaster in New England's maritime history is also among its least known. Only a handful of people have heard of the Dutch frigate *Erfprins,* yet when that ship went down off Cape Cod in 1783, she carried with her 303 members of the crew. Without question the disaster was accompanied by many acts of bravery, but except for a few brief accounts garnered from the few survivors, the loss of this Dutch vessel made hardly a ripple in the New England area.

The *Erfprins* was one of a convoy of three Dutch men-of-war that the Netherlands government provided to escort their newly appointed Minister Plenipotentiary to the United States. The new minister, Pieter Johan van Berckel, the brother of the Pensionary of Amsterdam, sailed from Texel on either the ship-of-the-line *Overijssel,* carrying sixty-eight guns, or the frigate *de Briel* of thirty-six guns. The *Erfprins,* with fifty-four guns, was the third ship-of-war. The brigantine *de Windhond* completed the convoy, which, according to plan, was to stay a unit during the voyage.

The minister reached his destination, and concerning his voyage the standard history of the Netherlands Navy says that nothing unusual happened except the loss of the *Erfprins*. This is a masterpiece of understatement in view of the magnitude of the disaster. What happened makes a most unusual story.

The *Erfprins* was not the most seaworthy of vessels. One of eight battleships of a squadron of the Netherlands Navy, it had fought on July 20, 1781, against heavy odds, with an English fleet off the Dogger Bank.* She gave shot for shot. The Dutch inflicted and received damage that forced both fleets to retire without victory. The *Erfprins,* the special target of the British, suffered seriously in the encounter. In the two years after the Dogger Bank engagement, other ships in the Netherlands Navy were coppered for safety, but as far as is known, the *Erfprins* was not repaired in any way.

When the convoy reached the English Channel on their voyage to America, the *Erfprins* sprang a leak so severe that all five pumps were needed constantly to keep the battleship afloat.** In spite of this overwhelming handicap Commander Louis Aberson began the long sail across the ocean. After a week at sea the water began to gain, and so the captain signaled to the squadron commander, Captain Riemersma of the *Overijssel,* for advice. The squadron commander told Aberson that the orders left no alternative; they must continue across the sea until they reached Philadelphia. The only concession Riemersma made was that each vessel could now choose its own route.

One by one the other ships left the *Erfprins*. It must have

* Located about due east of Newcastle, England, and about halfway to Denmark.
** J. C. De Jonge, *Geschiedenis van het Nederlandsche Zeewezen,* page 360.

been a trying period to the officers and crew as they watched the brigantine *de Windhond* slide over the horizon and out of sight. Soon the other vessels followed, until the leaking battleship was left alone on the wide expanse of ocean.*

The *Erfprins,* left to her fate, plodded along in clear weather for several weeks. On September 19, however, in latitude thirty-seven a violent storm battered the ship severely and left her decks a shambles. When the storm went down, the captain surveyed the damage and found the fore-topmast on the deck; the mizzenmast and mainmast had crashed overboard. Now wallowing in the trough of the sea, the *Erfprins* continued to receive a terrific battering from the waves, which swept headlong against the sides of the stricken vessel. Pumping furiously, the men on deck for the moment held their own against the water pouring in from more than a dozen locations.

The discouraged, disheartened commander ordered the rigging of a jury mast and had the ship made as seaworthy as possible. The sailors pumped day and night in their efforts to keep the *Erfprins* afloat, but it was developing into a hopeless task. Still out of sight of land, the ship drifted almost at the wind's will.

Then came the moment when the exhausted sailors could no longer maintain their own against the incoming sea and the water began to gain in the hold of the warship. Inch by inch the *Erfprins* sank lower into the ocean.

Finally the craft was nothing more than a hulk. For some unexplained reason she remained afloat. Nine long weeks this voyage of hopeless terror continued. Supplies grew low, water became unfit for drinking. Then the sea slowly, inexorably, again began to gain inch by inch. More storms hit the *Erfprins,* each gale leaving the man-of-war in a more hopeless condition. Finally, on November 25, 1783, the crisis came. By

* *Ibid.,* p. 361.

this date the ship had sailed and then drifted to a point only twenty-four miles from Cape Cod.* That afternoon the vessel reached a position so low in the water that she was making no headway at all. Captain Aberson, realizing that the *Erfprins* might go down at any moment, decided to try to reach land. Choosing thirty-nine picked men to form his longboat crew, he left the ship and ordered the longboat's sail up as the men pushed away from the battleship. Four minutes after they left the vessel, the *Erfprins* sank beneath the waves, carrying to their death 303 members of the ship's company.

Rowing strenuously for several hours, the captain and the longboat crew finally sighted a brig outward bound, hailed it, and were rescued. Shortly afterward they were transferred to a Gloucester-bound sloop, which landed them at Cape Ann some time later.

Just what happened to the survivors after the Cape Ann landing is not clear. The Gloucester records speak of the forty men who brought the news of New England's worst shipwreck; the Boston *Gazette and Country Journal* also reports the incident. Without question they all eventually returned to the Netherlands, but the details are lacking. Captain Aberson wrote a long letter to Van Kinsbergen in Holland that was printed in the *Nederlandsche Jaarb. 1784,* but other than brief mention of honors bestowed upon him for saving the thirty-nine men, nothing is certain. Whether he ever tried to find others aboard the *Erfprins* who might have escaped, how he returned to Holland, what parts of the coast he traversed on his journey, we can only surmise. No other members of his crew aboard the ill-fated man-of-war ever reached shore.

---

* Evidently this was the last reading of the sun which the captain obtained.

12

Four Incredible Tales

The four stories in this chapter are placed together because
of their unusual nature.

The Enchanted Silo

On a particularly rainy afternoon late in December 1943 I
was a patient in the multistoried Seventh General Hospital
in Oran, North Africa. The head nurse was almost at her
wit's end because of a few of the recalcitrant wounded officers
on the famous third floor there who were being particularly
boisterous and bothersome.

She decided to give the officers a new program with which
to occupy their minds, and arranged for several English-
speaking French teachers then living in Oran to tell us some
of the history of this interesting Mediterranean seaport.

The teachers would visit the various floors and give short
stories of unusual events in the history of the North African

coast. In this way I was told a story by Georges Berriere, who lived next door to the Oran hospital. The story that has always stayed in my mind was about the disappearance of several prisoners from the underground silos at the edge of town.

During the early French occupations, almost a century before, a group of captured Arabian fighters were so desperate in their struggle with the occupation forces that they had to be placed in the strange underground silos that surrounded the city.

In one particular silo there was a series of disappearances that had no conceivable explanation. There was absolutely no way to escape after the thirty-foot ladder had been removed, and the French became quite concerned.

The first man to disappear was one of the tribal chieftains. After he vanished they examined the silo with care. The only unusual part of the silo was about twelve feet up from the floor, where an aperture of about sixteen inches in diameter was noted.

Another native was then put in the silo and he also disappeared. When the following week a third native vanished it was decided to put a guard in the silo at night. Nothing happened for some time. Then, suddenly one evening, shouts were heard from the guard accompanied by screams of terror from the Arab prisoner.

As a first measure, the guards lowered a lantern at the end of a cord to light up the scene, but in a twinkling it was broken and nothing could be seen in the darkness. An immediate search was made for another light. By the time it arrived, the noise had ended and not a sound could be heard in the pit.

The officer of the guard then carefully descended on a ladder with the light and when he reached the bottom of the pit he beheld a horrible spectacle. The Arab prisoner and the Zouave who had remained there to guard him were found immobile on the bottom of the pit, half-crushed beneath the weight of two fragments of a large serpent.

The officer signaled to be hauled to the surface. Overcome with horror, he fainted as he reached safety. A moment later he revived, and spoke to the others.

"The anaconda—the anaconda!"

The soldiers of the guard, thinking that there must be some misunderstanding, went down the ladder in their turn. Only too quickly they realized the truth. Fortunately, however, the fearful reptile was dead. Their comrade was disabled, and the Arab, frightened out of his wits, was unconscious.

The constrictor and its victims were hauled to the surface, and there it was found that the serpent measured about twenty-nine feet. A contemporary drawing indicates that it was about this length.

The whole mystery of the enchanted silo was now quite clear. The serpent had surprised the prisoners, suffocating them in their sleep, then crushed and swallowed them, after which it had crawled back through its opening in the silo.

The Zouave who had been in the pit related, as soon as he recovered consciousness, that his attention had at first been attracted by the noise of clods of earth falling into the silo, and almost instantly the serpent had made its appearance.

The brave soldier, without losing his presence of mind, had simply drawn his short sword and slashed about him sturdily, shouting the while for help. At last he had succeeded in cutting the huge snake into two pieces, which writhed in horrible convulsions, bruising and wounding him.

The Arab lay ill for a week, and his experience so affected his mind that he was pardoned. In the picturesque language of his tribe he was nicknamed the Snake Man.

The Zouave was made a corporal and was subsequently decorated. The silo became known as the Trouau-Bou, or Boa Constrictor Hole, and new recruits mounting guard for the first time in the Casbah were invariably regaled with this cheerful narrative.

Before leaving Oran for England on the hospital ship *Amarapoora* I visited the outskirts of town where I had been told the underground silos could be found. Although I did see several silos, I never found the one called by the natives Trouau-Bou.

The *Myra B. Weaver*

With the limp, lifeless form of a half-naked woman dangling from the rigging and two dead men lashed to the mast, the *Myra B. Weaver* was towed into Boston Harbor by the tugs *Mercury, Zetes,* and *Juno* on November 12, 1900. It was one of the strangest sights in Boston waterfront history. I have talked with several persons who witnessed the weird scene that November morning and each one has told me that it filled him with horror.

One sailor declared that he vowed at that moment never to go to sea again. Though he later changed his mind, he never forgot that image of the girl dangling in the rigging, seventy feet above the sea, the girl he had tied there in a vain effort to save her life.

The 155-foot *Myra B. Weaver* had sailed from Fernandina, Florida, on October 16 with a load of 425,000 feet of hard pine. Before reaching the Delaware Breakwater, she ran into high winds and bad storms.

After anchoring at the breakwater for two days, she resumed her journey northward and entered the waters of Vineyard Sound on November 8, 1900. Later that afternoon, the *Weaver*'s captain, R. S. Vannaman, read the barometer and observed that the glass was falling rapidly.

Being a prudent mariner, Vannaman ordered both his starboard and port bower let go and prepared for the storm, believing himself safe because of the two anchors holding the *Weaver*. He feared that if the storm was a bad one, he would lose his deckload of lumber and, because of the heavy load, possibly his ship in the bargain.

Before dawn the next morning the entire Atlantic Coast was hit by a westerly gale of substantial proportions. Up off Yarmouth, Nova Scotia, the side-wheel steamer *City of Monticello* went to the bottom with the loss of thirty-four of the thirty-eight persons aboard.

Within a few hours the snow that had begun to fall changed to rain, and the rain in turn gave way to hail. Thunder and lightning occurred frequently and the temperature dropped from fifty-eight degrees to below freezing within a short time. The wind began to rise, and Captain Vannaman realized the possibility that the schooner was not going to weather the storm.

"All hands into the rigging!" he shouted.

There were two women aboard—Miss Mary Emerson and Miss Ella DuBois—and the crew carried them up to the crosstrees to escape the reach of the mighty breakers. A moment later the cables parted and the schooner began to drift. Smashing at the craft, the waves battered the lumber and scattered it about the deck.

The captain tied the girls to the masts with heavy lines to prevent their falling overboard, for as the giant seas smashed at the vessel they rolled her almost over on her beam ends. Miss Emerson could not endure the exposure in the rigging. Lapsing into unconsciousness, she died within an hour.

At three-thirty the next morning the drifting *Weaver* struck heavily on Handkerchief Shoals off Cape Cod, turning over on her beam ends until her starboard side and masts were under water.

The deckload of lumber floated free, allowing the schooner to right herself. But it was too late to save Captain Vannaman, Miss DuBois, and two crew members, all of whom drowned when the ship capsized. The mizzenmast, with the dead bodies of the captain and Miss DuBois, floated away and was never seen again.

First Mate John Kearney and three other sailors still clung for their lives to the mainmast. Suddenly, far in the distance, they heard the sound of a ship's whistle, and soon they could tell that a steamer was approaching.

It was the *City of Macon,* bound from Savannah to Boston. As soon as the *Macon* had come up with the *Weaver,* a lifeboat was lowered. A few minutes later the four survivors were taken aboard.

The tugs *Mercury, Zetes,* and *Juno* were sent out from Boston later that week to bring the *Myra B. Weaver* into port. Captain Kemp of the *Juno* located the schooner twenty-two miles southeast of Chatham, and the long tow to Boston began.

Incidentally, the *Weaver* was repaired and renamed *Pendleton's Satisfaction.* She was later lost off Islesboro, Maine.

The Seal of Clew Bay

The story which follows was told to me by a friend who lives in Northampton, Massachusetts.

About one hundred years ago a young seal was taken in Clew Bay, Ireland, and domesticated in a gentleman's home, which was situated on the seashore. It soon became tame. It would come at its master's call, and often played with the children of the household. As the old man later described it, the seal was as full of fun as a dog and as playful as a kitten. Soon it answered to the name of Prince.

The seal went out each day to fish for its own wants, and often brought back a salmon or turbot for its master. In the summer it basked in the sun, but when the chilly blasts of winter hit the coast, Prince would stay indoors. On occasion, Prince would flip into the large oven that formed a regular appendage of an Irish kitchen at that time.

When Prince had lived with the family four years, a cattle disease became prevalent. On consulting one of the village wise women, the master was told that the disease was caused by harboring an unclean beast, the harmless and amusing seal. She said the seal must be destroyed, or her charms against the disease would be of no avail and cattle would continue to die.

The superstitious master consented to having the seal taken far out to sea and thrown over the side. This was done, and the boat returned. That night the family retired as usual, but the next morning a servant awakened her master to tell him that the seal was quietly sleeping in the oven.

As another cow in the village was reported ill, Prince's master knew he would have to take further action. Looking about, he found a fishing boat which was to leave the next morning. The master of the boat agreed to carry off the seal and not put him overboard until he had sailed by Inisturk Island and was some leagues beyond the island known as Inishbofin.

This time a day and a night passed. Then, on the second evening, a servant heard a faint scratching on the door. Opening it, she discovered the seal. Weary but happy, the seal stretched out before the fire and fell asleep.

The master of the house realized he was indeed in trouble. He again consulted the old crone, who said that while it was unlucky to kill a seal, Prince could be blinded before being carried out to sea. This cruel order was carried out.

A week passed. Affairs in the village became worse instead of better. Cattle died rapidly, and the old crone was forced to admit that her arts were useless.

On the eighth night after the seal had been committed to the deep there was a tremendous windstorm, and the kitchen help said that the banshees were wailing. In the morning the door was opened, and there, lying dead upon the threshold, was the seal. It had perished from hunger, being unable to hunt in its blinded state.

The poor beast was buried in a sand hill. The misfortunes of the family increased. The old hag became involved in a killing shortly afterward and was eventually hanged for murder.

The master's sheep and cattle died, his corn was blighted, his children did not reach maturity, and he finally died, blind and miserable himself.

Sea Mysteries

While in St. John, New Brunswick, in the year 1949 I visited Miss Margaret Evans at the St. John Museum. Among other stories, she told me of Frederick Cochrane, the accountant at Holder's sail loft in St. John. In his spare time he was a painstaking investigator of the windships of New Brunswick. Mr. Cochrane studied old logbooks, perused age-yellowed newspaper files, and interviewed ancient mariners. On his death in 1938 he left the St. John Free Public Library the neatly typed notes that were the result of his lifelong hobby.

Going through these records, one may discover stories of mutiny, heroism, shipwrecks, and salvage. Two stories refer to craft involved in mysteries that have never been explained, the *Union* and the *Ann Currier.*

The *Union* was built in 1889 by four unemployed ship carpenters, John Kelly, George Cutten, Michael Kelly, and Nathaniel MacCumber. On her maiden voyage the *Union* delivered a cargo of piling to Boston, and her next assignment was to pick up lumber at Shulie, Nova Scotia.

After unloading the piling at Boston, the *Union* passed through the Gulf of Maine and approached the Bay of Fundy on her way to pick up the piling. Captain John Kelly had four in the crew, Frank McDonough, William Bradshaw, Nelson Smith, and Jack Dyre. The *Union* put into the breakwater at St. Martins so all could have a chance to visit their loved ones before reaching Shulie.

Jack Dyre, who had no relatives in the area, volunteered to serve as watchman while the others were ashore with their families. When they returned Monday morning, they found Dyre standing on the breakwater. Haggard and nervous, his luggage piled beside him, Dyre told a strange tale.

At ten o'clock Sunday night he had turned into his bunk since no one was around and everything seemed as usual, and soon he was fast asleep. He wakened with a start and heard a voice warning him to leave the *Union.*

He then looked for the source of the voice, but his search was in vain. He made up his mind that he had been dreaming and climbed back into his bunk. Hardly had he fallen asleep when he was reawakened by the same voice giving the same warning. Again he toured the *Union,* and again he failed to find anything unusual.

Asleep again, he was aroused by the eerie voice and the ominous words. This time he admitted defeat. Packing his belongings, Dyre retreated to the breakwater, where the others found him.

Although Captain Kelly tried to persuade him to forget

the strange experience, Dyre refused, and Kelly was forced to sign on Richard Bradshaw, a relative of William Bradshaw, already a member of the crew, to replace Dyre for the remainder of the voyage.

Dropping away from the breakwater at noon, the *Union* drifted up toward Shulie with the tide. As the tide ebbed, the *Union* came abeam of St. Martins again. The sails of forty becalmed vessels could be counted all around the *Union*.

As the afternoon wore on, black clouds gathered, but there was still no wind. Captain Kelly, his eye on the weather, walked into the galley, remarking that it looked like rain, and he thought he'd better be ready and don his oilskins.

Suddenly the *Union* gave a violent roll, and a moment later seemed to be falling through space. Captain Kelly then heard the voice of McDonough below telling everyone to come up on deck. The *Union* had capsized, turning completely over.

Smith, who had been with Captain Kelly in the galley, had dashed up the companionway as the ship went over, and leaped free. Captain Kelly, trapped in the galley, drew a deep breath and dived into the companionway, which by now was pointing down rather than up. He surfaced at the side of the ship, and Smith, who by this time was clinging to the keel, reached out and helped his captain to safety.

By this time a heavy rainstorm was pelting down, as the black cloud was directly over them. There was no sign of their companions, and later they discovered all had been drowned.

The schooner had gone over so fast that she was still full of compressed air, and every so often Kelly and Smith heard oakum blow out of her seams with reports like pistol shots.

When the rain stopped, fishermen put out in a small boat and rescued Kelly and Smith. The *Union* was towed ashore, righted, and repaired. Afterward she sailed for nearly twenty-eight years.*

Nobody ever did figure out what caused her to overturn that Sunday off St. Martins. After his interview with the survivors, Mr. Cochrane used to say that such a strange event couldn't have happened, but it did.

The other mystery, that of the *Ann Currier,* recalls the *Mary Celeste,*** another craft built in the Maritime Provinces.

The *Ann Currier* cleared New York for St. John on December 5, 1883, with a cargo of Christmas merchandise. Aboard were Captain William Vanwart, George Peck, Leonard Vanwart, and two other seamen.

Sometime later, off Nantucket Shoals, the *Ann Currier* was sighted by the crew of a fishing ketch, who noticed that she was lurching aimlessly and "acting mighty funny." The fishermen wondered what was wrong, maneuvered alongside, and hailed her. There was no answer, no sign of life, and so they boarded her.

Her foresail and jib were up, all was in good order, but there wasn't a soul on the ship. The only thing missing, apart from the captain and crew, was the lifeboat.

The fishermen took her into Vineyard Haven. The company that had insured her, represented by H. R. Ranney of St. John, paid them for salvage. Ranney hired a crew at Boston to bring the *Ann Currier* on from Vineyard Haven to St. John, with a Captain Beverly in command.

Captain Beverly brought her into the Bay of Fundy and would have reached St. John if a heavy gale hadn't blown up from the southwest, sweeping her beyond her destination. Finally Captain Beverly anchored in the shelter of Quaco

---

* In 1917 she was wrecked in a storm at the mouth of the Bay of Fundy. Abandoned, she was sunk by a French gunboat as a menace to navigation.

** See my *Mysteries and Adventures,* page 311, and *Mysterious Tales of the New England Coast,* page 114.

Head, but on the night of January 18, 1884, the wind hauled around to the southeast. Dragging anchor, the schooner piled up on White Rocks, and at low tide she was high and dry.

Captain Beverly and his crew got ashore, leaving with what struck some people as undue haste. Hiring a team January 19 to carry them to St. John, they were shipped back to the United States immediately. To add to the mystery, when the residents of the Quaco district went aboard the vessel, they found that the paneling of her cabin had been chopped away with an ax, and that boards and splinters lay all over.

Eighty-four years have gone by, and no word has ever been heard of the men who sailed from New York on the *Ann Currier* in December 1883. She has joined the *Mary Celeste* and the *Carrol A. Deering,* both of whose crews vanished forever.

13

The *Veronica* Pirates

The piratical mutiny that occurred aboard the bark *Veronica* was possibly more brutal and senseless than any of the other hundreds of piracies recorded on the high seas. Many do not realize the extent to which piracies and mutinies took place as late as the present century, but the voyage of the *Veronica*, which began in Biloxi, Mississippi, in the fall of 1902, ended at sea in mutiny, piracy, and death.*

At the turn of the present century the *Veronica* was owned by Thompson and Company of St. John, New Brunswick. During the middle of October 1902, she sailed from Ship Island, Biloxi, Mississippi, with a cargo of hard pine lumber for Montevideo, Uruguay, South America. The master of the *Veronica*, Captain Alexander Shaw, was a veteran of a lifetime at sea, but in recent years he had become extremely

* Constructed at St. John, New Brunswick, in 1879 by a builder named Rowan, the bark *Veronica* had the following vital statistics: registered tonnage 1137, length 186.4 feet, beam 37.8 feet, depth of hold 22.1 feet. Her owners in 1880 were Mills and Jago, with St. John her home port and surveying port. The *Veronica*'s rating that year was A minus. Her international code letters were SEGV, her official number 79983.

deaf. Although known as a kindly old man at his home in Canada, he was identified by many sailors who had shipped under him as a stern, cruel master.

Trouble aboard began when the two most dominant men in the crew, Pat Doran and Gustav Rau, fought with each other for the privilege of running the forecastle gang.

In the battle for control, Doran won and happily assumed his new honors as "boss-of-the-Fo'c'sle." Rau nursed his grudge, and two other Germans aboard, Otto Monsson and sixteen-year-old Harry Flohr, sided with their countryman. It was not long before a Dutchman, Willem Smith, was also won over to their way of thinking. These four men spent considerable time discussing Doran, and eventually they decided to kill him.*

By this time the *Veronica* had sailed beyond the West Indies. Reaching the outer fringe of the Doldrums, she was off Brazil when the situation aboard finally became serious. By this time Rau had convinced Smith, Flohr, and Monsson that Doran was in league with the captain and mates to make life a hell for the four "Dutchmen" aboard, although this was never substantiated in any way. Rau also spent much time complaining about the food. Nevertheless, it was no better and no worse than what was being supplied aboard scores upon scores of similar sailing vessels in and out of Atlantic seaports on both sides of the Atlantic.

On Sunday night, December 2, the *Veronica* was practically becalmed in the Doldrums. Doran, Rau's hated enemy, was standing out on the fo'c'sle-head. All that afternoon Rau had been complaining to his countrymen about the Irishman and

---

* The ship's company included Chief Mate Alexander McLeod of Prince Edward Island, Second Mate Fred Abrahamson of Sweden, the Negro cook Moses Thomas, and three Germans, Rau, Monsson, and Flohr, Smith from Holland, two Swedes, Julius Parsons and Gustav Johanssen, Alec Bravo, a Hindu, and Pat Doran, an Irishman.

the officers. Suddenly he pulled out his knife and handed the weapon to young Flohr.

"Stick it in Paddy's throat," he dared. Frightened by Rau's determined attitude, the German youth began to cry.

"I haven't the heart to kill a pig," he stammered. "How can I possibly kill a man?"

Rau and Smith then decided to do the job themselves. First Rau and then Smith picked up iron belaying pins. The two men, with Flohr trailing behind them, climbed up on the fo'c'sle-head to approach Doran, who was on watch.

"Well, Pat," began Rau in very friendly tones, "are you keeping a good look-out? Can you see the North Star?"

The Irishman, surprised at the apparent cordiality with which Rau spoke, stooped down under the foot of the foresail so that he could check on the position of the North Star. As he crouched there, first Rau and then Smith smashed him on the head with their iron belaying pins, but for some reason the two blows failed to knock Doran out.

He tried desperately to protect himself from the Germans, but they overpowered him and soon knocked him unconscious. Then they pulled him into the port paint-locker.

Hearing the scuffling, the chief mate rushed forward. Since there was no one on look-out, he shouted at the German leader, "Rau, who is on look-out?"

"Pat Doran was here," answered Rau. "Then we saw him fighting with some one."

Chief Mate McLeod hurried forward to investigate. As he came within range, the two Germans struck him a series of violent blows with their belaying pins, and he lost consciousness. During the scuffle in the darkness, Rau hit his friend Smith on the head by mistake, injuring the seaman severely.

With McLeod lying unconscious, Rau searched the officer's pockets. He found a revolver, which he kept.

"Overboard with him!" he now ordered.

Young Monsson dragged McLeod to the rail and tumbled him into the sea.

The moment had come to take over the *Veronica*. Rau, Smith, Monsson, and Flohr now went aft. Flohr chased helmsman Johanssen away from the wheel with a belaying pin, and as Rau and Smith came along the poop deck, Captain Shaw walked out of the after companion to find out why no one was at the helm. Confused, the master peered into the binnacle, and Smith hit him in the stomach with a belaying pin. As the captain fell toward Rau, the latter began to fire at him with the revolver. Staggering across the deck, Captain Shaw managed to reach the chartroom.

The next to be awakened by the scuffling and shooting was Second Mate Abrahamson, who ran up out of the cabin. Rau fired at the mate, hitting him in the stomach. Stumbling toward the chartroom, the mate joined Captain Shaw, and they shut and bolted the door.

The mutineers decided to entrap the master and mate in the chartroom. They nailed wood over the portholes, roped down the skylight, and fastened timbers across the entrance.

Next they turned their attention to Doran, the wounded Irishman, who had regained consciousness.

"Please, let me have a drink," he begged.

The two murderers smiled at each other.

"Yes," answered Rau, "we'll give you plenty to drink." They hauled him out and threw him overboard.

Next on the list was the cook. Thomas had shut himself in his berth, but when Rau fired several shots through the door, Thomas came out and surrendered. As the two met in the doorway, the German placed his revolver to the cook's head, intending to finish him. Smith stepped between the men, saying that Thomas was needed to prepare the meals.

Rau thought for a moment. Then, beginning to swear, he

ordered the cook into the galley, where Thomas set to work preparing coffee for the four men. Afterward the cook was locked in the sail room of the forward deckhouse.

The next few days passed without any more killings, but on December 11 Rau decided to turn his attention to the chartroom. Captain Shaw and the second mate had bound up their wounds as best they could and were awaiting Rau's next move. Badly wounded in the neck, shoulder, and lower part of his body, the master discovered that Abrahamson's stomach wound was also a serious one.

Rau now came to the skylight. Shouting down into the chartroom, he ordered the two officers up on deck.

"The captain is too ill to move," answered the mate. "He is dying."

"Dying or not," answered Rau, "I want him up here!"

Hearing Rau's command, Captain Shaw forced himself to get up from the floor. After rising to his knees, he crawled across until he was under the skylight.

"Give us some water and I'll let you have my gold watch," the old sea captain pleaded. Smith dipped out a bucket of water and lowered it down through the skylight and asked in return a sextant, chart, dividers, and parallel rulers.

With the exchange completed, Rau nailed down the skylight and left the two injured officers by themselves. Three long days were to elapse before another visit.

During that three-day interval, from December 11 to December 14, Rau was attempting to decide what his plan of operation should be. Finally he made up his mind to kill both the master and the second mate.

On December 14 he again approached the skylight. This time Rau shouted down to the second mate to come out. Rau and Monsson stood on the poop armed with revolvers, while Flohr had a belaying pin. When the mate staggered up on deck, he saw the mutineers waiting. Running from them as fast as his injuries would allow. Abrahamson reached the starboard side of the poop. Smith then took careful aim and shot the mate in the shoulder. Realizing he would probably be killed anyway, the twice-wounded officer leaped over the rail into the sea, where he began swimming away from the vessel. Hurriedly, Rau put the bark about to come up on the mate in the water and finish him off. The three pirates shot at the swimmer until he sank out of sight.

With the mate dead Rau ordered Captain Shaw up on deck. The captain refused. Rau decided to settle matters once and for all and gave the Hindu sailor Alec Bravo an ax.

"Get into the chartroom and drive out the captain," he ordered.

A few minutes later the old man tottered into the alleyway, and Rau called to young Flohr, "Shoot him, Flohr, shoot him!"

Flohr's heart sank when he saw the master's terrible condition, and the horrified lad ran away from the scene.

Rau went after Flohr. "If you don't shoot him, I have a bullet for you."

Flohr, trembling, then took the pistol and fired three times in the general direction of Captain Shaw, missing on each attempt.

"You are stupid," growled Rau as he snatched the revolver away from Flohr. "I'll show you."

Rau strode up to the captain, who was leaning against the companion hatchway with his hands before his face. Holding the gun against the master's head, Rau blew his brains out. The body fell down the companion steps, but they hauled it up and pitched it into the sea.

Gustav Rau now told the survivors that he was making himself captain of the *Veronica*. Smith would be his lieutenant, and Monsson, Thomas, Flohr, Bravo, and Johanssen the crew.

All this time Julius Parsons, who had refused to join the mutineers, was hiding in the forward deckhouse. For the moment the pirates left him alone.

Rau and his companions next began to discuss their plans for the future. At first they considered wrecking the *Veronica* at the St. Peter and St. Paul Islands, but now they abandoned this plan as far too uncertain. Their final decision was to burn the ship and let her sink.

In detail Rau's plan was to begin loading the longboat for a trip to the Brazilian coast, with the first step painting out the name on the longboat, VERONICA, ST. JOHN, N.B.

Rau then told all the survivors to memorize the story he concocted. He told them that after leaving port, the *Veronica* had encountered bad weather in the Florida Straits and the main-topsail-yard was carried away. While up aloft repairing it, Chief Mate McLeod had fallen to the deck and was killed. After this accident, so the story would go, yellow fever broke out aboardship and two of the crew and the second mate died. Rau was promoted to his place. Then while becalmed off the Brazilian coast, according to their story, fire began amidships so that they had to abandon the bark. Part of the crew got into the longboat while the master and others took the quarter-boat.

This fictitious account had to be rehearsed before Rau twice daily, but Bravo and Johanssen, being dull-witted, were unable to memorize the story correctly. Realizing that the two would expose the entire plot, Rau decided that they must die. He soon laid careful plans for disposal of both men.

The self-appointed captain now sent Johanssen out to stow the flying-jib. Hanging below the boom, the sail was just as it had been when run down. Johanssen clambered out to make the sail fast. As soon as he was out on the bowsprit, Rau and Smith riddled Johanssen with bullets, and the man fell overboard to his death.

Bravo was next. Rau ordered the Hindu to haul up the slack of the foresheet, which was trailing in the water. While the sailor hauled away, Smith went behind him and shot him in the back of the head. The Indian also fell into the sea.

Sixteen-year-old Flohr, evidently becoming hardened to the carnage, now aimed his pistol at the cook, but Smith interfered: "Who's going to cook for us if you kill him?" Smith thus saved the cook's life for the second time.

That midnight Julius Parsons, who had refused to take sides with or against the mutineers, attempted to escape from the deckhouse, but his body stuck when he got his head and shoulders through the tiny square window. In this position he was found by Monsson, who killed Parsons with his iron belaying pin, battering the sailor to death.

Rau, the inhuman monster, with success overwhelming him, now made his final plans. Hounding the cook from task to task, Rau told Thomas to bake a batch of bread for a long boat journey and forced him to provision the longboat. When ready to abandon ship, Rau ordered the cook to chop plenty of kindling wood and pile it up for a bonfire in the cabin and forecastle. The men then covered the kindling with mattresses and old clothing, on which kerosene was poured.

Next they hauled the longboat off the forward house and pulled it across the deckload for launching. After sliding her into the sea, they stowed more provisions and gear aboard her.

The pirates soon had the ship afire fore and aft. The four mutineers and the cook got into the boat, shoved off, and set sail. For a time they remained near the bark, fascinated by the sight of her going up in flames. Then they bore away south-southeast close-hauled to the prevailing trade wind, their destination the coast of Brazil.

It was December 21 when they set the *Veronica* afire, and on Christmas Day the longboat neared the coast. Rau now threw overboard all instruments and provisions in an effort to show that they had abandoned their ship in great haste. After rehearsing their story once more, they steered the boat for the shores of South America. Nearing the shore, the pirates made their last attempt to strengthen their tale, taking off their caps and tossing them into the sea, after which they protected their heads from the burning sun by removing their stockings and using them for hats.

The coast they approached proved to be a section of the Brazilian mangrove swamp near Cazniera Island, a port of call for a Liverpool line of steamers. On December 26 the mutineers, concealed in the mangroves, watched the S.S. *Brunswick* appear and come to anchor. While the ship was taking cargo aboard from a craft alongside, Rau decided to tell the *Brunswick*'s captain his story and then ask for help.

Rau's visit to the *Brunswick* and events which followed were later recorded by the ship's captain, George Browne.*

Boarding the steamer with the others, Rau asked to see the captain, to whom he told a story substantially as agreed upon beforehand. The other survivors kept quiet, listening attentively. Rau stated that they had spent eleven days in the boat and had only thirteen biscuits and a keg of water when they left the ship.

"This story appeared somewhat fishy to me," said Captain Browne afterward, "but the poor devils looked pretty hard up. I had to accept what they said and treat them as shipwrecked men. Accordingly, I gave them food, drink, and clothing."

Captain George Browne duly made an entry in the S.S. *Brunswick*'s log:

* I am indebted to Frederick William Wallace for Captain Browne's account.

From Lisbon towards Maranham. 1.1.03. Island of Cajueira Tutoia. Anchorage Brazil.

I have this day taken on board five members of the crew of the barque *Veronica* of St. John's, New Brunswick, which vessel was burnt at sea on the 20th December 02, they having arrived at the Island of Cajueira Barra de Tutoia Coast of Brazil on the 25th December 02 in a state of complete destitution being only partially clothed, and having been five days in the boat. Their provisions when they left the ship consisted of one small barrel of water, and eleven biscuits. There being no Consul at this place and no one to help them or give them food, as the island is only inhabited by native labourers during the stay of our vessel there, I have taken them on board in order to hand them over to their Consul at Lisbon to which port we are bound. I have examined several of them, and they all agree that the barque *Veronica* of St. John's, N.B., left Ship Island, U.S.A., on the 11th October 02 bound to Monte Video with a cargo of lumber. Alexander Shaw, Master. Crew 12 hands. All went well until about the 25 October. A seaman named Gustave Jansen, a native of Sweden died at sea and on or about 23rd November the chief mate Mr. MacLeod fell from the main topsail and was killed.

On the 20th December fire was discovered on board and the vessel soon became hopelessly on fire, and the crew abandoned the ship. The second mate and four men left in one boat and the captain and four men in the other. The boats separated and nothing has been heard of the captain's boat since to their knowledge or ours. I make this entry in the Official Log as being the only record on hand of the loss of the aforesaid vessel.

(Signed) George Browne, Master
John Clarke, Mate.

The "shipwrecked" men were the object of considerable sympathy. Coronel * Joaquin dos Santos, a benevolent Brazilian gentleman, offered to hire the men and give them good wages. An English cattle rancher also made them an offer. Nevertheless, Rau declared they all wanted to go to England and find out if the captain's boat had been picked up. Why he should have decided on this course is hard to understand. Had they stayed in Brazil, the true story of the *Veronica* probably would never have been told.

Captain Browne then made arrangements to take them to Liverpool and berthed the *Veronica*'s men in the forecastle with the *Brunswick*'s crew with the exception of Rau, the pirates' ringleader. As he had claimed that he was an officer, Rau was placed in officer quarters with an apprentice.

Nothing of importance occurred for ten days, and then, while off the Canary Islands, Captain Browne was aroused from an afternoon siesta by a soft but persistent tapping on the door. There he discovered Thomas, the *Veronica*'s cook, crouching on his hands and knees to avoid being seen by the officer of the watch. Trembling, tears streaming down his face, Thomas begged the captain to let him come into the chart room, as his life was in danger.

Captain Browne brought the man inside and asked why he was afraid of losing his life. "The *Veronica*," began Thomas, "was set afire by those fellows you have on board. They murdered the captain, his officers, and five others. Last night Gustav Rau came into the cabin where you put me with the cook, baker, and pantry man, when they were asleep, and tried to get hold of me. But I made a noise and the cook threw a boot at Rau, who ran out. I've made up my mind to tell you everything, as I know he will get me if he can."

Captain Browne cautiously locked the door and pulled the

* Coronel is an obsolete form of our present word Colonel.

blinds over the ports. Then after swearing Thomas on the Bible, he took down the cook's narrative.

Ordering the cook to complete secrecy, the master let him out of the chart room by another door. Nevertheless, as Thomas started out, he was seen by the officer of the watch, who afterward innocently commented on the visit to Rau.

Captain Browne realized that with four dangerous mutineers on board, he would have to plan his strategy carefully. There were a number of passengers on the *Brunswick*, including ladies and children, as well as a good many foreigners in his crew. Reluctant to put the *Veronica*'s men in irons on the cook's word alone, the master was also afraid of what the Germans in his own crew might do. After intensive consideration, he decided to act for the time as though he had heard nothing, and told no one of Thomas' revelations.

When he landed at Madeira, Captain Browne reported the loss of the *Veronica* by fire and stated that he had five survivors aboard, saying nothing about the mutiny. But when the *Brunswick* arrived at Lisbon, the captain revealed the entire story to the British consul, who advised him to keep quiet and carry the men to England, but to enter the story in the ship's log. Captain Browne made the following entry:

Moses Thomas of the barque *Veronica* of St. John's New Brunswick and one of the members of the shipwrecked crew on board this vessel did on the 12th day of January 1903 make a statement to me privately that the other four men led by Gustav Rau did before the barque was burnt kill the captain and mate and also attempt to kill him. This statement I have communicated to H.M.B. Consul at Lisbon who ordered me to make this entry in the Official Log and take the men to Liverpool and hand them to the authorities.

(*Signed*) George Brown, Master.

To allay Rau's suspicions, the captain arranged a shipboard concert for the castaways and collected quite a sum in cash for them.

When the steamer reached Liverpool, the police, already instructed by the British Foreign Office, were awaiting the pirates' arrival.

As soon as the ship was warped to the Liverpool Herculaneum Dock Wall, detectives clambered aboard the *Brunswick* to interview the murdering mutineers. The discussion between the *Veronica*'s survivors and the police had reached a point where the pirates asked if the captain's boat had been picked up. Suddenly the police snapped handcuffs on the mutineers. Taken by surprise, they were transported in a prison van to Dale Street Jail, Liverpool.

The cook, Moses Thomas, was brought before a magistrate, where he repeated the statement he had made to the master of the *Brunswick*. At first, the other four stuck to their pre-arranged story, but Flohr suddenly broke down and confessed, not knowing that Thomas had revealed the true story of the *Veronica*. Flohr was now given clemency to turn King's Evidence.

Smith, realizing that the game was up, tried to throw all the blame for the murders on the cook, declaring Thomas the ringleader, but Flohr's story refuted him. When on the stand, Rau declared that Flohr and Thomas were the ones who engineered the mutiny and did the killing, but this was easily proved false. Incidentally, it was ascertained that Rau, several years before on another ship, had attempted to murder his mate.

Rau, Monsson, and Smith were indicted—the murder charge being confined to the killing of Alexander Shaw, master of the *Veronica*, with an added charge of piracy on the high seas. Mr. Tobin, D.C., and F. E. Smith, later Lord Birkenhead, prosecuted. The mutineers were each defended by counsel, and the case was tried before Justice Lawrence, at the Liverpool Assizes, in St. George's Hall, May 12 to 15, 1903.

After the testimony ended, the jury took only twelve minutes in finding the accused men guilty.

Rau, Smith, and Monsson were sentenced to death. Monsson, a lad of eighteen, on account of his youth and previous good character, was recommended to mercy. Rau and Smith were duly executed in Walton Jail; Monsson escaped the gallows. Flohr, as King's Evidence, went free.

Captain Browne of the *Brunswick* had to undergo considerable chaff and criticism for the manner in which he handled his part of the affair, but actually he had been sitting on a powder keg from the moment he took the mutineers aboard until the *Brunswick* landed at Liverpool.

Justice Lawrence complimented him for his work and awarded him a "solatium" of ten guineas as compensation for the anxiety he had undergone during the passage.

14

————— ❦ —————

The *Erne*

In March 1967 I met Alfred Willis for the first time. Now believed to be the only man still alive who went to sea on the mystery ship *Erne*, the former able-bodied seaman related his experiences aboard and gave me his views concerning the strange disappearance of Captain Fickett and others from the vessel in the year 1912.

Before learning seaman Willis' story, let us discuss the *Erne*'s history. Indeed, the last voyage of the ship *Erne* is one of the most interesting unsolved mysteries of the Atlantic.

During the voyage preceding the final trip, a young artist named Worden Wood fell into the sea. On September 10, 1911, the British ship *Erne* was about thirty miles from shore near Lobos Island, South America. The *Erne,* under weigh at the mouth of the Plate River, was proceeding at nine knots, while Wood, serving as boatswain, and a sailor named Fred Hudson had been clearing the three-thousand-pound anchor in preparation for letting it go a few feet over the side.

Going over too soon, the anchor pulled Wood and Hudson with it to a position just under the cathead. Hudson held on, but Wood missed it and fell overboard, sinking down into the water.

His fellows sailors pulled Hudson back on board, but the *Erne* passed by Wood, who came to the surface just in time to make a frantic effort to snare the patent log line dragging astern. He managed to grasp it and hold on. By this time Captain Temple A. Fickett, master of the *Erne,* had noticed Wood's dilemma and began to haul in on the line. Wood was a husky lad, but the line snapped, leaving him to drift away. Captain Fickett tossed over a life preserver, but it floated diagonally away from Wood, who decided to rest on his back and await rescue.

It was fifteen minutes before the *Erne* could be headed into the wind, and by this time Worden Wood was a mile astern. He had already decided to make an effort to reach the life preserver, and gained it after a swim of a mile and a half.

Meanwhile his comrades were attempting to lower a lifeboat, but because the boat stuck on the davits, three quarters of an hour passed before it hit the water. The men then rowed energetically until they reached Wood, who was exhausted by his swim. In the water almost two hours by this time, he was grateful to his rescuers when they pulled him aboard, for his escape from death had been a narrow one.

On Saturday afternoon, December 23, 1911, Captain Fickett proudly sailed his beautiful ship in by the Boston Lightship and Boston Light, arriving in time for the Christmas holidays.

Boatswain Wood, bronzed and healthy from his long sea voyage, went down the gangplank to land once more. When he visited his friends he told of his experiences and of his narrow escape from death in the sea. He also informed them that he was going to continue as boatswain of the *Erne* for some time to come.

The *Erne* had been built in Grennoch, Scotland, in 1886,

and for years was actively engaged in the coolie trade between Calcutta and the West Indies.* She was 255.6 feet long, her beam was 38.3 feet, and the depth of hold 23.2 feet. Her net tonnage was 1528 and the gross tonnage 1692. Around 1911, Boston parties purchased her to engage in the lumber-carrying trade between Boston and the River Plate, although she still carried a British registry charter.

Captain Fickett, who hailed from Hampden, Maine, was about fifty years old, a capable navigator with an excellent rating as a master. For eight years he had been captain of the Emery-fleet barkentine *Allanwide*. After that he purchased a master's interest in the schooner *Miles M. Merry*, and for a time engaged in the coal-carrying trade. During the one trip when he stayed at home, the *Merry* was wrecked on the New Jersey coast. Shortly afterward he went to England, where he made arrangements to go aboard the *Erne*. His wife, who always traveled with him, was on this voyage, for the couple made their home aboardship.

Captain Fickett sailed back with the *Erne*, which was legally in the hands of the first mate, James Elliott of Liverpool. The mate had master's papers under British Registry. Thus Elliott was the technical captain while Fickett was the active master of the ship and the men.

At the end of this voyage, on a December day in 1911, Captain Mortimer Nickerson of the tug *Confidence* towed the *Erne* from Deer Island to Bird Island Flats, where she anchored. Captain Fickett had already frightened the first mate by sailing the *Erne* in from the vicinity of the Boston Lightship without a pilot in a thick, driving rain coming from the east southeast.

---

* According to Captain Frank H. Peterson of the Boston Marine Society: "The *Erne* was one of the coolie ships which brought the coolies out to work on plantations for three-year terms. The lower hold was full of rice and between decks it was full of coolies."

In January 1912, when the time came for the *Erne* to put on another load of lumber, Captain Fickett made his first mistake, deciding to violate British law. According to the British Merchants Shipping Act of 1906, no craft of British Registry is allowed to carry a deckload of lumber between October 31 and April 16, the winter season. This law was passed only after many sad experiences of disaster at sea because of deckloads.

Loading went ahead speedily at the Charlestown Mystic Docks, and by January 24 the cargo was aboard. There were 1,333,298 feet of white pine, 93,539 feet of oak, and 21,438 feet of poplar. The deckload was a substantial one.

Captain Fickett tentatively chose his crew, but one day Worden Wood discovered that the captain and the first mate had been quarreling; in fact, Wood declared later that "bad blood existed." Wood decided not to go on the trip, as did two others. This necessitated what amounted to shanghaiing three more men, Richard Fishwick, G. T. Keswick, and David Magnet. Other members of the ship's company were First Mate James Elliott of Liverpool, Second Mate Frank Cushing * of 9 Tufts Street, Somerville, steward George Ray of Brooklyn, cabin boy Russell Walker of 7 Hamlin Street, Medford, and seamen Samuel Mack, Andrew Almer, John Olsen, Harry Franklin, Nells Otteson, Magnus Lind, John Tolen, and Selin Wilen. Robert Hay, technically listed as the boatswain, actually was a passenger from Portland, Maine. Mrs. Fickett also made the trip with her husband. Thus there were eighteen persons aboard the *Erne* when she sailed.

On January 26, 1912, the *Erne* was towed down the harbor to Bird Island Flats, where ice delayed her departure. After being taken to President Road in Boston Harbor she was further delayed by adverse winds, finally sailing February 1. All went well during the first part of the voyage, but on

* Considered by his crew as a bad actor.

Saturday, February 3, when the *Erne* was seven hundred miles at sea, a tremendous northwest gale set in.

Soon gigantic waves were making a clean sweep of the overloaded *Erne*, causing extensive damage. The wind blew harder and harder, and the vessel, now under bare poles except for three storm sails, was driving before the gale as best she could. The deckload soon became a terrible handicap in the tremendous, raging seas.

Monday, February 5, was the worst day of the storm. Suddenly a giant wave hit the *Erne*, throwing the two men away from the wheel. She broached to, taking on another huge wave broadside which nearly engulfed her, destroying her bulwarks amidships.

Another sea washed through the break in the bulwarks, carrying a large portion of the deckload overboard through the opposite bulwarks, thus for all practical purposes cutting the ship in two. No one could pass either forward or aft through the breach, for green water from then on washed through almost continually.

Mrs. Fickett, her clothing soaking wet, suffered severely from seasickness at this time. Captain Fickett did what he could to comfort her and keep her as dry as possible. While she was resting in her cabin, a great wave swept right into the compartment, carrying her through a large plate-glass mirror into an adjoining compartment, from which she was swept by another wave a moment later. The captain found his wife and carried her into the chartroom in a fainting condition.

According to the seamen who survived, from the moment of the break through the bulwarks it was impossible to steer the ship, and she fell in the trough of the ocean. Most of the crew were forward with Chief Mate Elliott, while Captain Fickett, his wife, passenger Hay, Second Mate Cushing, and the cabin boy were aft. The break amidships separated the two groups. As the cabin boy says later in this chapter, he left the captain's party to get a fresh change of clothes and never saw the others again.

By now all the boats except one were swept away, and that boat remained at the break of the poop until about noon. It may have been there a greater length of time, but how much longer is a question.

On February 8, nine survivors, Russell Walker, Fishwick, Franklin, Mack, Almer, Magnet, Lind, Wilen, and Olsen, were sighted aboard the *Erne* by the captain of the Leyland Liner *Cuban,* and eventually rescued.

The survivors explained that the members of the crew who were in the forward part of the vessel had lashed themselves to the forerigging and the jibboom during the violent storm. They had stayed there from Monday night to Wednesday morning without food or drink. Several of the men, exhausted from exposure and lack of food, then slipped into the ocean to their death. The chief mate, in some manner, was hanged by the gaskets. The eight survivors had worked their way aft and reached the midships house, then the poop, and finally the chart room, the only safe and dry place on the ship. There they met cabin boy Walker, who had been alone on the after part of the vessel without seeing anyone for a good part of three days. It was the opinion of the survivors that the captain had taken the boat with his wife, the passenger, and the second officer, leaving the others aboard the stricken vessel.

When the *Cuban* reached Liverpool, the British government at first arranged to conduct a trial but later dropped these plans.

In Boston there was great excitement when the meager details of the disaster were learned. Various newspapers played up the exciting possibilities—mutiny, murder, desertion on the high seas. One theory easily discredited was that during a rush for the remaining lifeboat, the captain and the others with him were killed.

The theory of mutiny was almost universally agreed upon by New England seafaring men.

As the years have gone by there has been considerable discussion and argument as to what really happened on the *Erne*. In March and April 1954, after several years of research and interviewing, I re-examined all available evidence I could find concerning the *Erne*. Then I talked again with men of the sea whose viewpoints I respect. Personally I have yet to form an opinion as to what happened. All the facts, theories, and opinions available to me are presented here, and you must decide for yourself.

When the news of the disaster trickled back to Boston that February of 1912, among the first to make a statement was Oscar A. Fickett of Bangor, Maine. He had visited his cousin, Captain Fickett, aboard the *Erne* just before sailing. When informed of the disaster, Oscar Fickett stated: "I'm afraid that they've killed him." He explained that Captain Fickett and First Mate Elliott had serious trouble even before the voyage began. As a result of the trouble, Captain Fickett slapped the mate's face, after which Elliott had been overheard saying: "I'll get even with that son-of-a-gun!"

Horace A. Stone, a well-known shipowner and lifelong friend of Fickett, also visited the *Erne* just before the sailing.

"They've killed Captain Fickett," he announced when told of the tragedy. "Captain Fickett would never have left the ship and nine of his crew on board. I am positive of that! It would have been impossible for him and the second mate and Mr. Hay to have launched the heavy lifeboat alone in such a storm with those great seas running. It was eighteen feet long, and made of teakwood. Furthermore, they never would have taken their chances of freezing to death in an open boat in North Atlantic winter weather when they could have stayed aboard the ship, which was not in danger of sinking when the *Cuban* sighted her. I knew Captain Fickett well enough to be sure that he never would have deserted the ship. They killed him!"

Former Boastwain Worden Wood, who had fallen overboard from the *Erne,* as I have previously stated, also made a long statement after learning of the mysterious fate which befell the *Erne.* Having realized that serious trouble might develop on the coming trip, he had left the *Erne* a few days before she sailed.

Stating definitely that the lifeboat could never have been put over in a storm by only three men, he added that Captain Fickett would never have left the ship by boat unless it was under conditions similar to those forced on Captain Bligh of the *Bounty,* who was cast adrift by his rebellious crew.

Wood believed that there was a mutiny, and that because of bad feeling between Elliott and the captain, Fickett was surprised and overpowered.

"To my personal knowledge," said Wood, "Captain Fickett was in the habit of locking the heavy door which led to the main cabin, the captain's quarters, the pantry, the storeroom, and the spare cabin. Captain Fickett was armed with a seven-shot repeating rifle, a revolver of large caliber, and a magazine pistol. He could have prevented the stores from being seized for a time, without question. Probably First Mate Elliott got below while Captain Fickett was asleep and ordered him into the boat with his friends. Probably when they did get into the boat it capsized almost at once in the great seas then running. Furthermore, shortly before the *Erne* sailed, First Mate Elliott told me personally that he was going to get even with the captain before the trip ended. Apparently he did.

"The main topgallants were of wood, and the only way that I can account for these being gone and the sails in shreds is that they snapped in a blow either before or during the trouble aboard the ship, when there was nobody attending to the wheel."

When news of the disaster came, the derelict hunter *Seneca* of the Revenue Cutter Service was ordered to search for the *Erne* and obtain evidence of what had happened aboard her, but she never did catch up with her. When the *Cuban* left the *Erne*, the latter was reported as being in latitude 40° 27′ North, longitude 49° 36′ West, and was then drifting slowly to the south. On February 13 Captain Thomas of the steamship *Cestrian* sighted the *Erne*, which was then drifting in latitude 41° North, longitude 47° West, or almost nine hundred miles east northeast of Boston. Not quite a year later the *Erne* was sighted drifting bottom up off the east shores of Sable Island.

On several occasions I interviewed Russell F. Walker, the cabin boy of the *Erne*, who died two years ago. His voluntary statement follows:

"I went aboard the *Erne* about January 25, 1912. We sailed the first of February and were caught in the storm February fifth. It was three days later when the *Cuban* of the Leyland Line picked us up. Trouble started at twenty minutes of twelve on Monday, February 5, 1912. I was back in the cabin when it came. It was a giant wave, a big dallop that came right over the stern and washed two men from the wheel, coming down and pouring into the cabin. When I came up I went to the poop deck. When I got there I figured I was all set. The captain, his wife, the second mate, and Mr. Hay were all with me.

"The two sailors had managed to get forward after they lost control of the wheel, and the ship was wallowing in the trough of the sea. This rolled the sticks out of her. The captain then made the remark in my presence that although he had been going to sea for twenty-five years this storm was the dirtiest and the roughest of all, and it was the first time he had ever lost control of a ship.

"Captain Fickett was about six feet one inch and weighed around 230 pounds. He was a good fighter. I formed an opinion that he was a bad man to monkey with but nevertheless honest, good and square.

"Contrary to what you may have heard, First Mate Elliott always treated me well, and I found him a scholar and a gentleman. When he went forward that afternoon a gasket got loose and hopped around. This was about four o'clock, after the captain and his party had disappeared. Well, the mate got tangled up in that gasket, lost his hold on the rigging, and he went down, the gasket catching around his neck and hanging him before my eyes! It was an awful sight, nothing you'd wish to look at. Yes, I was terribly sorry when I saw First Mate Elliott hanged off the bowsprit.

"Sometime before then the captain and his party had disappeared. The way it happened we shall never know, but what I saw I'll tell now. Around noon I started away from the cabin toward the half deck for a change of clothes. The half deck was filled with water up to my knees.

"Now, on my way to the half deck I met the captain, his wife, mate Cushing and passenger Hay in the chart room. Watching my chances I reached the half deck, where I changed my clothes as best I could. Probably I remained there four hours. On my way to the half deck I noticed that the boat was knocked from the davits and was over on the half deck. On my return four hours later the boat was gone. Also missing were the four people I had met on the way down in the chart room, but at the time I thought that they had gone forward to the stump of the foremast to be with the others.

"The next day I reached the chart room, and the sea was

still there. I met no one in the cabin, which was gutted and had been awash. I came back from the cabin to the chart room by means of the crossjack arm, which had gone through the poop deck when she let go. I saw no one from the fifth to the seventh, being alone all day on the sixth and parts of the other two days.

"The storm finally went down, and the others visited me on the eighth. They asked me about the captain and the others. We never saw the missing ones again. When we were rescued by the men from the *Cuban,* we went over the side on ropes. By that time the lumber deckload had all washed overboard.

"At the time of the rescue the skipper of the *Cuban* asked us how it was that all the officers had been lost. Up to then I hadn't thought much about it. Years ago, Mr. Snow, when I first met you, you asked me about a blood-stained ax. I told you then I never saw any, and that question surprised me like the one the captain of the *Cuban* asked me. I just hadn't considered mutiny or the possibility of a blood-stained ax, and furthermore I didn't notice anything resembling a mutiny.

"As to how Captain Fickett and the three others were lost, perhaps he launched the lifeboat, for two men could have launched it. But the officers of the *Cuban* couldn't understand how Captain Fickett would leave his crew behind. I don't think Captain Fickett was that type unless there was no alternative. What might have happened is that green water came over the stern and took all four to their death in the sea. How they went I just don't know."

On Thursday, March 18, 1954, a meeting was held in the rooms of the Boston Marine Society,* 88 Broad Street, Boston. As the oldest marine society in America, it enjoys certain privileges of tradition in matters relating to the sea, and the

* The writer is a member of the Society, holding certificate No. 2738.

officers gladly agreed to conduct a survey of the *Erne* case, even though forty years had elapsed. Present at the meeting, among others who chose to remain anonymous, were Captain Frank H. Peterson, Captain Charles T. Snow, Captain William J. Keating, Captain Odber R. Farrell, and Theodore Shepardson.

At the beginning of the meeting I read the essential facts of the case, after which a tape recording was given of my interview with former cabin boy Russell Walker. Following the recording several captains, willing to express their own opinions, gave statements which were also recorded.

Captain Frank H. Peterson said that he'd "always thought there was something very peculiar about the whole affair. It doesn't seem reasonable that Captain Fickett would leave the ship. Green water might have washed them overboad with the boat, but why wasn't a survivor or the boat itself ever seen? I think that was actually happened will always be a mystery."

Captain Charles T. Snow said, "Captain 'Temp' Fickett would never desert his men, for it wasn't like him. The boat may have washed overboard, but Fickett would never have been in it."

One sea captain present there, who would not let me use his name, gave the most information concerning what he thought of the disaster, and a tape recording which I now have was made at that time.

"I have many definite objections to the statements of former cabin boy Russell Walker. First, why was the first mate down on the bowsprit anyway? What was he doing there? That wasn't the place for him.

"I think that the first mate killed Fickett, and then in some way met death himself. Back at Boston, you recall, the mate had made a statement and Fickett had slapped him. He got even all right, by killing the captain.

"Now here's another point. When they sent Fickett over to get the *Erne* he didn't have a master's ticket in Great Britain. The mate had the ticket and the mate was thus still the technical master, carried on the ship's papers as the master to satisfy the British law.

"Now when Fickett slapped the mate's face, he either had to get a new mate from England or someone else with a British ticket. This was impossible, and so Fickett made temporary peace with Elliott, who merely bided his time for revenge. Yes, Fickett was a bad man, a nasty devil to fool with. He shouldn't have slapped the mate, and when he did so he signed his own death warrant.

"Even when Fickett was in the little barkentine *Allanwide* he had a bad name. He was a hard case. Lots of times those fellows get a reputation as a driver. Now he was a nice, pleasant man otherwise.

"Regarding the disappearance, I know that Fickett would have tried to save his wife had he still been alive, but he had already been killed by the mate. Why would he leave the ship taking his wife, the second mate, the passenger, and no one else? Why didn't the rest of the crew see him abandon ship?

"Now I was master of the ship *Walden Abbey,* an iron ship of similar proportions to the *Erne,* so I know what I'm talking about. There are just too many questions. They crossed up their lines too many times. Fickett wouldn't leave his ship in that condition. There was foul play somewhere, mark me well! I think the yards got adrift, it must have been the foreyards. And what was the cabin boy doing for four hours on the half deck?

"I'd like to have the cabin boy explain how the men got the boat away in a gale of wind. The cabin boy says two men could have put the boat over. I dispute his statement. It couldn't be done. It was just a fairy tale. I think that the boy was too scared to remember just what happened. I will always think that the mate killed Captain Fickett!"

Another viewpoint is given by a man who had previously sailed on the *Erne*. I do not have permission to use his name, but his thoughts follow:

"R. L. Hay was not a passenger, but boatswain. It was Hay and Franklin who came to blows, starting the affair going. At no time during the mutiny did the storm reach the proportions claimed by the survivors, and the ship was never fenced off by shifting cargo. This was intentionally claimed later as an alibi.

"Captain Fickett was hanged along with the mate Elliott. They were fast friends at all times. The day after the hangings the captain's wife threw herself over the side. She had been badly injured by a fall down the ladder to where the two officers were hanging.

"Hay's body was tossed over and the captain's boat was stove in and jettisoned. The boy Walker, if still alive today, could show a scar four inches long on his left chest to remind him to forget what he witnessed on the "Salt Duck," as the *Erne* was called by her crew.

"The captain of the *Cuban* kept a bloodstained hatchet as a souvenir and its presence reminded him eternally to forget to remember anything he saw or heard when the crew of the *Erne* was brought aboard his ship."

Mr. Alfred Willis of Wollaston, Massachusetts, also sailed aboard the *Erne*. His remarks, made to me in March 1967, will close this chapter:

"My impressions of Captain Fickett of the *Erne* are that actually we saw very little of him, because he stayed in his quarters. Occasionally he was on deck. I never knew him to put a hand on a man, but I would say that we could have had more to eat by far. He was pretty hard on work. We used to work our afternoon watch below on the way home.

"The second mate's name was Mr. Phillips. I cannot recall the first mate's name. The name Elliott rings a bell.

"Worden Wood, a famous artist, was the bos'n on that trip. We came into Boston three days before Christmas, the year in my opinion being 1911. It was such a warm day that we washed decks barefooted.

"Pike was from Portland, Maine, I recall. I am sure he didn't go back again. He wanted to get home, as he had been in South America quite a while, and it wasn't a very nice place to be.

"I put in seven months in South America, in Buenos Aires, and some of the time pretty hungry. I walked from Buenos Aires to Rosario, hoping to find work, but as there was nothing there, I walked back again.

"I believe the *Erne* was a sister ship to the *Rhine* and possibly the *Avon*. The *Erne* was a main skysail yarder and during the trip home I put up a new pennant and painted the ball on the top of the skysail mast, probably two hundred feet above the deck.

"I think that Cushing was very abusive, got into trouble and got into a fight, and in all probability Fickett tried to take Cushing's part, and then had twelve men to deal with.

"It is my opinion that either Captain Fickett or Cushing found their way over the side with a little help. I think Mr. Elliott went forward with the men to get away from them. Whether Elliott met with an accident or the crew dealt with him, it is hard to say, for the crew never trusts officers.

"As far as the boat is concerned, I think that was an afterthought for the missing people. She was just swung out and let go.

"I think Elliott tried to get out of the way. Perhaps they

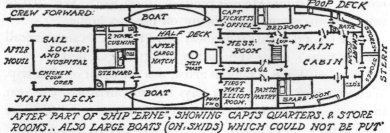

AFTER PART OF SHIP "ERNE", SHOWING CAPT'S QUARTERS. & STORE ROOMS. ALSO LARGE BOATS (ON SKIDS) WHICH COULD NOT BE PUT OVER BY THREE MEN

both went over the side, then later the crew tried to swing the boat out. Perhaps Elliott disappeared about that time.

"I repeat, a sailor never trusts the officers of a ship. He belongs aft and that thought is always in his mind. A mate or skipper will never come off the poop deck after dark. He is afraid he might not get back.

"There is no question in my mind that there was a mutiny on board the *Erne*. There are a lot of earmarks indicating a piratical outbreak there."

What really did happen? Apparently if Cushing was as abusive as is indicated, and Captain Fickett attempted to come to his rescue, the crew probably mutinied. Elliott and Mrs. Fickett and passenger Hay were also disposed of shortly afterward by necessity. The survivors now all swore each other to secrecy. The British authorities decided on a trial, as in the case of the *Veronica*, mentioned elsewhere in this book, but when they found so many American crewmen involved and a missing American captain as well, they abandoned their plans.

15

America's First Gentlewoman Vanishes

One of the most incredible occurrences in American history in the early nineteenth century was the disappearance at sea of Theodosia Burr.

Theodosia, the proud daughter of Aaron Burr, once Vice-President of the United States, was a talented, brilliant woman, possibly the most remarkable in her generation. While sailing to New York from the South in 1812, she and the ship on which she was traveling vanished completely, and people have been discussing her fate ever since. Some years ago I decided to investigate her career.

When I first pieced together my research results, it seemed too fantastic to be true, and I devoted much time and energy to finding any fallacies in the reconstruction. Not only did investigation prove the story accurate, but I was able to eliminate four other conflicting accounts as chronologically impossible.

Efforts to check the various clues led from state to state, and from lonely shores to the big cities of America. The story did not unfold itself suddenly, as have many others I have investigated. It resisted solution until the very end. The most unusual chase was from Nags Head, North Carolina, to Elizabeth City, North Carolina, and then to Amherst College, Massachusetts, and finally to New York City.

Theodosia Burr, the subject of our story, was born on June 23, 1783, the daughter of the Revolutionary hero Aaron Burr and his wife Theodosia. Early in life she was held high in the air by her proud father as they watched the British troops evacuating New York. Although Theo, as her father called her, was only five months old, she was even then considered a child of rare beauty.

Colonel Aaron Burr planned that his daughter should be given every possible opportunity to improve her mind. The descendant of two presidents of Princeton College should, if she could, become a great woman, for Burr was thoroughly disgusted with the frivolous education for girls at that time. Although many men of the day were well educated, it was not thought essential or even desirable that women should be their peers. There were only two acknowledge alternatives for a girl: marriage, or staying at home with her parents. Young women were prepared for life by learning to embroider, play the pianoforte, sing despondent love songs, and work samplers. All men had a chance to become famous, but they had no desire for a woman to be other than just a woman. The wives of many renowned Revolutionary leaders were illiterate, and few of them were cultured.

Aaron Burr, without neglecting Theo's feminine accomplishments, was determined that his daughter should be as well educated as any man of the period. He sat up one entire night reading Mary Wollstonecraft's book, *A Vindication of the Rights of Women,* and then determined that Theodosia should be brought up on the precepts of mental and moral development which the book emphasized. He told Theo of his plans early in her childhood.

By the time she was ten, Theo could read Horace and Terence in the original Latin and speak French with remarkable grace, and she had studied Greek. She played the harp and the pianoforte, rode, skated, and danced. At ten she was plump but very pretty; she hated cats, was full of pranks, and fond of telling fibs. She had a worshipful admiration for her illustrious father.

Theodosia's mother died the following year, in 1794, and father and daughter were drawn even closer together. In spite of the fact that, as a member of the United States Senate, he was away a great deal, Burr kept in touch with her constantly. Letters between the two became vital links, and this means of exchanging thoughts was kept up until Theodosia's death. One typical letter of Aaron's which precedes his wife's death suffices to show the remarkably close relationship between father and daughter.

I rose up suddenly from the sofa, and rubbing my head— "What book shall I buy for her?" said I to myself. "She reads so much and so rapidly that it is not easy to find proper and amusing French books for her; and yet I am so flattered with her progress in that language, that I am resolved that she shall at all events, be gratified." . . . I went into one bookseller's after another. I found plenty of fairy tales and such nonsense, fit for the generality of children of nine or ten years old. "These," said I, "will never do. Her understanding begins to be above such things"; but I could see nothing that I would offer with pleasure to an *intelligent, well-informed girl of nine years old.* I began to be discouraged. The hour of dining was come. "But I will search a little longer," I persevered. At last I found it. I found the very thing I sought. . . . It was a work of fancy, but replete with instruction and amusement. I must present it with my own hand.

> I am, my dear Theo,
> Your affectionate papa,
> A. Burr

At the age of fourteen Theodosia was rosy-cheeked, graceful, extremely self-assured and positive. With the death of her mother she gradually assumed the position of mistress of the household at Richmond Hill, Manhattan. In spite of her social duties and obligations, however, Theodosia was able to read two hundred lines daily from Homer, translate French comedies, and keep up with all the philosophical writers of her day. Her father's letters continued to mold her to his will, for her habits, her occupations, and even her features were under his guidance. He told her to avoid alike the sneer of contempt and the smile which was really a simper.

Colonel Joseph Alston, who later was elected Governor of South Carolina, became deeply interested in Theodosia late in 1800, and in December asked for her hand in marriage. Theodosia promptly referred Mr. Alston to Aristotle, and told him that Aristotle had said a man should not marry before thirty-six. "Pray, Mr. Alston," she ended, "what arguments have you to oppose such authority?" After a long and involved answer from Alston, Theodosia capitulated, and they were married at Albany, February 2, 1801, when he was twenty-two and she seventeen. Joseph Alston took his bride back to his plantation at the Oaks on Debordieu Island in the Waccamaw River, South Carolina. The following year their son was born, Aaron Burr Alston.

At the time of his daughter's marriage Colonel Aaron Burr was being considered for the highest office in the land.

Both he and Thomas Jefferson had received seventy-three votes for the presidency. This tie of votes created a deadlock, and there were thirty-five more attempts to elect a President before Alexander Hamilton assisted in an arrangement whereby Jefferson was elected to the presidency and Burr became Vice-President.

In July 1804 Theodosia received the shocking news that her father had killed Alexander Hamilton in a duel. Soon afterward he visited Blennerhassett's Island in the Ohio River in an effort to arrange with other conspirators to become Emperor Aaron I of Mexico. This plan met with opposition from the United States Government; Burr was accused of treason, and arrested on February 19, 1807. He was acquitted, however, at the trial. With the possibility of further charges to be brought against him, Burr fled to England, where he remained for four years.

Regardless of her marriage with Alston and the love she gave both her husband and her son, the most predominant factor in Theodosia Burr's life was her close relationship with her father. Aaron Burr worshiped her, and that feeling was more than returned by his daughter. But what seems amazing in this close relationship is the complete confidence between the two extending to matters that the average American father would hesitate to discuss even with his son. Aaron Burr had sent Theodosia his diaries for safekeeping, and he often asked her to look up some portion and copy it for him. The diaries contained some of the most scandalous passages devotees of Eros have ever recorded.

Theodosia found her father's absence a very hard burden to bear, though one which her husband was able to appreciate. Finally Burr wrote that he was sailing home. He left aboard the *Aurora,* disguised as a Mr. De Gamelli. Arriving in Boston, he further disguised himself with a wig and false whiskers. The government might be after him; he owed

thousands of dollars to various people; and there were many
political enemies who might still have grievances. Making his
way to Mrs. Goodrich's boardinghouse at Cornhill Square, he
obtained lodgings for the night. He had spent all his money
and did not have the means to engage passage to New York.
But he did have a trunkful of books acceptable at Harvard
College. President Kirkland of Harvard gave him forty dollars for several volumes, with the assurance that Burr could
redeem them at any time.

After several adventures on board the ship that carried him
to New York, he was finally taken ashore by "two vagabonds
in a skiff," who landed him in the city at half past eleven at
night.

The first night Burr was forced to sleep in a lodginghouse
garret with five other men, paying the sum of twelve cents for
his bed. He remained hidden in New York for three weeks
while his close friends attempted to sound out the government and the more pressing of his creditors as to his setting
up law practice again. Finally it was believed safe to insert a
small notice in the local paper announcing that Aaron Burr
had set up offices at 9 Nassau Street, New York, and was ready
for active practice. As a result of this notice, over five hundred friends and associates visited him before nightfall of the
first day, and before a fortnight had passed Aaron Burr had
earned two thousand dollars.

Unfortunately, a terrible blow was about to fall. He received a letter from Theodosia, dated July 12, 1812, shattering all his dreams for the future.

A few miserable days past, my dear father, and your late
letters would have gladdened my soul; and even now I
rejoice at their contents as much as it is possible for me to
rejoice at anything. I have lost my boy. My child is gone
forever. He expired on the 30th of June.

My head is not now sufficiently collected to say anything
further. May Heaven, by other blessings, make you some
amends for the noble grandson you have lost.

Theodosia

Theodosia soon became desperately ill. The Southern
climate, combined with her sufferings at the death of her
son and the fears she had for her father's welfare, finally
prostrated her. Eventually it was arranged for her to go
to New York, in the hope that the change of environ-
ment would benefit her. Burr sent his friend, Timothy
Green, to South Carolina to accompany Theodosia back
to New York by ship. Joseph Alston, now Governor of
South Carolina, was offended that Burr should think it
necessary to send a man from New York to assist his wife.
He felt that if Mrs. Alston had needed someone to attend her, either he or one of his brothers could have accompanied her. Alston had planned to charter a vessel for
Theodosia's journey northward, but, before this could be
done, Green obtained passage on another ship.

The name of the vessel was *Patriot*. She was a small, fast,
pilot boat which had often been used as a privateer. Theodosia Alston and Timothy Green boarded her at Georgetown, South Carolina, on December 30, 1812, and in so doing
took a step that ended in disaster. The pilot boat never
reached New York and neither Theodosia Burr nor anyone
else aboard the vessel was ever seen again. The mystery was
to remain with Governor Alston for the remaining three years
of his life, and with Aaron Burr until his death in 1836.

As the weeks passed and no information regarding the
Patriot came to them, the husband in South Carolina and the
father in New York exchanged many apprehensive letters.
Finally they decided to accept the inevitable conclusion that
Theodosia had died either at the hands of pirates or by

drowning. In February 1813, Governor Alston wrote to Aaron Burr:

"Your letter of the 10th, my friend, is received. This assurance of my fate is not wanting. Authentic accounts from Bermuda and Nassau, as late as January 30, connected with your letter from New York of the 28th, had already forced upon me the dreadful conviction that we had no more hope. . . . My boy—my wife—gone, both! This, then, is the end of all hope we had formed. You may well observe that you feel severed from the human race. She was the last tie that bound us to the species. What have we left? . . . You are the only person in the world with whom I can commune on this subject; for you are the only person whose feelings can have any community with mine. You knew those we loved. Here, none know them; none valued them as they deserved. The talents of my boy, his rare elevation of character, his already extensive reputation for so early an age, made his death regretted by the pride of my family; but though certain of the loss of my not less admirable wife, they seem to consider it like the loss of an ordinary woman. Alas! they knew nothing of my heart. They have never known anything of it. After all, he is a poor actor who cannot sustain his little hour upon the stage, be his part what it may. But the man who was deemed worthy of the heart of *Theodosia Burr,* and who has felt what it was to be blessed with such a woman, will never forget his elevation."

Governor Alston never recovered from the loss of both his only son and his devoted wife, and he died in the year 1816. Aaron Burr, made of stronger fiber, lived until September 14, 1836.

An interesting comparison can be made between the *Patriot* lost at sea with Theodosia Burr and the voyage of the brigantine *Mary Celeste.* I told in detail in my book *Mysteries and Adventures along the Atlantic Coast* the strange story of

the *Mary Celeste,* which sailed from New York in 1872 with
ten persons aboard, none of whom was ever seen again. The
brigantine itself was picked up a month later, abandoned at
sea, with no indication of what had caused the ship's company
to leave, and the mystery of the *Mary Celeste* has never been
fully explained. The case of Theodosia Burr and the *Patriot*
rivals and in some respects even surpasses that gripping story.

In analyzing events on the *Celeste,* I could only prove the
solution I believe correct by circumstantial evidence. The
mystery of the *Patriot* was at first even more difficult to solve,
for there was no way of telling whether a schooner that
washed ashore at Nag's Head later was actually the *Patriot.*
However, by the time all evidence had been collected and
evaluated and the story made ready for telling, there were
many sworn statements and much tangible evidence to rein-
force my theories. Although there have been several other
versions of the fate of the *Patriot,* I believe I can prove none
of them is accurate.

With all my information at hand, I made my way out to
the great barrier beach on which the community of Nag's
Head stands. The lonely stretches of beach grass, the curved
hills and irregular valleys and hollows attracted me, and the
long sweep of the outer shore and the wild surf drew me on.
What an impressive geographical phenomenon this outer
beach is, running all the way from the Little Life Boat Station south of Virginia Beach through False Cape, Kitty
Hawk, Oregon Inlet, Rodanthe, past Cape Hatteras to reach
Ocracoke Island and finally Cape Lookout, located out to sea
from Beaufort, North Carolina. This 180-mile barrier reef
protects Currituck Sound, Albemarle Sound, Pamlico Sound,
and Core Sound from the furies of the ocean.

Countless shipwrecks have occurred along the beach, and
many pirates and buccaneers sailed in the vicinity. Black-
beard himself considered the region his particular cruising

ground, and he met his death at the hands of fearless Lieutenant Robert Maynard inside Ocracoke Inlet, not too far
from the place where I was walking. The shipwrecks included
such famous names as the *Metropolis, Aaron Reppard,
Henry P. Simmons, Carl Gerhard, Lizzie S. Haynes,* and the
Elizabeth. All of them took place many years after the *Patriot*
had come ashore two miles below Nag's Head.

I had much to accomplish in my visit and hardly knew
where to begin. My first two leads turned out to be hoaxes,
but, to help some reader who may know about them and believe them to be true, I include them here.

The first hoax concerns the alleged son of Aaron Burr,
whose mother, he claimed, remarried after Burr's death in
1836. In 1902, at the age of 108, Charles Henry Burr Crosby
(he had adopted his "stepfather's" name) came forward with
the claim that he was Aaron Burr's son. He also claimed to
know something about the death of his "sister," Theodosia.

Crosby said that in 1813 he had shipped aboard the sloop
Independence as a cook, and in the course of the voyage the
ship had picked up two men adrift on a raft. Their names
were Gibbs and Wansley, and they claimed to be shipwrecked
merchants. One night Crosby overheard them talking. Gibbs
was telling Wansley that they never should have made Theodosia Burr walk the plank after their pirate captain captured
the *Patriot.* Wansley agreed with his friend but added that
their captain would have killed them if they had disobeyed.

Realizing that these two men were pirates who had helped
to capture the *Patriot* that same year, Crosby notified his
captain. The two pirates were placed in irons for the rest of
the voyage. Then, according to Crosby, they were taken
ashore in New York and prosecuted by Aaron Burr. Burr
won his alleged case, and the pirates were convicted and
hanged. Crosby's confused story thus attempted to solve the

mystery of what happened to Theodosia. However, it is almost certain that he actually was not Burr's son.

Moreover, Crosby chose the wrong pirates with whom to implement his yarn. Actually there were two such pirates (I mention them in my book *Pirates and Buccaneers*), but that is where the truth of Crosby's story ends. Charles Gibbs and Thomas J. Wansley never met each other until the year 1830, when they plotted the capture of the brig *Vinyard*. After scuttling the ship off Coney Island, New York, they rowed ashore at Pelican Island and there they were arrested. Later they were tried for piracy, and both were hanged April 22, 1831.* The brig they captured in 1830 could have no connection with Theodosia Burr, who died in 1813, and Crosby's story can therefore be discarded as a hoax.

The second spurious tale concerns a mysterious grave in the St. Paul's Episcopal Cemetery at Alexandria, Virginia. The inscription on the stone reads:

To the memory of a female stranger whose mortal sufferings terminated on the 14th day of October, 1816, aged 23 years and 8 months.

This stone is placed here by her disconsolate husband, in whose arms she sighed her last breath and who under God did his utmost to soothe the cold, dread fear of death.

Romantic tradition in Alexandria says that the woman buried with this inscription was Theodosia Burr. According to the adherents of this story, Theodosia left the *Patriot* with her lover, a man she secretly (and bigamously) married. Many persons saw the two when they arrived in Alexandria. The woman, a creature of rare beauty, soon became very ill, and

---

* Part of Gibbs' body was preserved in a bottle and presented to the Harvard College Medical School.

her frantic husband called a doctor. When the doctor opened the door of the sick room, he found that the husband of the beautiful lady had placed a brace of pistols on the table.

"Do not be too inquisitive," the husband said. "Ask her no questions about her family, but cure her if you can. If you ask her a single question about who she is, I'll blow your head off." Although the doctor was terribly frightened, he did his best to administer to the woman. She rapidly grew worse, however, and died the next day. The husband contracted for the strangely worded tombstone and left Alexandria. Two years later he returned and paid a short visit to his wife's grave. For many years his visits continued, but he always refused to reveal either his identity or that of the woman.

The legend that he was the husband of Theodosia Burr quickly sprang up and has been repeated for more than a century and a half. But the age given on the tombstone was twenty-three, and Theodosia would have been more than thirty when the lady of the mystery died in Alexandria in 1816.*

Now let us return to the actual circumstances that followed the embarkation of Theodosia Burr and her escort, Timothy Green, from Georgetown,** South Carolina, on December 30, 1813. When Captain Overstocks guided the pilot boat *Patriot* out to sea, her guns were stored below deck. The *Patriot* was a speedy sailer and the voyage was expected to take no more than five or six days. The captain carried a message from Governor Alston himself, asking that, because of her illness, his wife be allowed passage through the British blockade to New York. Two days later the British warships intercepted the pilot boat, the message was presented and honored, and the *Patriot* sailed through the blockade and continued until she was out of sight of the Brtish men-of-war.

* New evidence indicates the couple were a John Trust and his wife Ellen.
** Many mistakenly believe that the *Patriot* sailed from Charleston.

That very night a terrific gale lashed the Carolina coast, and the British officers believed that the little pilot boat must have foundered with all on board. Actually, the pilot boat did stay afloat, but she had been dismasted and damaged considerably by the gale.

On the morning after the storm, January 3, 1813, the battered *Patriot* was sighted by Captain Dominique You, former second mate for pirate Jean Lafitte. According to his later confession, he quickly bore down on the helpless vessel. There was no need for the firing of cannon, and the pirate captain and his crew soon took over the schooner. The captured men could not be allowed to live and provide the testimony which would hang the pirates later. Every one of them, including Captain Overstocks and Timothy Green, was hustled up on deck, lashed to the mast, and executed. According to eyewitnesses, in ransacking the vessel the buccaneers discovered Theodosia Burr in her cabin, seized her, and brought her up on deck to face the giant pirate captain.

"What is your name?" the ruffian asked.

"Theodosia Burr, the daughter of Aaron Burr, former Vice-President of the United States. I am also the wife of Governor Joseph Alston of South Carolina."

"A grand conquest," exclaimed one of the pirates, "and we shall have a jolly time with her." He began to advance toward Theodosia.

"Back, all of you," shouted Dominique You, and gave the speaker a tremendous blow with his huge fist. "Now you know that she must die. Death is the bond I signed, but never rape. Back, then, all of you." The men murmured at first, but the huge captain made another threatening gesture, and the pirate crew sullenly retired to their quarters.

Dominque You then told Theodosia Burr that he had no alternative but to execute her as he had all the others, and she agreed that it was better to have it done at once. She went over to the side of the pirate craft, where the plank had been tied across the center of the taffrail. A moment later, with two pirates to assist her, she walked up to the middle of the plank. There she paused, balancing on the plank over the taffrail.

Then, with eyes uplifted, and with arms outstretched, Theodosia Burr walked calmly down the slanting plank into the sea.

The pirates spent the next few hours ransacking the pilot boat, gathering together their spoils, and preparing to return to the ship. A sail on the horizon hurried them, however, and their original plans to burn the *Patriot* had to be abandoned. Much of the material in Theodosia's cabin was left behind, including an oil painting of herself and a trunkful of dresses. At a roar from the captain the pirates transferred to their own ship, hoisted sail, and were soon far away.*

A short time later the pirates were practically wiped out when they attempted to capture another ship, and only three or four escaped.

The day after the pirates left the *Patriot,* she drifted within a few miles of Nag's Head, North Carolina, and wreckers from the area sailed out and boarded the abandoned vessel. She was in battered condition because of the storm and could only stay afloat a few hours, but the men removed whatever they could before she went to the bottom. While they were exploring the *Patriot,* the wreckers observed several things: the rudder was fastened; breakfast was set on the table in the cabin; and the berths were not made up. Although the cabins were all in disorder, there was no trace of blood or violence.

One wrecker named Mann, who had a sweetheart at Nag's

---

* A surprising corroboration of my findings is a sworn statement made February 14, 1903, by Harriette Sprague before Notary Freeman Atwell at Cass County, Michigan, of the confession in 1848 of Frank Burdick, who admitted that he was one of the pirates who murdered Theodosia Burr in 1813. The story agrees essentially with my account.

Head, took as his share of the salvage a trunkful of dresses, some wax flowers, and a woman's portrait in oil which he had found on a locker. Everything in that particular cabin indicated that its occupant had been a lady of refinement and elegance. Apparently she had been the only woman passenger aboard the pilot boat.

When Mann went ashore that afternoon, he presented his sweetheart, Lovie Tillet, with his share of the spoils from the *Patriot*. Lovie lived in a shack made from the timbers of half a dozen shipwrecks, thatched with reeds and oakum. To brighten her surroundings, she hung the oil painting against the wall of her hut, where it remained for many years. Then she placed the wax flowers on the rude table and put the dresses away in a trunk.

Something went wrong with the romance between Lovie Tillet and young Mann, and Lovie married a rival suitor, John Wescott. Many years later, when she was an old woman and had gained a great deal in weight, Lovie fell ill and required medical treatment. Dr. William Gaskins Pool of Elizabeth City was called to treat her. After he had finished with his patient, Dr. Pool glanced across the room at the portrait on the crude wall.

"Where did you get that?" he asked the old lady.

"My young man gave me that over fifty years ago," she answered, "but I married someone else after all."

Dr. Pool strode across the room and brushed aside the cobwebs that festooned the picture. In the semidarkness he saw the striking face of an unusual woman. The incongruity of finding such a fine portrait on the wall of this ramshackle hut impressed the doctor.

"Do you know who it is in the painting?" he asked Mrs. Wescott.

"All I know is that they went out to the wreck of a pilot boat and brought the painting back along with a lot of other things. The picture came from a woman's cabin on the vessel. The other things are in the trunk over there."

Dr. Pool showed such interest in the painting that old Mrs. Wescott ordered her family to open the trunk. They pulled out two soft black silk dresses and a lovely black lace shawl. The apparel was that of a gentlewoman. The dresses had very full skirts gathered at the waist, low-cut bodices, and short sleeves.

At the conclusion of his visit Dr. Pool invited Mrs. Wescott to come to his home when she recovered from her illness. Some time later she accepted his invitation, arriving in a tread cart that was none too big for her oversized body. Lovie Wescott was a tall woman weighing over 250 pounds, but she had altered one of Theodosia's gowns for the occasion by ripping the garment apart in the back and inserting a homespun gore. A lace shawl, held together over her shoulders with a long steel hairpin, at least partially concealed the gore. In her hands she carried her most prized possession, the Theodosia Burr portrait, and she presented it to Dr. Pool in appreciation of his professional services.

Later a careful examination revealed that the portrait had been executed by an outstanding artist, John Vanderlyn. The color work was very good, executed with advantage to the pink cheeks, red lips, piercing black eyes, and hair tinged with auburn. The subject wore a white muslin gown of an empire cut. But it was the round full jaw that seemed to indicate beyond any reasonable doubt that it was indeed a painting of Theodosia Burr, probably done in 1811 or early 1812 when she was twenty-eight or twenty-nine years old. In its emphasis on the vigorous jaw, the painting is quite similar to an earlier portrait also by Vanderlyn.

The painting found on the *Patriot* and given to Dr. Pool by Mrs. Wescott has been exhibited for many years and copied many times, and no one has ever claimed that the subject was anyone other than Theodosia. A dozen members of her family have expressed the opinion that it *could* be no one else.

In July 1888, Mrs. Stella E. P. Drake, fourth cousin of Theodosia Burr, visited Elizabeth City to examine the painting at the home of Dr. Pool, and a local writer interviewed her. He was amazed by the resemblance between Mrs. Drake and the subject of the painting. The two women had the same piercing black eyes, and the same brunette complexion. Mrs. Drake, in turn, thought that the painting was truly a likeness of Theodosia.

Dr. Pool kept the portrait for the remainder of his life, and when he died his daughter, Mrs. Anna Overmann, acquired it. According to Lovie Wescott's grandson, it was on exhibition in a museum around 1905. Some years later Mr. Herbert Lee Pratt of Glen Cove, New York, purchased the painting. At his death in 1945 his collection was broken up, and while Amherst College received the bulk of his art treasures, his immediate family kept the Theodosia Burr portrait, which is now officially listed in the Frick Art Reference Library as a Theodosia Burr portrait by John Vanderlyn.

The final episode in my visit to Nag's Head came three days after my first arrival there. I had walked all around the ancient settlement looking for the old shacks and huts that had been built out of the wrecks of ships. They had vanished, however, with the advance of Nag's Head as a flourishing summer resort.

Visiting the Coast Guard Station, I met Chief Boatswain's Mate Nevin Wescott. I asked him if he had ever heard of the Theodosia Burr painting that had been found in a hut.

"I sure have," he replied, "and if you go over to Manteo, my father'll tell you the whole story."

An hour and a quarter later I had reached Manteo, and soon found the residence where John Wescott, a retired coastguardman, lived on Water Street. I told him Theodosia's story in full, and he listened attentively until I had finished.

"Well, Mr. Snow, you sure have come to the right place. My own grandmother was the woman who gave Dr. Pool the painting. Her name was Lovie Tillet when she got the painting and the dresses. One of the young wreckers down the beach was mad about her and gave her the dresses, wax flowers, and the painting which he'd taken from the pilot boat. But it didn't do him any good. Later on she married John Wescott, who, of course, was my grandfather."

Although the fate of Theodosia Burr is no longer a mystery, there remains one question that will always remain unanswered.

In the early part of January 1813, there drifted ashore at Cape Charles, Virginia, the dead body of a young woman, whose clothes and general appearance gave every indication of refinement. She was buried on a farm a short distance away, and is still there, unidentified and undisturbed.

Was it the body of Theodosia Burr?

16

The Last Real Pirate

Lone voyagers who crossed the ocean in the last hundred years can be counted by the dozen, but undoubtedly the most viciously desperate of them all was Franz Palow, whom the late marine writer Fred Hunt called "thief, smuggler, murderer, and pirate."

One day Fred told me that he considered Franz Palow the last "dyed-in-the-wool" pirate in history to set sail from a New England port.

Fred Hunt himself was an adventurer of the sea. After several years of deep-water fishing and merchant-fleet service, he became associated with the *Patriot Ledger* of Quincy, Massachusetts, where his sea stories from time to time were classics in newspaper reporting.

Fred also admired several other men who either alone or with one other companion crossed the often stormy Atlantic in small craft. Fred's special heroes were William Hudson, F. E. Fitch, Alfred Johnson, W. A. Andrews, J. W. Lawlor, and Joshua Slocum. Fred often told me of his deep admiration for these small-craft sailors.

By far the most remarkable of them was Joshua Slocum, whose singlehanded journey around the world in his yawl *Spray*, a Connecticut oyster smack, was an epic of the sea. He left Boston on April 24, 1895, arriving back in America in the year 1898. On a later trip in the winter of 1909 he was run down and drowned off an island in the Lesser Antilles.*

Then there was the *Red, White and Blue,* a tiny, ship-rigged craft measuring only twenty-seven feet in length. Six feet in beam, she displaced two and a half tons. Captain William Hudson and F. E. Fitch sailed her across the Atlantic, leaving New York on July 12, 1866. Far at sea, on the fifth of August, the *Red, White and Blue* was hailed by the bark *Princess Royal* of Nova Scotia. On the very next day she was nearly lost in a gale, but managed to survive, reaching England at the Bill of Portland on August 14. From there she was towed to Margate and then on to London. The two sailors had a single passenger, a dog named *Fanny.*

On June 15, 1876, Alfred Johnson started from Gloucester, Massachusetts, in the *Centennial,* a sloop-rigged dory twenty feet long. He landed on the Welsh coast on August 11, 1876.

Captain Asa W. Andrews and his brother sailed from City Point, Boston, Massachusetts, on June 3, 1878, heading for France. Their dory, the *Nautilus,* was the smallest craft ever to attempt a crossing up to that time. Nineteen feet overall, she had a depth of twenty-seven inches. Her mast was eighteen feet high, with a lateen sail of twenty-five square yards.

Since they had scarcely any knowledge of navigation, the adventurers were fortunate to meet several ships on the way over, which helped keep the *Nautilus* on the right course. Forty-five days after leaving City Point, they landed at Mullion Cove, Cornwall, England.

On June 17, 1888, Captain Andrews tried the crossing alone in a fifteen-foot boat, sailing from Boston. After sixty-

* See my *Mysterious Tales of the New England Coast,* pages 174–185.

eight days at sea, during which time he was battered by a
series of severe storms, he was picked up only 150 miles out!

In 1891 Captain Andrews and J. W. Lawlor raced each
other across the Atlantic in fifteen-foot dories. Andrews gave
up before his goal was reached, but Lawlor landed in England
safely. Although his trip was successful, he had been capsized,
righted, and had had to "lie to" with a sea anchor for a full
day of the journey.

In 1894 Captain Andrews sailed the fifteen-foot *Sapolio*
from Atlantic City to Spain. Seven years later, in 1901, he
attempted a crossing with his wife in the fourteen-foot *Flying Dutchman*. After sailing from Atlantic City, they were
never heard from again.

Nevertheless, in spite of Fred Hunt's admiration for the
courage and fortitude shown by the heroes of the deep I've
mentioned, his all-time favorite ocean crosser was the man
he called the last real pirate, Franz Palow.

Fred Hunt always believed that the two incredible "loner"
cross-Atlantic trips of murderer Franz Palow, first from Spain
to Cuba and then from Quincy, Massachusetts, to his death
on the shores of Holland, make Palow the most amazing character in Atlantic crossing history.

The Massachusetts aspect of the story began in July 1931
at the Motor Mart Garage in Boston's Park Square, where a
workman calling himself Pollo was apprehended while stealing cameras and ladies' apparel from parked cars.

Discharged from his duties, Pollo changed his name to
Palow and soon sought out the companionship of car-washer
Albert B. Hitchcock. Living at 23 Milford Street, Boston,
Hitchcock had been a patient at the National Soldiers Home
in Togus, Maine, until the preceding October.

One afternoon the pair walked across to Boston Common.
There on a park bench Franz Palow told Hitchcock the fasci-

natingly horrible account of his life. Born in 1892, he grew up to become a sailor. In 1916 he stole a small sailboat in Spain and in it crossed the Atlantic only to fall asleep off Cuba and wreck the craft on the shores of that island.

Then he had sailed aboard large craft for several years, ending up on the West Coast where he murdered a man. Given a life sentence, Palow was sent to Walla Walla State Penitentiary in Washington. Committed June 20, 1918, to life imprisonment, he was pardoned conditionally on August 21, 1924, the condition being that he would leave the United States forever. He did set up a bicycle shop in Germany after returning there, but became bored and went to sea again.

After several voyages, early in 1931 he landed in Boston. Without references he was lucky enough to obtain a job in the garage.

As the two friends sat in the warm sun on the Boston Common park bench, Palow decided to reveal his plan.

"I'd like to take another sailing boat for a long trip. Perhaps you'd go with me this time as crew. How about it?"

Hitchcock replied that he was willing to give up his car washing and joined the murderer. They decided that their next step would be to visit Quincy, where they could pick out a boat from one of the yacht clubs.

Reaching Quincy a few days later, they hiked down to Hough's Neck. There they saw a red canoe owned by a summer resident named MacCurdy. The craft was pulled up above the high-tide mark near 137 Sea Avenue.

That afternoon they visited Nut Island peninsula and later looked across the Bay to Peddock's Island, where they noticed a score or more cottages at Central Hill there.

Palow now told Hitchcock that they would steal the red canoe, break into a grocery store for supplies, and paddle across to Peddock's Island. There they would pick an unoccupied cottage, gain entrance, and make their final plans for the trip in stolen sailing craft to Germany, where they might be able to sell the boat for a substantial sum.

Waiting until after midnight, the two men returned to the Sea Avenue area, where they carried the canoe down to the water's edge.

Not familiar with canoes, Hitchcock was hesitant. Palow, however, was at home in any sort of craft. He put Hitchcock in the bow, the stolen groceries amidships, and began the perilous predawn paddle across the Bay to Peddock's Island, which they reached an hour later.

With the coming of sunrise they visited the island's Central Hill and looked over the houses and cottages that had been erected years before by the Portuguese families who were evicted from Long Island. They broke into one cottage that apparently had not been used that summer.

In the afternoon the two men enjoyed the first meal in their new home. Well fed and feeling contented, they now began making plans for the immediate future.

During the next few days and nights the men were very active, going ashore to steal groceries for their future needs and viewing sailing craft, one of which Palow would pick out to cross the Atlantic. During this period Palow located a skiff behind one of the Peddock's Island cottages and appropriated it.

Rowing near the Quincy Yacht Club one morning, Palow decided that he would steal one of two sailing vessels he admired, a Friendship sloop named *Duffer II*, or another beautiful sailer named *Gladiator*. The *Duffer II* was owned by Clark Saville, while Captain Bill Kemp owned the *Gladiator*. Breaking into both craft, they appropriated what they desired.

Meanwhile, alterted by Mrs. MacCurdy's report of the theft of her canoe, the Quincy police went ashore at several inhabited islands in the area. Across at Grape Island they interviewed caretaker Captain Billy McLeod, who told them he had noticed unusual midweek activities at Peddock's Island. Finally, on July 24, Quincy police officers E. P. Cunniff and John Flaherty went ashore at Peddock's and discovered Mrs. MacCurdy's canoe behind a cottage.

A short time later they captured Hitchcock, who was hiding near the canoe. Within a few minutes Hitchcock broke down and made a partial confession. Strangely enough, at that very moment Palow was rowing the skiff across from Hough's Neck!

In the canoe were found cushions stolen from the other craft, while the building where the men had lived was found to contain a supply of canned goods, and several other articles, including a raincoat, a blanket, and a camera.

While this was going on, Palow noticed the police launch and realized that all was not well. He now started to row toward Fort Andrews on the eastern end of Peddock's Island. Actually, during this period, he was observed from the mainland. Finally landing on the northern side of Central Hill, he pulled the skiff up on the shore near Silva's Rock, behind which he hid.

Of course, the policemen knew nothing of this, and left Peddock's Island with Hitchcock their prisoner.

The very next morning the Friendship sloop *Duffer II* was found to be missing from her mooring off the Quincy Yacht Club.

Although we shall never be sure, it is probable that Palow realized his time was running out. Indications are that he waited for darkness before he started for the mainland. Going ashore the last time at Hough's Neck, he probably stole enough canned goods and other supplies to last him several weeks.

Making his final rounds of the area some time between midnight and dawn, Palow must have gone aboard the

Duffer II at least two hours before sunrise to sail her out to sea before daybreak.

Without question, when those at the Quincy Yacht Club that morning noticed the Friendship sloop missing from her mooring, Palow was far at sea, either with or without the help of the Universal motor that the *Duffer* carried. At least the *Duffer II* was never reported again in Massachusetts waters.

There are those who believe that the brutally clever mind of Franz Palow planned another murder a short time later off the shores of Connecticut, a murder which occurred about the time Palow could have been in that area.

On Thursday, September 10, 1931, Benjamin P. Collings, an inventor of Stamford, Connecticut, disappeared from his yacht, the *Penguin,* while the craft was in Long Island Sound.

The cabin cruiser was sighted at two-thirty in the morning by a fishing party entering Oyster Bay. At the time the *Penguin* was slipping out to sea with the tide off Lloyd's Point, Long Island. The aimless drifting of the *Penguin* attracted the attention of those in the fishing craft, who at the same time heard a splashing in the water such as a swimmer might make. The fishermen thought they could see the head and arms of a man in the water, but before they came alongside, the swimmer had vanished. Boarding the unlighted cruiser, they called out for the captain. There was an answer.

"I'm not the captain. I'm Barbara."

A little five-year-old girl then came out of the cabin and told them that her father had gone swimming with his clothes on. Her mother had also disappeared, according to Barbara.

Shortly after dawn a fisherman off Cove Neck heard a woman calling for help from a small boat anchored off shore. He rowed to the boat and found it was the *Bo-Peep.* The woman identified herself as Mrs. Lillian Collings, wife of Benjamin P. Collings. Mrs. Collings told of how her husband had been tied up and thrown overboard. Her husband was never seen alive again, and no solution to the mystery was ever announced. Later his lifeless body was recovered, the hands and feet securely tied.

Nevertheless, Quincy residents who knew of the theft of the *Duffer II* in Quincy Harbor have written to me as late as January 1966 suggesting that it may have been Palow who caused the murder of Collings. Of course, the truth will never be known.

Nothing official was heard from Palow from that August day when he stole the *Duffer II* until October 12, when he was sighted in the English Channel where he hailed a British freighter, asking for a position fix.

"Where are you heading?" the freighter captain asked Palow.

"I'm going around the world on a bet, and my next stop is Kiel," was the astounding reply.

But adventurer-murderer Palow was never to come into Kiel. Hardly had the freighter exchanged greetings with the *Duffer II* than there was a complete change of weather. What had been a pleasant, sunny Columbus Day morning out on the ocean developed by afternoon into a bad storm with raging seas. By midnight an English Channel gale had hit the area, and the next day a fearful hurricane was battering the coast. All that morning and evening the seas built up higher and higher.

By Wednesday, October 14, even the big liners and tankers were finding conditions extremely difficult.

No one will ever know how Palow attempted to ride out the hurricane, because he perished in the storm. His lifeless, battered body came ashore on the coast of Holland a few hours after the gale abated, tied to the remains of Clark Saville's beautiful sloop *Duffer II.*

The shipwreck of the *Duffer II* and the discovery of the remains of her occupant presented quite a problem to the local Dutch police. To find a solution, the Netherlands authorities tried to piece together the story of how Palow met his death. It was decided that the pirate-murderer had attempted to anchor offshore. Probably the anchor began to drag. Knowing that he was doomed unless he could stop the drift, Palow wrenched the engine * from its bed and bent it to the anchor cable. When this did not stop the drifting *Duffer II*, he seized the Shipmate range and bent the stove on as well. Nothing, however, prevented the *Duffer II* from entering the breakers, and soon it was all over.**

Excerpts from the letter of the American consul general at Amsterdam, Charles L. Hoover, follow:

"Reports from the burgomaster of the town of Ulrum, state that the yacht had apparently been lying at anchor, but seemingly the anchor was too light to keep the vessel from drifting, and the man had apparently unshipped the motor and attached it, as well as the stove, to the anchor chain. . . . It seems probable that the man on this boat was the one who hailed a British vessel a few days before in the Channel to state that he was sailing around the world on a wager and that he had been at sea two years. This is just such a statement as he would be likely to make after having stolen the vessel. The burgomaster of Cosdongeradeel stated to this office that no money was found on the body, which was buried on October 16."

Later Superintendent Clarence E. Lovey of the Washing-

---

* A ten-horsepower Universal.

** On the body was found a registry receipt issued in Boston July 3, 1931, and a New York chauffeur's license belonging to Frank Palow, 369 Vernon Avenue, Brooklyn, with a date of birth April 14, 1892.

ton State Penitentiary at Walla Walla announced that without doubt the drowned man was Franz Palow, Number 8575, who served a term for first-degree murder.

Fred Hunt told me that in a way he secretly envied Palow, who probably could not slip by a yacht-club membership committee, but who would have been an abler and far more entertaining shipmate than some of those who would blackball him. Entertaining, that is, if he would open up in the quiet watches of the night and spin yarns out of his rousing past.

"Dig down deep in the soul of any yachtsman," Fred concluded, "and you'll find something of Dampier, Lolonois, and Teach."

17

Morro Castle and *Yarmouth Castle*

Every so often, almost with tragic regularity, a disaster occurs out on the Atlantic, and the public soon reads about it in the newspapers. In the last third of a century three marine disasters, two of similar nature, have impressed me because of the needless sacrifice of human life. They are the holocausts aboard the *Morro Castle* in 1934 and the *Yarmouth Castle* in 1965, and the sinking of the *Andrea Doria* in 1956.

In 1952, while writing the story of the great fire that overwhelmed the beautiful, palatial liner *Morro Castle* on September 7, 1934, I stated that the very marine board which approved the vessel as being in satisfactory condition the month before the disaster, conducted the hearings that included a review of its own neglect. I reminded the reader that the "American public has a fatal flaw in its character—the failure to follow through in matters pertaining to its own safety." *

* In *Great Gales and Dire Disasters.*

Later, in the year 1956, shortly after the collision between the *Andrea Doria* and the *Stockholm* * I recorded in my *Legends of the New England Coast* that a "great marine disaster causes many people momentary wonder as to how such a calamity could happen. . . . Then the inevitable lassitude creeps in, and only those with a fixed purpose in the matter are left 'crying alone in the wilderness' for reform in marine procedure, and so it goes until the next disaster." Nothing in the intervening years has changed my belief as expressed in either book.

The *Yarmouth Castle* was built in 1927 and named *Evangeline*. Under that name she was well known around Boston Harbor. As the *Evangeline,* the ship has a special place in my memory, for at the time we were acquainted with her my wife and I were first exploring the bay, gathering information on all the islands and lighthouses for the books I wrote later. It seemed for one period of several weeks that we were always crossing in our canoe just ahead or a few hundred yards astern of the *Evangeline.*

Then World War II came. After the conflict we occasionally learned of the *Evangeline*'s whereabouts, and finally discovered that her name had been changed to *Yarmouth Castle,* and that she was a cruise ship out of Miami.

The next we heard about her was on that fatal day in November 1965 when it was reported that she was in trouble at sea while en route from Miami, Florida, to Nassau in the Bahama Islands. Then running under the Panamanian flag, she was making good progress toward her destination when a fire broke out after the hour of midnight. Spreading to the

---

* At 11:22 P.M. on July 25, 1956, the *Stockholm* ran into the *Andrea Doria* south of Nantucket. The *Andrea Doria,* after remaining afloat for more than nine hours, sank at 9:08 the next morning. Fifty-one persons were lost.

ship's staircase area forward, the blaze soon enveloped the amidships passenger section and the bridge.*

On November 19, 1965, Admiral E. J. Roland, Commandant of the U. S. Coast Guard, convened a Marine Board of Investigation on the fire, sinking, and loss of life on the *Yarmouth Castle*. This was done at the request of the government of the Republic of Panama.

On February 23, after weeks of intensive study, the Marine Board reported its finding to the Commandant, placing heavy blame on the captain and ship's officers of the *Yarmouth Castle*.

The report also listed the presence of combustible materials and the chimney effect of a stairway as probable contributors to the tragedy. Nevertheless, the actual discovery of a cut hose line may remove the catastrophe from the category of disasters based on "acts of God" to those willfully planned by human beings. It is even possible that conditions existed aboard the *Yarmouth Castle* similar to those aboard the *Morro Castle* back in 1934, as will be explained later in this chapter.

Incidentally, the conclusions drawn by the board in the *Yarmouth Castle* report emphasized human error far more than any other reason for the disaster.

No general alarm was ever sounded, even by means of the public address system, nor was a complete "abandon ship" signal warning given at any time, the inquiry board reported. Of course, the officers, not wishing to alarm the passengers, probably waited too long and were cut off by the flames before they could act.

* Historian Walter S. Ehrenfeld of York, Pennsylvania, has been very active in going through the hundreds upon hundreds of pages of testimony concerning the disaster to the *Yarmouth Castle*, now in the Coast Guard files in Washington. He has generously allowed me to examine all of his fiindings. Much of the following material was taken from his records.

The details I have been able to piece together form a particularly tragic picture. It was approximately five o'clock at night, November 12, 1965, when the *Yarmouth Castle* departed on her biweekly trip from Miami to Nassau. The subsequent passage was not unusually eventful until about half an hour after midnight, November 13, 1965. At that time the course of the S.S. *Yarmouth Castle* was one hundred and one degrees true, and her speed was fourteen knots. She was then steaming in the Northwest Providence Channel of the Atlantic Ocean between Great Isaac Light * and Great Stirrup Cay.

On board the *Yarmouth Castle* were 376 passengers and 175 members of the crew. West and behind her, on course one hundred and one degrees, speed fourteen knots, was the Panamanian S.S. *Bahama Star* at a distance of about twelve miles. Speeding at thirteen knots, ahead and east of the S.S. *Yarmouth Castle,* on course one hundred degrees true, was the Finnish M.V. *Finnpulp* about eight miles away.

The master of the *Yarmouth Castle,* Captain Byron Voutsinas, had retired to his cabin. On the bridge were Second Mate José L. Rams de León, the helmsman, and two watchmen. One watchman had started his security patrol thirty minutes after midnight. He completed his rounds twenty minutes later and returned to the bridge to relieve the helm. Incidentally, the watchman in making his rounds skipped the area around Room 610, where the fire originated.

Although it was not known on the bridge, first indications of fire were noted by the officer and crew of the vessel sometime after midnight and before one o'clock. During that period a member of the engine-room crew advised the chief engineer by word of mouth that there was smoke coming into the engine spaces through the regular draft ventilation system.

---

* In my *Mysteries and Adventures* I tell a weird story of the lighthouses at Great Isaac and the ghost of a drowned woman who haunted the area.

Immediately the chief engineer started a search in the pantry-galley-bakeshop area, but the search resulted in negative findings that were not reported to the bridge. The chief then proceeded to the main entrance lobby (purser's square on the main deck) where he met the night cleaner, Whyley. The workman reported that he also had detected smoke when he visited the men's toilet on the promenade deck. Frightened, the night cleaner and the chief engineer ran up to the promenade deck and forward via the port passageway to the men's toilet opposite Stateroom 702.

The chief engineer opened the door, looked inside, and smelled smoke, after which he closed the door and proceeded forward. The night cleaner ran aft to awaken the crew in their quarters. Hurrying through the main entrance lobby on the main deck, he shouted to the gift shop operator, Charlie Agero, about the fire and its location. Mr. Agero later testified that it was then 12:45 A.M. A moment later Agero proceeded to the men's toilet on the promenade deck.

Meanwhile the radio operator, who left the radio room at 12:48, smelled smoke at his station on the sun deck and started looking for the fire.

From this time on, many people were involved in attempting to discover the source of the smoke but there still is considerable confusion as to what did happen. The cruise director, the master, the chief mate, the switchboard operator, the first assistant engineer, and a passenger of Cabin 634 named Lloyd Lann all searched for the fire, running back and forth in and out of the area. Fire and smoke were found or observed by these individuals in Room 610 on the main deck and in the men's toilet directly above 610 on the promenade deck. Several fire extinguishers were brought into play to no avail.

A fire hose was run out. The chief engineer sent the first assistant engineer to notify the engine room to start the fire pump. By this time the fire in Room 610 appeared to be extremely hot and well advanced. When the door to this room either fell or was pushed in, the fire, heat, and smoke broke out into the passageway and then quickly advanced into the forward staircase and aft in the hallway, a raging inferno by this time far out of control.

The master, leaving the chief engineer in charge, returned to the bridge. After fighting the fire for a brief period, the chief engineer gave the hose to an unidentified crewman and went to the engine room to close off the mechanical ventilating system and to see that all machinery was operating. The chief engineer then rushed about the decks closing scuppers.

The chief mate did not tarry at the scene of the fire but went forward on the outside of the house on the promenade deck. With other crew members he began assisting passengers through their stateroom windows and breaking out fire hoses to subdue the spreading holocaust.

The radio operator made his way back to the bridge. All the others went aft, pounding on stateroom doors to awaken passengers and crew. Members of the crew were never officially alerted to the fire emergency and off-watch personnel at no time ever formed a fire emergency organization—their mandatory task on the *Yarmouth Castle.*

When the master reached the bridge, there was heavy smoke and flame in the chartroom immediately aft and he ordered, "Stop the engines." * One minute later his command was, "Close the watertight door in the engine room, and turn to port." No attempt was made to use the public address system.

At about this time the radio officer reported for orders. The master directed him to transmit a distress message. Making his way to the radio room, the radio officer was met by a wall

* The time was one-twenty.

of flame, so that he could not send out the S.O.S. When he returned to the captain, the radio officer was directed to transmit a distress signal by flashing light.

All his efforts failed, however, and he was unable to communicate with either the S.S. *Bahama Star* or the M.V. *Finnpulp* in any way! Nevertheless, with the engines stopped the flaming *Yarmouth Castle* was soon sighted by the *Bahama Star* and the *Finnpulp*, for a fire at sea is easily detected by craft many miles away.

During this time bridge personnel were forced by smoke and flame to the open forward deck of the wheelhouse. Then, at approximately one twenty-five the master ordered the abandon-ship signal sounded. Fire and smoke again interfered with the orders being carried out. Although the second mate broke the wheelhouse window in an attempt to sound the whistle by electrical control, the roaring flames prevented him from entering the bridge to set off the general alarm. Actually, the abandon-ship signal of seven shorts and one long was begun but never finished!

Within a few minutes Captain Voutsinas, together with the second and third officers and the watchman, abandoned the forward deck of the bridge. All, with the exception of the master, went to motor lifeboat number 3, which contained the emergency radio.

At this time the second electrician, together with four passengers, Mr. and Mrs. James T. Heigel, from Stateroom W-1, and Mr. and Mrs. Carl M. Apuzzo, from Stateroom 835, released a lifesaving apparatus into the sea and jumped from the sun or top deck into the water. Mrs. Heigel testified later that her watch, which had stopped at one-thirty, indicated the time she entered the water.

Proceeding to lifeboat number 1, the master found it already contained several passengers. The smoke and flames were now dangerously close and Captain Voutsinas decided to lower the boat. In this act he was assisted by the chief boatswain, Ines Gozan-Pinder, who had come to the boat deck from the forecastle. The boatswain descended in the boat and the master went down on the life lines. At this time Staff Captain Panagiotis Menegatos appeared and came down to the boat on the lifelines. The time by best estimate was 1:45 A.M.

About two hours after the fire was discovered, the *Bahama Star* and the *Finnpulp,* proceeding under forced draft, reached the scene. The *Star* rescued 240 passengers and 133 crewmen and the *Finnpulp* 51 passengers and 41 crewmen.

Without question, the story of the cruise ship's last night is one of incredible confusion. Fire must have originated in either Room 610 or the nearby closet. After reading all available testimony from the Coast Guard investigation, I believe that a "jury rigged" lighting circuit, human carelessness with a cigarette, or the placing of mattresses near a raw open light in Room 610 was the cause of the disaster.

As far as can be estimated, word of the fire was passed along a human chain and did not reach the bridge until twenty-five minutes after the discovery. By this time crewmen and even passengers were running around the ship in search of the fire's source.

Because Room 610 was the probable location of the start of the fire, details concerning it follow:

Located on the Main Deck (referred to as Upper C deck on original construction plans) on the inboard side of the port passageway, Room 610 was immediately forward of the pipes which led down to the boiler room. The steel galley vent trunk on the forward side separated the room from the forward passenger stairwell.

On the starboard side of the room was a ladies' toilet. The boiler room was below, and above was a men's toilet on the promenade deck and directly above was another toilet on the boat deck.

At the forward and after ends of this room were natural ventilation ducts which extended vertically from this room to the top of the superstructure. These ducts also served the two toilet rooms above and opened directly into those rooms. Additionally, a mechanical exhaust duct served these rooms.

Room 610 had been built as a toilet room and was of steel construction, and when the sprinkler system was installed in 1947 no sprinkler head served this room. At some later date the room had been converted to a ship's hostess stateroom, but still no sprinkler head was installed.

The first indication of fire came to the ballroom-bar area aft on the boat deck at one-five when Miss Erna Groeger, a passenger from Stateroom 832 on the same deck, burst in screaming, "Fire!" Shortly thereafter a badly burned passenger came into the bar. There was no smoke in this area at the time and the lights were on.

Meanwhile other passengers who had escaped from the amidships section and the passengers in the after staterooms were proceeding to the stern of the vessel. The members of the crew in the after crew's quarters came up and mingled with the passengers in this area. Some of these assisted the passengers in finding life jackets. Others broke out fire hoses and directed water on the fire forward of the after staircase and others assisted in preparing the after lifeboats for lowering.

The Coast Guard Investigation Board found most of the ship's lifesaving and fire-fighting equipment to have been adequate had they been used properly. Nevertheless, the reader should not forget that one hose had been cut through, as testimony proved.

"The magnitude of loss of life stemmed from failure of early use of the general alarm or the public address system and failure of windows and shutters on outside staterooms to be maintained in a condition so they could be easily opened," the board's report stated in part.

The board also found that not only was there no sprinkler system outlet in the closet where the fire began, there were too many valves open, including the main one to the swimming pool, thus reducing pressure at the fire hydrants. It is also stated that with one possible exception no fire doors were closed.

According to the testimony recorded by the Coast Guard, a hostess of the *Yarmouth Castle*, Mrs. Ruth Marie Wright, had been serving in similar capacities on ships for several years. Her position included actually singing in the stage show in addition to the usual hostess duties. She had served continuously on the *Yarmouth Castle* since it had come out of dry dock in October.

On the night of the fire Mrs. Wright dressed for dinner. Later the manager of the gift shop, Charles Agero, met her at the dinner table. During their conversation Charles complained about the bed he slept in, saying that he was anxious to get a better mattress than the one he was using.

"I told him where he might find one, and after dinner I would show him where they were. . . . I took him around to 610. I showed him what the mattresses in there were, and told him that if there was a comfortable one for him and if he wanted it, he could take it, and he said yes."

Just above the mattresses was an aperture in the steel hull of the ship, an open vent stack. At the stack in the wall was some wood siding. More wood was on the floor, and there was a piece of electrical cable spliced to the conduit for a light bulb of at least 150 volts. It was raw light, and it burned all the time, never being turned off. The light or a carelessly disposed burning cigarette may have caused a mattress first to smolder, and then burst into flame.

Ruth Wright went "upstairs" at 7 P.M. and Charles Agero returned to his duties. When he retired he discovered that a steward had transferred the mattress he had chosen to his own stateroom. Ruth Wright went to her room about nine o'clock, retiring about midnight, when she heard "a little commotion and a noise and a fire door being closed," but paid no attention because often the door would be closed to keep people off the floor while it was wet or waxed.

Hearing more noise above, Ruth reached for her light, but it would not turn on. Half-dressing, she opened her door when she heard someone call, "Fire!" and put her head out the porthole. The entire bridge was aflame.

Later she was able to escape. She jumped overboard, swam back to the *Yarmouth Castle* and hung on to the bumper strip. Eventually Ruth Wright was saved by one of the two rescue vessels.

The question of whether or not a fire hose was cut on the *Yarmouth Castle* has been brought up on several occasions. I have conclusive proof that someone did cut a fire hose on the *Yarmouth Castle*.

I now quote from the testimony of Panagiotis Menegatos of Zanatha, the Island of Cephalonia, Greece, who had earlier identified himself to the board as the staff captain, a position he had held for twelve days:

Q. And then what did you do?
A. They brought the hose—When they pulled the hose they found that the hose had been cut right at the faucet—just a little bit below, but it was completely—it was a clean cut.
Q. Captain, refer to your deck plan and show me the station where this hose was located.
A. I went on the *Yarmouth* and checked it and I remember that the number is 14.

Q. The hose was cut at the hydrant, is that correct?
A. Yes. About five or six inches below the hydrant.

The above three questions and answers settle for all time whether or not a hose was cut. I agree with the Coast Guard Board that this single example of a cut hose should not necessarily by itself be considered definite evidence of arson or sabotage.

Nevertheless, if the hose was cut, as the above testimony so indicates, it is possible that sabotage or arson was attempted on the *Yarmouth Castle.*

Followers of marine history should not forget that in the year 1934 the luxury liner *Morro Castle* burned at sea off the New Jersey coast, with the loss of 134 persons. When writing about the incident in 1952 I mentioned Chief Radio Operator George W. Rogers,* who was regarded as the hero of the disaster. He later appeared on a vaudeville tour to tell the "inside story" of what happened aboard the *Morro Castle,* and was paid several times what he had earned on board ship. However, when the excitement died down, Rogers gave up the sea, and joined the Bayonne, New Jersey, police force.

Actually Rogers had a long record of crimes of various sorts, acts which before the *Morro Castle* disaster included almost every unmentionable perversion. So far he had never been caught in murder, but two years after joining the police force he planned even that.

As a member of the Bayonne police force, and possibly anxious to be promoted to his superior officer's position, Rogers set up an infernal machine to kill Lieutenant Vincent Doyle, but the blast failed in its objective to end Doyle's life. At the trial which followed, Rogers was convicted and sen-

---

* *Great Gales and Dire Disasters,* page 73.

tenced to from twelve to twenty years in prison for the attempted murder of Lieutenant Doyle, his superior.

When World War II came, he was paroled to enter the armed forces. No service wanted him, however, and he went back to his old position as radio operator, this time on a freighter.

With the war's end he returned to Bayonne, where his friendship with Mr. William Hummel and Hummel's daughter Edith ended in his murdering both of them. He was caught, convicted and sentenced. Then followed life imprisonment.

While in jail, Rogers occasionally discussed the *Morro Castle* disaster. The other prisoners soon received the impression that Rogers knew how the blaze started. According to Rogers an incendiary fountain pen began the holocaust, but he never admitted that it was his pen. Rogers died in prison in 1958, his secret still untold. Incidentally, a book published in 1959, *Fire at Sea* by Thomas Gallagher, leaves one with the definite impression that Rogers without question knew that the *Morro Castle* fire was of incendiary nature.

Nevertheless, when I wrote my story of the *Morro Castle* in 1952 the government investigation had resulted in commendation of Rogers rather than condemnation. However, in my opinion it should now be generally accepted, because of facts set forth in Gallagher's outstanding book, that the *Morro Castle* fire was incendiary and that Rogers knew about it.

Do not read into my words something which is not there. At this moment I am not claiming that arson was the cause of the *Yarmouth Castle* blaze. What I am asking is that the reader should agree that as someone cut the fire hose there was a reason for this act, and that an arsonist acting on a plan could easily have been the one who cut the hose. Possibly in a few years, another case similar to that of Rogers on the

Morro Castle may be revealed. Remember, at the trial of the *Morro Castle* crew in New York, Rogers came out as the hero, but when he died in 1958, almost a quarter century later, he was no longer regarded as a hero, but as a probable arsonist with the deaths of countless people on his hands.

Although most of the passengers aboard the *Yarmouth Castle* were eventually rescued, ninety people lost their lives.* The vessel capsized and went to the bottom at three minutes past six in the morning, sinking in the Northwest Providence Channel, in twenty-five degrees fifty-five North Latitude, seventy-eight degrees zero-six West Longitude, roughly thirteen miles from Great Stirrup Cay.

The Coast Guard report stated that the vessel's skipper, Byron Voutsinas, demonstrated "negligence, abandonment of command responsibility and an over-all failure to approach and cope with the difficulties" in leaving the ship "allegedly" to go to a rescue vessel and assure the sending of a distress signal.**

* A list of those lost on the *Yarmouth Castle* follows:

Nathan Barkin	Helen M. Hier	Louis W. Neher	Pauline I. Tomasini
Norman J. Barton	William Hier	Margaret E. Neher	Warren Tomasini
Frances M. Best	Henry A. Hughes	Elsie M. O'Connell	Charles E. Vincent
Andrew J. Best	Mary Hughes	Charles E. Polm	Salle A. Vincent
William H. Burleigh	Anne M. Jackson	Mary A. Polm	Betty Wand
Elsie Burleigh	Louise Jackson	Herman Pollock	Stella M. Wiehe
Anna E. Cirlincione	Robert W. Johnson	Minnie Pollock	Alice Weible
Frank A. Cirlincione	John A. Karnes	Omar D. Quay	Steven W. Wright
George R. Crawford	Alice Karnes	Della Quay	Joseph T. Wright
Sarah J. Crawford	George D. Keen	Charlotte M. Reich	Florence B. Wright
Dena A. Duffy	Catherine Keen	Vivian St. Clair	Carlos Davis
Silvia Ebner	Arthur H. Lehr	Helen St. Clair	Carmen Davis
Hal M. Eberle	Nathan Lehr	Bertha Salke	Allen M. Gillan
Helen E. Eustice	Stella Lehr	Edith R. Schneider	Lynda Ann Gillan
Samuel Frankel	Clarice Lobel	Frank Silver	Castillo F. Hurtarte
Rose Frankel	Myrtle P. Lowe	Elmer E. Stanley	Leonie Pellowski
Estelle M. Franc	Morgan I. Lowe	Juan P. Stanley	Eduardo Pinedo
Fred R. Franc	Florence B. Lucchesi	Mabel Straub	Maria Pinedo
Wanda B. Gang	Ann J. Marple	Ralph D. Storrs	Mercedes Vila Sole
Agnes Hill	Edna Matias	Winfield W. Thomas	Lisardo Diaztorrens
William Hill	John Mazzarisi	Ethel L. Thomas	Phillis Hall
Jonathan A. Hamilton	Jessie Mazzarisi	Flora G. Tiefenthaler	
Mary Hall	Gayle M. Musson	William C. Tiefenthaler	

** In fairness, I quote P. Lantz, lawyer for Captain Voutsinas, who stated later that "Captain Voutsinas found it necessary to temporarily abandon his command in order to effect the greatest possible saving of lives under the circumstances and who, after seeing to the sending of a distress signal, promptly resumed his command."

The two craft in the vicinity soon discovered that the *Yarmouth Castle* was afire.

Actually, those aboard the M.V. *Finnpulp* noticed a red glow in the sky at the same time the radar picked up a following vessel seven and eight-tenths miles aft on the port quarter.

The captain of the *Finnpulp* was called to the bridge at once, and ordered the vessel to be turned and headed back to the blazing craft, which proved to be the *Yarmouth Castle*.

The radio officer aboard the *Finnpulp* attempted at 1:40 A.M. to reach the *Yarmouth Castle* but never accomplished his purpose. His next step was to communicate with the Miami Coast Guard and he succeeded at one fifty-four, when he told the Coast Guard that a ship was on fire at sea close at hand. On a course of two hundred eighty degrees, with speed increased to seventeen knots, the *Finnpulp* came within one third of a mile of the *Yarmouth Castle,* where towering flames were seen forward of the ship's stack and engulfing the bridge area.

The *Finnpulp*'s lifeboat was cleared and lowered into the water, while the starboard gangway was lowered just in time to receive a *Yarmouth Castle* lifeboat, in charge of Captain Byron Voutsinas. Passengers in the lifeboat were taken aboard, while Captain Voutsinas returned to the blazing ship. Eventually fifty-one passengers and forty-one of the crew came aboard the *Finnpulp*.

Meanwhile those on the *Bahama Star,* following the *Yarmouth Castle,* noticed a glow in the sky at two-five that morning, and the captain ordered the helmsman to "come left and steer for that ship."

Twenty minutes later the *Bahama Star* was alongside the burning craft after having passed two or three lifeboats in the water.

The *Yarmouth Castle* was then afire from her stack forward, including her bridge and radio shack, through all the decks to the main deck. The forecastle was not burning, neither was there fire aft.

As fast as possible, the *Bahama Star*'s officers and men put fourteen lifeboats into the water and as a result by 4:15 A.M. had saved 240 passengers and 133 members of the crew.

However, by three o'clock there had been a five-degree list to port, and the *Yarmouth Castle* was down by the head. At four o'clock the list had increased to eight degrees, with the sea pouring into the open cargo sideport. The vessel increased her list until three minutes past six that morning, when she rolled over bottom up and sank beneath the waves.

Although the 5002-ton steel vessel was built in Philadelphia in 1927, it did not conform to several safety rules later adopted.

The board urged a study aimed toward a federal law to require ships built before May 27, 1936, to use noncombustible materials, as is necessary on ships built since then.

The board also recommended that the United States seek to have all signers of the 1960 International Convention for Safety of Life at Sea upgrade the safety of vessels that now contain large amounts of combustible material.

In the interim, the board said, the United States should consider bilateral safety agreements with nations whose flag vessels carry passengers from American ports.

The board also recommended that the ships *Bahama Star* and *Finnpulp* be commended for their rescue work "in the highest traditions of the sea."

The greatest loss of life occurred on the boat deck. Fifty-two of the passengers and crew lost were assigned staterooms on this deck; twenty-two were assigned staterooms on the promenade deck; and thirteen were assigned staterooms on the main deck.

Testimony of several witnesses who occupied outside staterooms on the night of the fire indicated that they could not open the windows and shutters in their staterooms.

In summary, certain thoughts are suggested:

The fire originated in Room 610, on the main deck. The room contained a number of combustible items including mattresses, discarded bulkhead paneling, and broken chairs. The fire smoldered and increased in intensity for an unknown period of time before it was noticed.

The cause of the great loss of human life was failure of early detection of the fire in a ship with combustible materials in her structure. When the fire spread from Room 610, the wooden interior and inflammable paint together with the chimney effect of the forward stairway permitted a rapid, uncontrolled progress of fire and smoke to the overhead of the boat deck and forward passageways. Aiding the rapid spread of the fire was the mechanical exhaust system connecting Room 610 with the toilet spaces on the port side of the main deck.

Contributing to the failure of early detection was the security patrolman's not knowing that he was *not* following the prescribed route and thereby increasing the possibility of a fire's going undetected. A further factor was the absence of a sprinkler head in Room 610 which contained combustible materials.

The magnitude of loss of life stemmed from failure of early use of the general alarm or the public address system and failure of windows and shutters on outside staterooms to be maintained in a condition so they could be easily opened.

President Johnson mentioned the *Yarmouth Castle* disaster in a message to Congress March 2, 1966, asking for creation of a department of transportation.

He said that although the *Yarmouth Castle* was exempt from American safety standards, as it was built before 1937, he promised to submit legislation which would "improve safety measures and guarantees of financial responsibility on the part of owners and operators of passenger-carrying vessels sailing from our ports."

In spite of lessons learned because of the great marine tragedies of the twentieth century, including the *Titanic, Morro Castle, Andrea Doria,* and now the *Yarmouth Castle,* the seas are not safe today.

Not until all nations combine to pass and enforce sensible marine laws of safety in all types of weather, including fog and hurricane, will passengers be able to go aboard cruise liners, secure in the knowledge that all precautions have been taken for a safe passage to their destination.

18

―――――――❦―――――――

Cape Cod Mysteries

On more than one occasion Cape Cod has been the scene of strange, incredible occurrences such as the fantastic murder story of Ansell Nickerson,* Charles Freeman's horrific sacrifice of his daughter Edie in 1879, the peculiar marine death of shipwreck survivor Samuel Evans, and the mysterious disappearance of ten men from the fishing schooner *Commerce*. I'll tell Freeman's weird story first.

In 1877 Charles Freeman joined a group of Cape Codders who lived in Pocasset. Interested in an unusual type of religious fanaticism, the members so impressed Freeman that there were fatal results two years later. Freeman and his wife joined the fanatics, becoming sincere followers of the faith, but Freeman without question eventually found the religion too much for him.

In May 1879 Charles Freeman awoke late one night, believing that he had seen a vision of the Lord. The Lord told him, as Freeman later related, to make a sacrifice, and the sacrifice,

―――――――

* Nickerson's strange account is in my *Tales of Sea and Shore*, pages 36–51.

which Freeman eventually carried out, was the killing of his four-year-old daughter, Edith.

The disturbed Freeman awakened his wife, who was completely dominated by her husband. In an effort to solve their horrible problem, the couple knelt in prayer. Freeman asked God to stay his hand at the last minute as He had done with Abraham over Isaac. The Cape Codder prayed, however, that if he had to kill his daughter, he would be allowed to do so at once.

Commanding his wife to hold the lamp, Freeman walked to little Edith's bed, a sheath knife in his hand. Then Freeman acted, plunging the sheath knife into his daughter's side. The poor girl, awakening, gave one last look at her father. A moment later she was dead.

When the authorities took Freeman and his wife away from their little home, Freeman told them that he had done right. Perplexed and enraged, the policeman who arrested Freeman, Constable Redding, asked him if it were right to murder his poor little daughter. The confused fanatic attempted to explain that he had not committed murder, for Edith would rise again in three days.

She was buried in a tiny coffin on which was printed: *Little Edie—lived only 57 months. She shall surely rise again. John vi. 39.*

After the funeral Freeman's wife was released and Freeman was sent to a hospital for the insane. Allowed to leave the hospital in 1887, Freeman went west, where, it is said, he caused no more trouble for the rest of his life.

The story of Samuel Evans is of a far different nature. In February 1892 he sailed out of England on the ship *Jason* with a load of coal for Zanzibar. The captain's wife was aboard. Three days afterward, the *Jason* collided with the steamer *Trilawie* from St. Ives. After limping back into port for dry-dock repairs at Queenstown, the *Jason* was boarded by a work crew. Four weeks later she started again for Zanzibar.

The *Jason* encountered a terrific gale while rounding the Cape of Good Hope, during which time one of the men high in the rigging lost his hold, fell overboard, and drowned in the sea. At Zanzibar the ship discharged her cargo and then started for Calcutta. In the harbor of Calcutta another sailor fell overboard and also drowned.

Finally, with a great cargo of jute on board, the *Jason* sailed for Boston. Strong gales began to lash the ship, and they soon increased to hurricane winds. Suddenly a terrible gust hit the *Jason,* and over she rolled on her beam ends. One by one the masts all went by the board. At the height of the excitement, the captain broke his leg.

When the storm came to an end the crew rigged a jury mast and sailed to Mauritius, where they arrived ten days later. Once in port, the members of the crew found that they would be in Mauritius for several months while the *Jason* was repaired. Meanwhile the injured captain went back to England with his wife.

For those who claim a woman aboard a ship brings bad luck, it is only fair to say the *Jason* ran into even worse luck when the captain's wife was safely off the ship and ashore.

After a total of six months spent in repairs, the *Jason* sailed away from Mauritius under a new captain. Before she was fairly at sea, the jute cargo below began to swell. Conditions soon became so serious that the captain turned back to port and left two hundred bales of jute on the dock. Sailing again for America, the *Jason* finally arrived off the coast of New England on December 1, 1893. It had been more than a year and three quarters since the *Jason* had left England.

Although the captain did not realize it, he was approaching Cape Cod in such a way that he was about to enter the dangerous, often fatal triangle of Pollock Rip Shoal, Chatham, and Highland Light. Once inside this area, whenever a strong northeasterly gale is blowing, a ship's doom is sealed, for there is no room to veer around and escape.

With the wind from the northeast, a driving rain now began. Almost at once the rain turned to sleet, with a hard snowstorm shutting the ship in. Nauset Three Lights was the first landfall the *Jason* made, late that afternoon of December 5. Now on a lee shore, the *Jason* was heading for inevitable disaster.

With the knowledge of impending doom, all along the Cape Cod shore the life-saving stations cleared their decks for action. Every member of every crew without exception from Nauset Beach to Race Point hauled out gear to await the shipwreck they knew must take place. One by one they reported.

Down at Chatham, Captain H. F. Doane telephoned the other stations that the *Jason* had gone by. Then came the message from Captain James H. Charles at Orleans. "I've missed her," he said as he watched the *Jason* edge on up the coast.

Some time later Captain Daniel Cole at Cahoon's Hollow came through with "She's gone by our station."

Finally came the last report. "I've got her," shouted Captain David Rich of Pamet River over the wires. "She's stranded off the beach."

By the time the crew of the Pamet Station had pulled the beach cart to the scene they noticed that the *Jason*'s mizzen-mast had gone by the board and the shore was piled high with wreckage. Even above the whistling wind the slatting of the *Jason*'s sails could be heard. Setting up the lifesaving gun on the shore, the surfmen took careful aim. Adjusting the lines in the faking box to the shot, Captain Rich made sure all was in readiness. A moment later he fired, and the twelve-pound projectile, followed by the line, landed safely on the deck of the *Jason*. There was no response out on the *Jason*, for the lines lay untouched. No one was alive!

Out on the *Jason*, just before the mast broke in two, Samuel Evans had come up from below. Before he could join the others in the mizzen shrouds, a great sea swept him overboard. Strangely enough this saved Evans from death. His life belt secure, Evans grasped at a bale of jute, obtained a firm hold, and lapsed into unconsciousness. A great wave caught him and the bale, flinging them up on the shore. When the lifesavers found him, Evans opened his eyes.

"Be I saved?" he asked as he came to.

"Yes," was the answer, "but you're the only one." Twenty-six other men had been engulfed by the storm.

The great jute cargo of the square rigger continued to come ashore, and soon it was littering the beach for miles. As the days went by the foremast of the *Jason* continued to show out of water, prompting the observation that if the crew had chosen the foremast, many of them probably would have been saved.

Sole survivor Samuel Evans returned to England, his mind filled with the memory of the *Jason*'s strange voyage. It is said that when he sailed again in another vessel shortly afterward, he fell from his bunk in the forecastle and was killed.

There are those who believe that every man aboard the *Jason* when she left on her last voyage was doomed the moment the vessel reached the open sea off England and that Evans' death was delayed only a short time longer than the others.

Although this sad tale of bad luck and the subsequent disaster of the *Jason* holds an unusual place in the minds of the Cape Codders, it must yield in pure mystery to the tale of what happened to ten men of Cape Cod on a calm day coming ashore from a fishing schooner.

The event which for sheer incredibility and never-to-be-explained conjecture surpasses almost all others of similar nature in Cape history occurred on Sunday, September 15, 1844.

Late in August 1844 the schooner *Commerce* had sailed from Truro on a fishing voyage to the George's Banks. Returning early Sunday, September 15, the schooner carried a cargo of mackerel. The *Commerce* anchored off the shores of Truro, and all ten men * aboard left the schooner to row ashore.

Captain Solomon Lombard, master of the *Commerce,* was a young man of "excellent character and much promise." For several years he had followed the sea, fishing out on the George's Banks. The sailors of Captain Lombard's crew, mostly neighbors, were all members and prominent supporters of the Methodist-Episcopal Church in South Truro.

When arising on Sunday, September 15, the Truro inhabitants found it was a beautiful day. Historian Shebnah Rich tells us that the first charming touches of early autumn brightened the landscape with the valleys "in soft sunshine." The brown hills were indeed lovely, and the blue water of the bay was particularly attractive to the observer. Far out on the sea several craft could be identified, in almost every case becalmed by the lack of wind, with only the current moving them ever so slowly along the glassy surface of the Atlantic.

The *Commerce* was well known in Truro. On the next day, Monday morning, when the boats went out of the harbor, the

---

* The men on the *Commerce* were Solomon H. Lombard, master, thirty; James H. Lombard, a brother, twenty-five; Reuben Pierce, thirty-nine; Solomon P. Rich, thirty-six; son of Charles Wesley Rich, twelve; Elisha Rich, sixteen; John L. Rich, thirteen; Thomas Mayo, twenty-three; Ezra Turner, twenty; and Sewell Worcester, of Wellfleet, about thirty.

sailors aboard saw the schooner lying at anchor in the road-
stead off the Truro shore, as was customary in fine weather.

At the time it was believed that she had come in during the
night, for there was no small boat out at the *Commerce,* and
the residents correctly decided that the crew had left the
schooner. Later that morning, when not a single sailor belonging to the schooner was seen ashore, with the boat still
missing, one of the neighbors went to Captain Lombard's
house and knocked at the door. He was greeted by Mrs.
Lombard.

Surprised at the neighbor's visit, Mrs. Lombard explained
that the captain had not come home from the mackerel-
fishing expedition. She added that she had received no news
from either the captain or any member of the crew since the
Commerce sailed away more than two weeks before!

The men of Truro then boarded the fishing schooner. She
was found carefully secured and all gear was in "Bristol
fashion." Evidently the crew had started for shore in the
schooner's boat, but something of serious nature must have
taken place. An investigation was begun and it was revealed
that the *Commerce* had been seen by several persons during
the daylight hours of Sunday, but not in the location where
she eventually anchored.

When noticed by those on the shore, she had been lying
abeam of a high hill near the captain's house, but she had not
been observed at this anchorage by any of the friends or relatives of those aboard. The residents of the entire area then
began an organized search.

It was not until noon on Monday that they discovered the
schooner's boat, waterlogged on the shore about a mile to the
south of the anchorage of the *Commerce.* Several men pulled
her high on the beach and when they turned the boat over
they discovered a plank started from her bilge.

Even now there was no sign or indication of what had happened to the ten fishermen. All except one or two were expert swimmers, yet apparently they had simply vanished.

Ten days later a body washed up on the beach and was identified as one of the crew. From time to time after this, during the following two weeks, the remains of all the other nine sailors came ashore, scattered for thirty miles along Cape Cod's Massachusetts Bay shore. The unfortunates received the sacred rites of burial, with solemn services, and were committed "dust to dust."

The incredible drowning so impressed Shebnah Rich,* that when he wrote about it more than four decades later, he stated that in "mystery and agonizing detail" the disaster simply paralyzed the community. No one has ever been able to explain the deaths of these ten men.

More than 132 years later, in January 1967, I joined members of the Massachusetts Marine Historical League with President Arthur J. Cunningham of Lynn, and journeyed to the Pine Grove Cemetery in Truro. With the help of Horace Snow of that town we visited the tombstones of the nine Truro men buried there. The other victim of the disaster, Sewell Worcester, had been interred in his home cemetery of Wellfleet.

Shebnah Rich, to whose grave I made a pilgrimage during my hike around Cape Cod in 1946,** wrote a poem about the ten men who disappeared so mysteriously. I quote below:

> Upon the breezy headland, the fishermen's graves
> they made;
> Where, over the daisies and clover bells, the oaken
> branches swayed;

---

*Shebnah Rich, *Truro, Cape Cod, Landmarks and Sea Marks.*
** While gathering material for the book *A Pilgrim Returns to Cape Cod* I covered 265 miles, visiting all fifteen Cape towns.

> Above them the birds were singing in the cloudless
>   skies of fall,
> And under the bank the billows were chanting their
>   ceaseless call;
> For the foaming line was curving along the hollow
>   shore,
> Where the same old waves were breaking, that they
>   would ride no more.

On the occasion of the M.M.H.L. Truro visit in the winter
of 1967, I copied the gravestone inscription of Solomon P.
Rich, and repeat it now to end this chapter:

> SOLOMON P. RICH
> drowned in Cape Cod
> bay Sept. 15, 1844.
> —•—
>
> Adieu my friends weep not for me
> Long have I stem[m]ed life's troubled sea
> But now redeem'd from sin and woe
> I rest where peaceful waters flow.

19

━━━━◦◦◦◦◦◦━━━━

America's First Canal

One of the most unusual situations in all New England coastal history concerns part of the shoreline of Plymouth County in Massachusetts. More than three centuries ago, the people of Plymouth, Duxbury, Kingston, and Marshfield banded together to reduce the dangers of marine communication in the area by digging America's first canal from Plymouth Bay to Green Harbor, Marshfield. In addition to this human activity, natural changes had been taking place in the region long before the Pilgrims landed in Massachusetts, in fact even before Columbus made his trip across the Atlantic.*

The North River, the South River, and the Cut River all figure in both the natural and the artificial changes along the Plymouth County coastline.

The North River, before the year 1600, had its mouth or opening into the sea where it is at the present time. Nevertheless, the mouth of the North River has changed within the memory of man at least four times. Even before the Pilgrims reached the New World there had been an area desig-

---

* Most of this chapter appeared in *Yankee,* March 1966.

nated as Old Harbor, located between what is now known as the Third Cliff and the Fourth Cliff in Scituate.

During the great gale of 1635, which according to historians brought a tide twenty feet high, the river mouth between the Third and Fourth Cliffs was sealed and the river forced its way miles to the south into the sea.

This new river mouth lasted until 1723. Then, during the terrible November gale of that year, the ocean again broke through between the Third and Fourth Cliffs and for a time the North River had two different mouths several miles apart. Gradually, however, the southern mouth became deeper and the Third Cliff–Fourth Cliff area dried out. For more than a century and a half, or during the major period of North River launchings, the North River retained its southern opening.

Although the beach between Third and Fourth Cliffs effectively kept back the ocean, it was by only the thinnest of margins. Then, during the 1898 Portland Gale, with its several hours of demoniacal fury, a new mouth was formed between the Third and Fourth Cliffs and the old mouth at the Marshfield boundary line gradually silted in with sand.

It is true that in 1851 and again in 1888 the mouth of the river moved a few hundred yards both north and south to create a deltalike formation, but it was not until 1898 that the river mouth moved bodily several miles to the north to reoccupy the area it had occupied in the seventeenth century.

On the other hand the Cut River, which the Pilgrims made into America's first canal, although it changed the location of its mouth from time to time, was almost entirely an inland project.

Late in April of 1965 I revisited this little-known waterway variously called Cut River, the Breakthrough, and the Canal. At one time it was used almost daily by the Pilgrims of Plymouth. (The portion of the Cut River from Green Harbor north seems to be known now as the Green Harbor River.)

New England mariners from almost the beginning of Pilgrim history have dreaded rounding the Gurnet Peninsula in bad weather as they entered or sailed from Plymouth Harbor. After losing several vessels of their colony, the early Pilgrims decided to attempt digging a canal from the north part of Duxbury into southern Marshfield.

After laborious efforts, the Breakthrough, or Cut River, as it has been called since, was completed. Probably it saved the lives of scores of boatmen by offering a quiet inland waterway between Plymouth, Kingston, Duxbury, and Marshfield, thus avoiding the dangers of the North Atlantic.

I believe I had the honor of making the last complete trip by anything resembling a sailing craft all the distance through the Cut River region. That was in the year 1956. In my sailing canoe, my family and I left Scituate, Massachusetts, near the Old Oaken Bucket well and started out into the North River. There were several stops and portages until we actually reached the Cut River, but from then on it was relatively easy sailing and paddling.

We paddled just off Trouant's Island, which is opposite the North River, and went into the old North River opening, the area that is now known as the South River. We were wise enough to choose the highest tide of the year and after a portage of 155 yards were soon paddling into the Green Harbor River and on down to the Brant Rock region. We reached the Cut River and started toward the Duxbury border. From this place we paddled and sailed all the way to Plymouth Rock without a single additional portage.

All this time we were meeting people whose summer residences bordered the Cut River—but of the Cut River they knew nothing. It was quite an experience explaining to the people whose back yards we and the high tide had invaded that this was actually the earliest waterway in New England history. Again and again people would come running down to us as our sailing canoe passed by their homes. I should have printed a circular to hand out, because I repeated my story so often that both Mrs. Snow and our daughter Dorothy were tired of hearing my raucous voice explaining what we were doing.

Finally, we arrived at the little creek in back of Duxbury Park, which widens as it flows under the Powder Point Bridge. We had to take the mast down to get under the bridge, and the various fishermen who were catching flounders, sculpins, and codfish shouted encouragement as we passed under the bridge. Reaching an area abeam of Clark's Island, we soon doubled Duxbury Pier Light. The tide by this time had definitely started to go out, and so we went ashore briefly to view the bones of the *General Arnold* on the flats. Her wreck cost the lives of more than a hundred American soldiers and sailors in the year 1778.

Far in the distance we could see the columns that surround Plymouth Rock; one hour later our sailing canoe grounded on the shale just below the Rock itself. Beside the Rock we made the final picture of our trip, and then went up to eat a hearty meal at a nearby restaurant.

From a historical point of view, the records indicate that the Pilgrims thought long and carefully about digging this first American canal.

Quoting from the *American Magazine* for the year 1837:

"The Cut River, so called, is in the town of Marshfield, county of Plymouth. It is not a large river; generally from three to five rods in width; and it extends (in a very circuitous course like most other rivers and creeks) upwards of three miles. Its general course is from west and northwest to the east and southeast. Within fifty years, the bed of the river near the sea, and the outlet (which is into the ocean about half way from the Gurnet, at the entrance of Plymouth harbor, and Scituate) has been changed and entirely filled up at the distance of eighty or one hundred rods.

"It is believed few such changes have been known in this country. There has been, indeed, a change of the beach and harbor of Chatham, on the back side of Cape Cod; but to what extent we have not been informed. The alteration both of the river and beach near the outlet, may be stated with a good measure of accuracy, as follows—for the distance of about five rods next to the mouth of the river, or its junction with the ocean, the river was made to take a more southerly direction, and the channel or deepest part, was removed farther west than it had before been. The cause of this change is found in the sand of the beach, on the east and northeast of the river but adjoining it, being forced inwardly into the side of the river next to it, by the waves of the ocean, in times of high winds and storms.

"The beach itself thus became gradually changed, being, in the course of several years, some rods more westerly than it had been. The bed or channel of the river (we speak of the lower part near the ocean) was therefore constantly changing, and being in or over a spot farther west than formerly.

"By this process, in about thirty years, the spot or meadow over which the river ran was quite different from its former course; and the sand of the beach occupied the old bed of the river. The moving of the sand of the beach also gradually filled up the old outlet to the ocean; and forced the river so to run as to find an outlet about seventy rods south of the ancient mouth. But after several years, the second mouth or outlet was also choked up; and the waters of the river overflowed some new lands and became stagnant."

Actually, the Pilgrims were able from the very beginning, during periods of new moon and full moon, to navigate (at high tide) shallow-draft craft from Plymouth to Green Harbor, Marshfield. Even before 1630 they were anxious, nevertheless, to cut through with enough depth in the canal to make America's first artificial waterway practical during all times except extreme low water.

I have spent hour upon hour delving into the records of the early Pilgrims and believe that I have uncovered most of the material that explains how the men of the seventeenth century dug the canal so that it could be used twenty hours out of the twenty-four.

The most important period of canal construction was in the winter of 1636. At the General Court held at New Plymouth in that year it was ordered by the court "that the Cut at Green Harbor for a boat passage shalbe made eighteene foote wide and sixe foote deepe. And for the manner how the same shalbe donn for the better ordering thereof it is referred to the Governr and Assistante with the help of John Winslowe Jonathan Brewster John Barnes Christopher Waddcsworth as well to portion every man equally to the charge thereof as also to order men that shall worke thereat, than tenn men may worke together there at once, and the Gounor or whom he shall appoynt shall oversee the same that it may be well formed."

Year after year, especially after great storms swept the coast, the Cut River had to be "cleaned out" and, by the time of the article already quoted from the *American Magazine,* the later-day Pilgrims were having their troubles keeping the waterway navigable.

By 1850 most craft were large and substantially built, enabling them to go around Gurnet Light and thus avoid the Cut River altogether. Nevertheless, the first American canal in history is a pleasant reminder today of early Pilgrim industry.

20

---◦◦◦---

The *Andrea Doria*

On the afternoon of July 25, 1956, many of the 1706 people aboard the New York-bound Italian luxury liner *Andrea Doria,* then approaching Nantucket Lightship, noticed that fog was building up around the 29,000-ton vessel. Because of the fog Captain Piero Calamai knew that there were certain decisions he'd have to make in the next few hours. He realized that with the Lightship more than a hundred miles away, the fog might get much worse as they approached land. Four hours later his worst fears were realized and by ten o'clock that night the fog was overwhelming, but his decision was to keep up his speed and make New York on time.

Meanwhile, several miles away, the 12,165-ton Swedish-American liner *Stockholm* was beginning her first night at sea on her journey from New York to Europe. Soon each vessel located the other on its radarscope. Actually, if each craft had continued on its own course, the liners would not have come within two miles of colliding. Unfortunately, as each sighted the other, they gradually turned into the other's path, slowly coming closer and closer.

At exactly eleven-nine that night of July 25, the *Stockholm* plowed into the starboard side of the *Andrea Doria* just abaft her flying bridge, inflicting a wound partly below the water-line.

Holding together for a split second, the two liners then seemed to leap apart in a dazzling shower of sparks. The *Stockholm*'s sharp bow, which had been rebuilt for use as an icebreaker, had dealt the *Doria* a fatal blow.

Captain Piero Calamai, master of the *Doria,* was in command of the situation, and ordered an appeal for help sent out at once over the ship's radio.

Hundreds of passengers, asleep in their bunks and beds, had been hurled about their cabins at the impact of the crash. Out in the corridors smoke and dust from the collision began to settle over the masses of baggage already assembled for the New York landing, and it was a weird scene that greeted the frightened passengers scrambling out of their staterooms.

A list developed almost at once in the ill-fated Italian craft. Soon the cant to starboard reached twenty-five degrees. By the time the angle was forty-five degrees it was impossible to launch any of the port lifeboats.

The fog now lifted to reveal the *Île de France,* all lights blazing, standing by, while the *Stockholm,* although her bow had been crushed, was still seaworthy and also standing by to help.

Other craft attracted by the appeal for assistance were the *Robert E. Hopkins,* the *Pvt. W. H. Thomas,* the *Cape Ann,* and the *Edward H. Allen.* All assisted in the rescue of those escaping from the sinking liner, some sending lifeboats, others motor tenders. Within a few hours everyone who could escape was safe aboard one of the several rescue craft.

At eight-fifteen on the morning of July 26 the Coast Guard cutter *Evergreen* took command of the situation. Captain

Calamai had left his craft at seven that morning, giving up his unequal struggle with the sea.

Shortly before nine o'clock an observer could notice the change in the *Andrea Doria*'s position in the water, for the sea was then lapping around the liner's starboard rail. The port propellor could easily be seen above the surface. The top deck of the *Doria* was now awash, and six lifeboats ripped loose one by one and came to the surface. Giant geysers spurted forth from the amidships section, with the great vessel slowly going down by the bow.

At the very last moment she simply slid over and went under, leaving lifeboats and other wreckage swirling around on the surface. Fifty-one persons lost their lives.

During the years that have elapsed since the *Andrea Doria* went down, I have received more than fourteen hundred letters from people interested either in trying to bring her up to the surface again, or in actually visiting her at the bottom of the sea. I have also received correspondence from people anxious to learn the history of the name of this ship.

The *Andrea Doria* was named for an Italian admiral born in Oneglia, Italy, in 1468. He became one of the greatest naval heroes of his age. This noble Genoese served in the guard of Pope Innocent VIII, after which he protected Genoa against the Spanish. Some credit Andrea Doria as the first to master the art of sailing a ship against the wind.

After a long career spent protecting Genoa and Genoese ships from Barbary pirates, he retired at forty-one, but was called back into service in 1513 to save his beloved city of Genoa from the French. In 1529 Andrea Doria was given the title of "Father of Peace" and awarded the principality of Melfi. He put down a final uprising in 1547 and died in 1560 without offspring. He was then ninety-three.

Several ships have been named after this famous admiral, but few people are aware that the early American Revolutionary Navy carried the name *Andrea Doria* on one of its smaller warships. On November 2, 1775, Congress placed $100,000 at the disposal of the Marine Committee, which then consisted of Silas Deane, Christopher Gadsden, John Langdon, Stephen Hopkins,* Joseph Hewes, and Richard Henry Lee. These six men were the real originators of the American Navy.

Among the committee's first purchase was a brig that the group named *Andrea Doria* for the famous Italian sailor.

This *Andrea Doria* participated in the first battle in the history of the United States and acquitted herself handsomely. Aided by another American craft, the *Alfred,* the brig *Andrea Doria* eventually forced the retirement of an English battleship, which fled into Newport.

On May 16, 1776, the brig *Andrea Doria,* under Captain Nicholas Biddle, was ordered to sea. For four months she cruised between the capes of Delaware and the coast of Maine. During that time she captured ten transport prizes, all but one of which reached port safely.

Eleven years have passed since the year 1956 when the Italian luxury liner *Andrea Doria* sank into the depths after the *Stockholm* collided with her.

Through the years hundreds of people have dreamed of bringing up the *Andrea Doria,* but of those hundreds, only a few have visited her on the bottom of the sea. After tragic diving results suffered in the first few months following the sinking, the *Andrea Doria* was not visited for some time.

Then, national publicity was given two ideas to raise the liner, but neither idea was even attempted. However, several Massachusetts scuba divers, without fanfare, quietly went ahead with their own plans to visit the *Andrea Doria.*

Early in August 1964, Paul Harling, a Gloucester school-

---

* About whose ancestor Stephen Hopkins I have a chapter in this book.

teacher, went down with two other scuba divers, Joseph Paynotta of Gloucester and Robert Laverdiere of Dedham. They found the sunken liner lying on her starboard side.

"All of us stood at the bottom and looked directly at the keel of the ship. The starboard side is buried in ten to fifteen feet of muck," Harling explained. "It took some real effort on our part to recall that the ship sank more than eight years ago and not within the last three or four weeks."

Mr. Harling, who had been diving for a number of years, believed it impossible to raise the ship. At the time he did not intend to take part in further salvage operations.

The six dives made by Mr. Harling with Paynotta and Laverdiere were the first that had "actually brought back any evidence" of real success. They pulled to the surface a section of the liner's running lights, a large floodlight, a small radar set, and a bridge tyro compass. After cleaning and minor repairs, all were in workable condition.

The radar set served definitely to identify the ship, as it was specially numbered as a demonstration model for the *Andrea Doria.*

The diving group were said to have used twin air tanks that enable divers to stay underwater for one hour. The New Bedford *Standard Times* reported that the divers were able to stay on the bottom only twenty minutes and had to allot thirty minutes for decompression on the return to the surface. However, they found no current whatsoever on the bottom, and diving conditions in general were termed excellent.

On August 23, 1964, the salvage ship *Top Cat* berthed at the State Pier in New Bedford with a life-size bronze statue that the divers said they had recovered from the sunken liner *Andrea Doria.* Four divers reported that they had made fifty-four dives to the hull before the statue was freed. They were unable to detach it from its pedestal, and so they had to saw through the legs just above the ankles.

Captain Turner of the *Top Cat* indicated that the recovery of the statue merely concluded the preliminary salvage operations, and that their intention was to refloat the 697-foot liner.

The bronze statue, its finish hidden by a thin sand-colored crust, was removed from the liner's main lounge. While the scuba divers were operating, several sharks appeared, and two divers had to be hauled up so quickly that they required six hours in a decompression chamber.

Many rumors circulated about offers made for the statue, including one offer of $1,000,000, and an indication of interest from the Italian Government. However, at the time the captain stated that the statue was not for sale. A spokesman from the Italian Line, former owner of the vessel, said the line had "no intention of having anyone from its staff examine the statue."

Other rumors abound as to the contents of the ship's safes and deposit boxes, with estimates going as high as $3,000,000.

Late in September 1964, the statue, which had been standing at the end of the bar at the National Social Club on Union Street, left New Bedford for Baltimore, where it was to be unloaded. However, nothing has been heard as to the statue's final destination, although some said it was eventually to be set up in Washington, D. C.

21

My Ancestor, a Piratical Mutineer

In March 1948, I stood at St. Catherine's Fort, Bermuda, looking out on the ocean toward the area known as Sea Venture Shoals. More than three centuries before that day my ancestor Stephen Hopkins had been one of 150 people wrecked offshore on a great ship, the *Sea Venture*. Virginia-bound, she had battered her way into the Bermuda area and finally slid onto an underwater ledge just in time to save herself from going down with all on board.

Historian Will Zuill told me that same day in 1948 there was a possibility that some fragments of wreckage from the *Sea Venture* remained in the area. Although I was willing and anxious to recover artifacts and curios from the craft that brought my ancestor Hopkins to the Bermudas, I never found anything I could prove within reason as coming from the *Sea Venture*.*

* The *Sea Venture*, part of a fleet of nine ships destined for Virginia, left Woolwich, England, on May 15, 1609, and was joined at Plymouth by Sir George Somers. Delayed in loading until June 2, the fleet got under weigh on June 8. Gates and Somers, both rival leaders, compromised by sailing together on the flagship *Sea Venture*. Eight of the nine vessels reached Virginia, but the *Sea Venture* did not.

More than ten years after my 1948 visit, on October 18, 1958, the *Sea Venture*'s skeletal ribs were discovered three quarters of a mile off the Bermuda shore by diver Edmund P. W. Downing of Franktown, Virginia. All that summer of 1958 he had explored the sea bottom off Fort Saint Catherine without success, just as I had failed ten years before.* Then on that October afternoon scuba diver Downing went over the side of a ladder attached to his forty-four-foot launch *Yachet*. The results were eminently gratifying.

Approaching the bottom thirty-five feet down, Downing first identified several piles of flint, a common substance used as ballast in the seventeeth century. Then he saw the faint outlines of the keel and ribs of a ship, plainly discernible in the sand. From that moment on he was sure that he had discovered a very old craft.

Bermuda Archivist L. D. Grurrin had given him a clue when the historian suggested Downing look for a crevice at least twenty-five feet wide in the underwater reefs, a crevice which would wedge a ship and hold her fast.

Following this discovery Downing and Teddy Tucker, famed Bermuda diver with whom I am associated on the Foul Anchor Archives advisory board,** did extensive diving at the wreck.

Incidentally, the ship's bow when found by Downing was facing toward a small sandy beach where tradition says the survivors landed in small boats. Actually, after the colonists had removed everything which could be taken ashore, the lightened *Sea Venture* without assistance had slid

---

*While my interest in the *Sea Venture* developed because of Stephen Hopkins, who later landed at Plymouth, Massachusetts, on the *Mayflower*, Downing was anxious to find the wreck because of his ancestor, George Yardley, also aboard the *Sea Venture*. Yardley later became Governor of Virginia.

** Others on the board include Robert F. Marx, Caribbean; Arthur McKee, Jr., Florida; John S. Potter, Jr., Spain; Walter Remick, Great Lakes; Alarich Walton, Oak Island; Clyde Hubbard, Mexico; Harry Grunthal, W. J. Robertson, Peter Stackpole, and Robert I. Nesmith.

off the wedge-shaped ledge to sink to the bottom in sand where Downing found her centuries later.

History records that for four days before the shipwreck the *Sea Venture* had been in danger of going down. Luckily, at the very moment when the expedition leaders Sir George Somers and Sir Thomas Gates feared the *Venture* was about to sink, they sighted Bermuda. Superhuman efforts in pumping and bailing enabled the sailors on the *Sea Venture* to keep her afloat as the craft approached relatively close to shore. Luckily the cradlelike reef caught her. Time was vital if everyone was to get ashore before the *Sea Venture* sank. The boats were run back and forth all afternoon from ship to shore, across the distance of about three quarters of a mile. Finally the last survivor landed on the beach.*

A camp was set up on the beach below St. Catherine's Point, but of all the 150 persons in the ship's company, only Sir George Somers, Sir Thomas Gates, and Captain Newport knew that they were wrecked on "the Isles of Devils," Bermuda.

When Strachey, the secretary-elect of Virginia, learned where he had landed, he was fearful, writing that "Bermuda is a place so terrible to all that ever touched on them." Indeed, the Devil's Islands were feared and avoided by all superstitious sea travelers of the period above any other place in the world.

Nevertheless, in spite of their fears, everyone found Bermuda delightful. Incidentally, as many of my readers know already, Bermuda is said to be the scene of Shakespeare's *Tempest.***

---

* I am greatly indebted to Sister Jean de Chantal of Bermuda for her efforts in helping to gather much of the material in this chapter, and recall with pleasure our visit with her to St. Catherine's Fort.

** I offer three excerpts from the pen of William Strachey, the secretary-elect of Virginia, and compare them to similar thoughts in William Shakespeare's *Tempest:*

When ashore, Stephen Hopkins and his family looked for an area where they could establish a temporary abode. We are told by Bermuda historian William Zuill that cabins of palmetto leaves were quickly put together by securing the leaves of the palm tree to cedar posts and placing leaves on top of the edifice for a roof.

Somers himself provided the first meal, catching enough fish for everyone. Still in command, Lieutenant General Gates started things off by setting up an orderly, disciplined camp.

As the days went by after the wreck, the sailors visited the *Sea Venture* again and again bringing ashore bread, beer, hardware, and even spars and riggings. Luckily the island already had a good supply of birds, birds' eggs, wild hogs, and fish.

Historian Strachey tells us that one of Sir George Somers' men inaugurated an unusual system of catching the wild boars. He would hide with some of the pigs which they had brought ashore from the wreck. When the boars on the island were attracted to the pigs, the Englishman would wait until the boar was close at hand, and then with lightning speed fasten a rope with a slip knot to the boar's hind leg to capture

---

The first is the word "glut." Strachey says, "The glut of water was no sooner a little emptied and qualified, but instantly the windes spake more loud." Shakespeare only uses the word "glut" once in all of his works, and that is in the *Tempest* when he copies the idea of Strachey in "Though every drop of water gape at widest to glut him."

Also, the spirit Ariel speaks in the *Tempest* as a flame which "boarded the King's ship; now on the beak; now in the waist, the deck, in every cabin I flamed amazement."

Shakespeare copied the thought from Strachey, who said that "Sir George Sommers being upon the watch, had an apparition of a little round lite, like a faint starre, trembling, and streaming along with a sparkling blaze, half the height upon the main mast, and shooting something from shroud to shroud." The light is also called St. Elmo's flame.

Strachey says that the meat of sea turtles is "such as a man can neither absolutely call fish nor flesh. . . ." In the *Tempest*, Shakespeare asks, referring to turtles, "What have we here, a man or a fish. . . ."

the animal. This unusual Englishman worked the same stunt successfully time after time, adding substantially to the food supply.

The men also trained the ship's dogs to hunt the boars. Chasing and capturing the boar, the dog would fasten his jaws on the boar's hind leg and delay the animal just long enough for the men to catch up and secure the beast.

When winter came to Bermuda the boars had become very thin and scraggly and not worth killing. Fortunately, the sea turtles which arrived offshore in November were captured in substantial numbers and eaten with great enjoyment. Strachey says the meat was good, as one turtle gave more food than three fat boars. Turtle meat tastes like veal. Incidentally the early friars were not sure if a turtle could be called a fish as it might be "abjured as meat."

Strachey writes that the shipwrecked men went down on the shore at low tide to discover lobsters under rocks and in crevices. Crabs and oysters were also abundant. The birds were plentiful, robins of all colors, herons, snipes, crows, hawks, bald-cootes, owls, and bats. All were eaten.

There was a fearsome thunderstorm in March which produced "the mightiest blast of lightning and the most terrible rap of thunder that ever astonished mortal man."

It had been agreed that an attempt should be made to reach Virginia so that the others in the fleet would know that those on the *Sea Venture* had had a safe arrival in Bermuda. The remaining longboat was prepared for the journey with Mate Henry Ravens in command. Sailing away from Bermuda on August 28, just a month after the wreck of July 28, 1609, he carried a crew of seven.

Two nights later he returned, for the mate had not been able to find his way out of the reefs for his start for Virginia. Trying again on Friday, September 1, Ravens said that he would return during the next moon. When the moon arrived, fires were lighted on St. David's Hill * to guide Ravens in. Unfortunately Henry Ravens and the longboat were never heard from again.

Now that the last craft had sailed away, plans had to be made for any eventuality. As is often the case, the two factions representing land soldiers led by Gates and naval sailors under the command of Somers did not see eye to eye, and from time to time incidents occurred. Sir George Somers realized that with Ravens gone he would have to build his own craft in order to leave Bermuda. He had a conference with Gates, asking the other leader for two carpenters and twenty men. Taking them to a separate island, Somers and his men eventually built a small craft which they called the *Patience*. Meanwhile Gates began the construction of a larger vessel which was named *Deliverance*.

Trouble developed as soon as Sir George moved from the main camp to the island. Some of the sailors left behind began to grumble, saying that if the two craft they were building did reach Virginia nothing "but wretchedness and labour must be expected. . . ." About the first of September a conspiracy was discovered. Six ringleaders were detected who had agreed to do no work at all for the building of the vessel. On discovering the plot, Somers punished them by banishing the six to a lonely island. After a reasonable time he pardoned them, and it is said they were glad to return.

Weeks later, on January 24, 1610, my ancestor Stephen Hopkins talked with Sam Sharpe and Humfrey Reed. Evidently, enjoying the relative freedom of the islands he had many ideas he had to talk about. He stated that it was not a breach of honesty to refuse obedience to the captain or leader after a shipwreck, as "his authority ceased" when they were wrecked. From that very moment, stated ancestor Hopkins, they were free men and not under anyone's authority as far

* Where the lighthouse now stands.

as conscience had anything to do with it. Incidentally, his opinion is still being argued today, 357 years later.

There were two good reasons, Hopkins declared, for staying right on the island of Bermuda where "God's providence" had provided an abundance of food. First, if they reached Virginia, they no longer would be free and they might be hungry.*

Talking together, Sharpe and Reed decided to warn Thomas Gates as to what Hopkins was doing. Hopkins, extremely religious and already clerk to Master Bucke, was regarded as a step above the others, and a man to be respected. On receiving the news of Hopkins' statement, Gates sounded the ship's bell which had been erected on shore. Assembling the whole company, he ordered Hopkins, now manacled, to be tried for piratical, mutinous statements.

At the court proceedings the two witnesses gave evidence. Hopkins' reply, if anything, was rather weak. He stated he was full of "sorrow and teares, pleading simplicity and deniall." Penitent, he was worried about how his wife and children would survive if he were hanged as a pirate. Nevertheless, the verdict was death!

His impassioned appeal had moved the hearts of "all the better sort," so they joined in seeking his pardon, and Gates postponed the execution. Strachey himself and Captain Newport were among those who went to Sir Thomas Gates and stayed with the leader until Gates agreed to pardon Hopkins.

As Zuill said of Gates in 1959, "He let them have their way, forgoing his better judgment. It was a mistake."

Nevertheless, if it were a mistake, as a descendant of Hopkins I am one who is pleased that Gates made it that portentious day in 1610.

---

* Indeed, unknown to Hopkins, there was a very strong argument in favor of his remarks, for it was later found that one of the men who landed in Virginia had become so starved that he had killed his wife and eaten her.

Then another incident occurred. On the night of March 13, Henry Paine, a man trusted for guard duty, not only shouted insults at his captain but ended up by striking him. Others warned Paine that if Gates learned of this "it might be as much as his life was worth," and he proclaimed that the governor "had no authority to justify upon anyone, no matter how mean, an action of that nature" and therefore dared the governor to perform an act which at best was embarrassingly indecent.

Gates soon found out what Paine had said. With Hopkins' case still fresh in everyone's memory, the leader realized that the time to put down the mutiny was at hand. The incident was made a test case. The evidence was clear enough, for everyone told the same story. In the eyes of the entire company Gates condemned Paine and sentenced him to be hanged immediately. Now, with the angel of death hovering over him, Paine was just as full of remorse as Hopkins had been. He realized that there would be no pardon, and begged that a final wish be granted. Instead of being hanged, he asked to be shot to death. This was agreed upon, and in the words of Strachey, Paine had his desire immediately, "the sunne and his life setting together."

The weeks went by and finally the two craft were completed for the long trip to Virginia. The expedition sailed from Bermuda May 10, 1610, arriving at Jamestown 580 miles away fourteen days later. In this way all those except six people who died at Bermuda and two others who fled into the woods reached Virginia.*

Stephen Hopkins did not stay long in Virginia after his arrival there, although the details of his life are missing for the next few years. Eventually returning to England, this restless, scripture-quoting Englishman became a London mer-

---

* The two men were Christopher Carter and Robert Waters. Staying behind, they became the first settlers of Bermuda.

chant, but his love for exploration, colonization, adventure, and freedom probably was a factor in his taking steps which led to his embarking with his family aboard the *Mayflower* in 1620.

By this time his first wife was dead. When he went aboard the *Mayflower* he was one of only twelve passengers entitled to have the title or prefix Mr. or Master attached to his name. Others in his party, which was one of the two largest groups aboard, included his second wife, Elizabeth, two children by his first wife, Constance and Giles, and eventually a babe, Oceanus, born at sea. Two indentured servants, Edward Leister and Edward Doty, completed the party. Hopkins' second marriage is duly recorded in St. Mary's Whitechapel, London:

> *Stephen Hopkins et Eliza: ffisher, March, 1617*

Stephen Hopkins was a man of more than ordinary force of character and influence and played an important part in early Plymouth history. His restless spirit, still yearning for the freedom England could not give him, must have soared that day in the cabin of the *Mayflower* as he realized that the compact was being drawn up. There were others aboard imbued with the same spirit of freedom, men such as Carver, Bradford, Brewster, Standish, Winslow, Alden, and Warren.

As the *Mayflower* was maneuvering off the tip of Cape Cod about to enter Provincetown Harbor, Stephen Hopkins and the university man William Brewster probably were making their decisions as to the wording of what many call America's first Declaration of Independence. Hopkins, his mind still on freedom, which he had briefly but joyously enjoyed at Bermuda before he was sentenced as a piratical mutineer, probably may have wished for a definite statement stressing freedom of spirit but also emphasizing the necessity of joining together for controlled action.

Already there was talk that once landed the individual

groups would be free from the "government" of any one else.

And so it was that Hopkins and Brewster sketched the outline for the covenant which all able-bodied leaders signed. They agreed to "combine ourselves together into a Civill Body Politick and by vertue hereof to enacte, constitute and frame such just & equall lawes . . . from time to time, as shall be though most meete and convenient for ye generall good of ye colonie."

Incidentally, Moore in his *Lives of the Colonial Governors,* says: "Of the Pilgrims who remained in 1634, Stephen Hopkins, Miles Standish, and John Alden were the most prominent individuals. Hopkins was then one of the principal magistrates."

D. C. S. Lowell tells us that Hopkins "was one of the signers of the first Declaration of Independence in the New World—the famous Compact, drawn up and signed in the cabin of the *Mayflower,* November twenty-first, 1620; it has been called 'the nucleus around which everything else clustered—unquestionably the foundation of all the superstructures of government which have since been reared in these United States.'

"He was a member of the first expedition that left the ship to find a place for landing ('Ten of our men were appointed who were of themselves willing to undertake it'); he was in the first party that went ashore at Plymouth Rock; he was the first white man of the colony to entertain an Indian at his house over night; he went (with Gov. Winslow and Squantum) on the first embassy sent to Massasoit to conclude a treaty; he was a member of the first Council of Governor's Assistants after the incorporation of Plymouth—a position to which he was chosen for three years in succession (1632–1635); and to this we may add that his two servants, Edward Leister and Edward Doty, fought the first duel on record in New England."

Hopkins heads a list of persons chosen to arrange for trade with outsiders—a sort of chamber of commerce; he is added to the governor and assistants in 1637 as an assessor to raise a fund for sending aid to the Massachusetts Bay and Connecticut colonies in the impending Indian war. In the same year he and his two sons, Giles and Caleb (three Hopkinses, more than of any other name), are among the forty-two who volunteered their services as soldiers to aid these same colonies—a fact in noteworthy contrast with the statement of three "carpet knights" that they will "goe if they be prest."

We find him repeatedly mentioned as an appraiser of estates, administrator, guardian, and foreman for the jury. Fairly prosperous, Hopkins near the close of his life purchased a share in a vessel of forty to fifty tons, valued at two hundred pounds sterling.

On June 6, 1644, Stephen Hopkins made his will. The exact date of his death is unknown; but it must have been before July 17, for then his inventory was taken. The will was witnessed or "exhibited upon the Oathes of" Governor Bradford and Captain Standish. In the will he passes by his oldest son Giles to make Caleb, the only son of his second wife, his heir and executor.

Indeed, a summary of Hopkins' life offers quite a career. Clerk aboard the *Sea Venture,* wrecked at Bermuda, later a piratical mutineer, he was then sentenced to be hanged. Pardoned, he reaches Virginia, makes his way back to London, and marries again in 1617. Leaving on the *Mayflower,* he becomes a leading Plymouth citizen, and meets his death in 1644, leaving more than ten thousand descendants today of the Hopkins and Snow lineage in the United States.*

* Writing around the year 1650, Bradford tells of Stephen Hopkins and his family. "Mr. Hopkins and his wife are now both dead, but they both lived above 20. years in this place, and had one sone and 4. doughters borne here. . . .

"His doughter Constanta is also married, and hath 12. children, all living, and one of them married."

Nevertheless, Stephen Hopkins has a special niche in the hall of Bermuda's history and in the hearts of all Bermudians. He was the first Englishman publicly to declare, at the risk of his own life, that it was his wish always to remain in the beautiful isles of Bermuda rather than sail away! How many of us have agreed with him since?

Constance Hopkins married my ancestor Nicholas Snow, who came to Plymouth on the ship *Ann* in 1623.

INDEX

Index